CAMBRIDGE LIBRARY COLLECTION

Books of enduring scholarly value

Travel and Exploration

The history of travel writing dates back to the Bible, Caesar, the Vikings and the Crusaders, and its many themes include war, trade, science and recreation. Explorers from Columbus to Cook charted lands not previously visited by Western travellers, and were followed by merchants, missionaries, and colonists, who wrote accounts of their experiences. The development of steam power in the nineteenth century provided opportunities for increasing numbers of 'ordinary' people to travel further, more economically, and more safely, and resulted in great enthusiasm for travel writing among the reading public. Works included in this series range from first-hand descriptions of previously unrecorded places, to literary accounts of the strange habits of foreigners, to examples of the burgeoning numbers of guidebooks produced to satisfy the needs of a new kind of traveller - the tourist.

Observations of Sir Richard Hawkins, K^{nt} in his Voyage into the South Sea in the Year 1593

The publications of the Hakluyt Society (founded in 1846) made available edited (and sometimes translated) early accounts of exploration. The first series, which ran from 1847 to 1899, consists of 100 books containing published or previously unpublished works by authors from Christopher Columbus to Sir Francis Drake, and covering voyages to the New World, to China and Japan, to Russia and to Africa and India. Volume 1, published in 1847, contains Sir Richard Hawkins's account of the voyage by which in 1593 he planned to sail to 'the Ilands of Japan, of the Phillippinas, and Molucas, the kingdomes of China, and the East Indies, by the way of the Straites of Magelan, and the South Sea'. The version of the book printed in 1622 was edited by Captain C.R. Drinkwater Bethune of the Royal Navy, a member of the Council of the Hakluyt Society from the year of its foundation. It includes an editorial preface, explanatory footnotes and an index.

T0370648

Cambridge University Press has long been a pioneer in the reissuing of out-of-print titles from its own backlist, producing digital reprints of books that are still sought after by scholars and students but could not be reprinted economically using traditional technology. The Cambridge Library Collection extends this activity to a wider range of books which are still of importance to researchers and professionals, either for the source material they contain, or as landmarks in the history of their academic discipline.

Drawing from the world-renowned collections in the Cambridge University Library, and guided by the advice of experts in each subject area, Cambridge University Press is using state-of-the-art scanning machines in its own Printing House to capture the content of each book selected for inclusion. The files are processed to give a consistently clear, crisp image, and the books finished to the high quality standard for which the Press is recognised around the world. The latest print-on-demand technology ensures that the books will remain available indefinitely, and that orders for single or multiple copies can quickly be supplied.

The Cambridge Library Collection will bring back to life books of enduring scholarly value (including out-of-copyright works originally issued by other publishers) across a wide range of disciplines in the humanities and social sciences and in science and technology.

Observations of Sir Richard Hawkins, K^{nt} in his Voyage into the South Sea in the Year 1593

Reprinted from the Edition of 1622

EDITED BY
CHARLES RAMSAY DRINKWATER BETHUNE

CAMBRIDGE
UNIVERSITY PRESS

CAMBRIDGE UNIVERSITY PRESS

Cambridge, New York, Melbourne, Madrid, Cape Town, Singapore,
São Paolo, Delhi, Dubai, Tokyo

Published in the United States of America by Cambridge University Press, New York

www.cambridge.org
Information on this title: www.cambridge.org/9781108007986

© in this compilation Cambridge University Press 2010

This edition first published 1847
This digitally printed version 2010

ISBN 978-1-108-00798-6 Paperback

WORKS ISSUED BY

The Hakluyt Society.

———×———

THE

OBSERVATIONS OF

SIR RICHARD HAWKINS.

M.DCCC.XLVII.

THE

OBSERVATIONS

OF

SIR RICHARD HAWKINS, K^{NT}

IN HIS

VOYAGE INTO

THE SOUTH SEA

IN THE YEAR

1593.

REPRINTED FROM THE EDITION OF 1622.

———

EDITED BY

C. R. DRINKWATER BETHUNE,

CAPTAIN R.N.

LONDON:

PRINTED FOR THE HAKLUYT SOCIETY.

M.DCCC.XLVII.

THE HAKLUYT SOCIETY.

Council.

EDITOR'S PREFACE.

MANY of the early voyages to the Spanish possessions in South America, are open to the charge of having been conducted more upon buccaneering principles, than on those that should guide nations in their intercourse with each other.

Even Sir Francis Drake, on his return from one of the most memorable, endured the mortification of being considered little better than a pirate, and it required all the honors conferred on him by Queen Elizabeth, to set him right in public opinion.

This is not the proper place to discuss the question, whether England was justified in allowing such expeditions to leave her shores; it is sufficient to state, that our author is not liable to any animadversion, as his voyage was undertaken under the authority of the Queen's commission; and his conduct was marked throughout by humanity and benevolence.

We can hardly appreciate too highly the adventurous daring of these early navigators ; but while we give due credit to them for attempting such long voyages into almost unknown seas, in vessels of small burthen, we must not imagine that they were utterly unprovided for the nature of the expected service : on the contrary, great care seems have been taken both in selecting proper crews, and in providing them with everything needful.

Sir Richard Hawkins, at page 12, alludes generally to his own preparations ; and we read in the accounts of Sir Francis Drake's expedition, "that his vessels were plentifully furnished with all manner of provisions and necessaries for so long and dangerous a voyage ; and such as served only for ornament and delight were likewise not forgotten. For this purpose he took with him very expert musicians for several instruments. His furniture of all kinds was rich and sumptuous ; all the vessels for his table, and many in the cook-room, being of pure silver, curiously wrought, and many other things whereby the magnificence of his native country might be displayed."

We find even more detail in the *North West Fox, or Fox from the North-west passage*, London, 1635: a work professing to give an account of all Northern voyagers, commencing with King Arthur, and ending with Captain Luke Fox. We quote from the preface to the latter voyage:—

" The ship of his Majesties, was (of my own chusing, and the best for condition and quality, especially for this voyage, that the world could afford), of burthen eighty tonnes, the number of men twenty, and two boyes, and by all our cares was sheathed, cordaged, builded, and repaired; all things being made exactly ready against an appointed time. My greatest care was to have my men of godly conversation, and such as their years, of time not exceeding thirty-five, had gained good experience, that I might thereby be the better assisted, especially by such as had been upon those frost-biting voyages, by which they were hardened for indurance, and could not so soone be dismayed at the sight of the ice. For beardless younkers, I knew as many as could man the boate was enough; and for all our dependances was upon God alone, for I had neither private ambition or vaine glory.

"And all these things I had contractedly done by

b

the master, wardens, and assistants of the Trinity House. For a lieutenant I had no use; but it grieved me much that I could not get one man that had been on the same voyage before, by whose counsaile or discourse I might better have shunned the ice. I was victualled compleatly for eighteene months; but whether the baker, brewer, butcher, and other, were master of their arts, or professors or no, I know not; but this I am sure of, I had excellent fat beefe, strong beere, good wheaten bread, good Iceland ling, butter and cheese of the best, admirable sacke and aqua-vitæ, pease, oat-meale, wheat-meale, oyle, spice, sugar, fruit, and rice; with chyrugerie, as sirrups, julips, condits, trechisses, antidotes, balsoms, gummes, unguents, implaisters, oyles, potions, suppositors, and purging pills; and if I wanted instruments, my chyrugion had enough. My carpenter was fitted from the thickest bolt to the pumpe nayle, or tacket. The gunner, from the sacor to the pistol. The boat-swaine, from the cable to the sayle twine. The steward and cooke, from the caldron to the spoone.

"And for books, if I wanted any I was to blame, being bountifully furnisht from the treasurer with money to provide me, especially for those of study there would be no leisure, nor was there, for I found work enough."

Besides this abundant preparation of all things needful for the body, rules for good discipline were not wanting, which we also transcribe, considering they have some relation to the matter in hand.

"May 7, anno 1631.—The voyage of Captaine Luke Fox, in his Majesties pinnace the *Charles*, burthen seventy tonnes, twenty men, and two boyes, victuals for eighteen months, young Sir John Wolstenholme being treasurer.

" Orders and articles for civill government, to be duly observed amongst us in this voyage.

" Forasmuch as the good successe and prosperity of every action doth consist in the due service and glorifying of God, knowing that not only our being and preservation, but the prosperity of all our actions and enterprizes doe immediately depend upon His Almighty goodness and mercy; of which this being none of the least, eyther of nature or quality. For the better governing and managing of this present voyage, in his Majesties ship the *Charles*, bound for the North-west Passage, towards the South Sea, May 7, 1631, as followeth:—

" 1. That all the whole company, as well officers

as others, shall duly repaire every day twice, at the call of the bell, to heare publike prayers to be read (such as are authorized by the Church), and that in a godly and devout manner, as good Christians ought.

" 2. That no man shall swear by the name of God, nor use any prophane oath, or blaspheme his holy name, upon pain of severe punishment.

" 3. That no man shall speak any vile or unbeseeming word, against the honour of his Majestie, our dread soveraigne, his lawes or ordinances, or the religion established and authorized by him here in England, but as good subjects shall duly pray for him.

" 4. That no man shall speake any doubtfull or despairing words against the good successe of the voyage, or make any doubt thereof, eyther in publique or private, at his messe, or to his watch-mate, or shall make any question of the skill and knowledge eyther of superiour or inferior officer, or of the undertakings ; nor shall offer to combine against the authority thereof, upon the paine of severe punishment, as well to him that shall first heare and conceale the same, as to the first beginner.

" 5. That no man do offer to filch or steale any

of the goods of the ship or company, or doe offer to breake into hould, there to take his pleasure of such provisions as are layd in generall for the whole company of the ship; nor that any officer appointed for the charge and oversight thereof, doe other wayes than shall be appointed him, but shall every man bee carefull for the necessary preservation of the victuall and fuell conteyned in the hould; and that also every officer be so carefull of his store, as hee must not be found (upon examination) to deserve punishment.

" 6. That no man doe grumble at his allowance of victuall, or steale any from others, nor shall give cross language, eyther to superior or equal, in reviling words or daring speeches, which do tend to the inflaming of blood or inraging of choller; remembering this also, that a stroke or a blow is the breach of his Majesties peace, and may not want his punishment therefore, as for other reasons.

" 7. That at the boatswaine's call, all the whole company shall appeare above decke, or else that his mate fetch up presently all such sloathfull persons, eyther with rope or cudgell, as in such cases deserves the same. The quarter-masters shall look into the steeridge, while the captains, masters, and mates are at dinner, or at supper.

" 8. That all men duely observe the watch, as well at anchor as under sayle, and at the discharge thereof, the boatswaine or his mate shall call up the other ; all praising God together, with psalme and prayer. And so committing our selves, both soules and bodies, ship and goods, to God's mercifull preservation, wee beseech him to steere, direct, and guide us, from the beginning to the end of our voyage: which hee make prosperous unto us. Amen."

Sir Richard Hawkins followed the profession of a seaman from an early age. Brought up in stirring times, under the eye of his father, one of the most experienced naval commanders of his time, he appears to have inherited a knowledge of sound principles of discipline, and to have become imbued with that indomitable courage, tempered with prudence, essential to the character of a good sea officer. In 1588, Captain Hawkins commanded the *Swallow*, a Queen's ship of three hundred and sixty tons, and assisted in her at the destruction of the Spanish armada. He appears at that period to have attained a certain consideration, as he was employed as Queen's Commissioner, to settle some prize claims. He next undertook the voyage the history of which is recounted in the following pages. After his return from his detention in the South Seas, we find him, in 1620, in the *Vanguard*, of six hundred and sixty tons, vice-admirall of Sir Robert Mansel's expedition against the Algerines. He died suddenly shortly afterwards.

Admiral Burney, in his *History of Voyages and Discoveries in the South Seas*, alluding to this work, says, " it might with propriety have been entitled a book of good counsel; many of his observations being unconnected with the voyage he is relating, but his digressions are ingenious and entertaining, and they frequently contain useful or curious information": and Mr. Barrow, in his *Memoirs of the Naval Worthies of Queen Elizabeth*, thinks that the " *Observations* must take their station in the very first rank of our old' sea voyages."

Similar considerations led the council of the Hakluyt Society to select it, though not exactly a rare work, for early publication; and it is submitted to the Members, with a confident hope that it will repay an attentive perusal.

The editor has confined his labours to reproducing the text of the original, with only such slight alterations as were necessary where the sense

of the author had been obviously marred by a misprint; giving such explanations of obsolete words
and technical terms as might embarrass an unpro-
fessional reader; identifying the places visited with
their modern appellation, where practicable; and
adding such remarks as occurred to him while
correcting the proof sheets.

C. R. D. B.

Nov. 1847.

THE
OBSERVATIONS
OF
S^{IR} RICHARD HAVV-
KINS KNIGHT, IN HIS
VOIAGE INTO THE
South Sea.

Anno Domini, 1593.

Per varios Casus, Artem Experientia fecit,
Exemplo monstrante viam.—Manil. li. I.

LONDON
Printed by *I. D.* for Iohn Iaggard, and are to be
sold at his shop at the Hand and Starre in Fleete-streete,
neere the Temple Gate. 1 6 2 2.

MONGST other neglects prejudiciall to this state, I have observed, that many the worthy and heroyque acts of our nation, have been buried and forgotten : the actors themselves being desirous to shunne emulation in publishing them, and those which overlived them, fearefull to adde, or to diminish from the actors worth, judgement, and valour, have forborne to write them; by which succeeding ages have been deprived of the fruits which might have beene gathered out of their experience, had they beene committed to record. To avoyd this neglect, and for the good of my country, I have thought it my duty to publish the observations of my South Sea Voyage; and for that unto your highnesse, your heires, and successors, it is most likely to be advantagious (having brought on me nothing but losse and misery), I am bold to use your name, a protection unto it, and to offer it with all humblenes and duty to your highnesse approbation, which if it purchase, I have attained my desire, which shall ever ayme to performe dutie.

Your Highnesse humble

And devoted servant,

RICHARD HAWKINS.

TO THE READER.

HAD *that worthie knight, the author, lived to have seen this his Treatise published, he would perhaps himselfe have given the account thereof: for by his owne directions it was put to the presse, though it pleased God to take him to his mercy during the time of the impression. His purpose was to have recommended both it and himselfe unto our most excellent Prince Charles, and himselfe wrote the Dedication, which being imparted unto me, I conceited that it stood not with my dutie to suppresse it.*

Touching the discourse it selfe, as it is out of my element to judge, so it is out of my purpose to say much of it. This onely I may boldly promise, that you shall heere find an expert seaman, in his owne dialect, deliver a true relation of an unfortunat voyage ; which howsoever it proved lamentable and fatall to the actors, may yet prove pleasing to the readers : it being an itch in our natures to delight in newnes and varietie, be the subject never so grievous. This (if there were no more) were yet worthy your perusall; and is as much as others have with good acceptance afforded in relations of this nature. Howbeit besides the bare series and context of the storie, you shall heere finde interweaved, sundry exact descriptions of Countries, Townes, Capes, Promontories, Rivers, Creeks, Harbours, and the like, not un-profitable for navigators ; besides many notable observations, the fruites of a long experience, that may give light touching marine accidents, even to the best captaines and commaund-ers : who if they desire to learn by precepts, shall here find store : but if examples prevaile more with them, here are also aliena pericula. *If you believe mee not, reade and judge.* Farewell.

THE OBSERVATIONS

OF

SIR RICHARD HAWKINS, KNIGHT,

IN HIS

VOYAGE INTO THE SOUTH SEA.

———

SECTION I.

WITH the counsels consent, and helpe of my father, Sir John Hawkins,[1] knight, I resolved a voyage to be made for the Ilands of Japan, of the Phillippinas, and Molucas, the kingdomes of China, and East Indies, by the way of the Straites of Magelan, and the South Sea.

The principall end of our designements, was, to make a *The necessary use of discoveries.* perfect discovery of all those parts where I should arrive, as well knowne as unknowne, with their longitudes, and latitudes; the lying of their coasts; their head-lands; *Of travaile.* their ports, and bayes; their cities, townes, and peoplings; their manner of government; with the commodities which the countries yeelded, and of which they have want, and are in necessitie.

For this purpose in the end of anno 1588, returning *Of shipping.* from the journey against the Spanish Armado, I caused a

---

[1] Sir John Hawkins was one of the most distinguished men of his period. He was a noted commander at sea forty-eight years, and treasurer of the navy for twenty-two years; and it was generally owned that he was the author of more useful inventions, and introduced into the navy better regulations, than any officer before his time.

ship to be builded in the river of Thames, betwixt three and foure hundred tunnes, which was finished in that perfection as could be required; for shee was pleasing to the eye, profitable for stowage, good of sayle, and well conditioned.

The day of her lanching being appoynted, the Lady Hawkins (my mother-in-law) craved the naming of the ship, which was easily granted her: who knowing what voyage was pretended to be undertaken, named her the *Repentance*: what her thoughts were, was kept secret to her selfe; and although many times I expostulated with her, to declare the reason for giving her that uncouth name, I could never have any other satisfaction, then that repentance was the safest ship we could sayle in, to purchase the haven of Heaven. Well, I know, shee was no prophetesse, though a religious and most vertuous lady, and of a very good understanding.[1]

Yet too propheticall it fell out by Gods secrete judgementes, which in his wisdome was pleased to reveale unto us by so unknowne a way, and was sufficient for the present, to cause me to desist from the enterprise, and to leave the ship to my father, who willingly tooke her, and paid the entire charge of the building and furnishing of her, which I had concorted[2] or paid. And this I did not for any superstition I have in names, or for that I thinke them able to further or hinder any thing; for that all immediately dependeth upon the Providence of Almightie God, and is disposed by him alone.

Yet advise I all persons ever (as neere as they can) by all meanes, and in all occasions, to presage unto them-

---

[1] Possibly her ladyship's thoughts may be explained by the consideration that she compared the objects of the proposed voyage with those followed out by her husband. He was the first Englishman who engaged in the inhuman traffic of slaves, and was granted the unenviable addition to his arms: " a demi moor proper ; bound."

[2] Incurred ?

selves the good they can, and in giving names to terestriall
workes (especially to ships), not to give such as meerly
represent the celestial character; for few have I knowne,
or seen, come to a good end, which have had such attributes. As was plainely seene in the *Revenge*, which was
ever the unfortunatest ship the late queenes majestie had
during her raigne; for coming out of Ireland, with Sir
John Parrot, shee was like to be cast away upon the
Kentish coast. After, in the voyage of Sir John Hawkins,
my father, anno 1586, shee strucke aground coming into
Plimouth, before her going to sea. Upon the coast of
Spaine, shee left her fleete, readie to sinke with a great
leake: at her returne into the harbour of Plimouth, shee
beate upon Winter stone; and after, in the same voyage,
going out of Portsmouth haven, shee ranne twice aground;
and in the latter of them, lay twentie-two houres beating
upon the shore, and at length, with eight foote of water in
hold, shee was forced off, and presently ranne upon the
Oose: and was cause that shee remained there (with other
three ships of her majesties) six months, till the spring of
the yeare; when coming about to bee decked,[1] entring
the river of Thames, her old leake breaking upon her,
had like to have drowned all those which were in her. In
anno 1591, with a storme of wind and weather, riding at her
moorings in the river of Rochester, nothing but her bare
masts over head, shee was turned topse-turvie, her kele
uppermost: and the cost and losse shee wrought, I have
too good cause to remember, in her last voyage, in which
shee was lost, when shee gave England and Spain just
cause to remember her. For the Spaniards themselves
confesse, that three of their ships sunke by her side, and
was the death of above 1500 of their men, with the losse See Master
Hacluits Re-
lations.
of a great part of their fleete, by a storme which suddainly
tooke them the next day. What English died in her,

---

[1] Docked ?

many living are witnesses : amongst which was Sir Richard Greenfeild,[1] a noble and valiant gentleman, vice-admirall in her of her majesties fleete. So that, well considered, shee was even a ship loaden, and full fraught with ill successe.

The *Thunderbolt* of Loudon.

The like wee might behold in the *Thunderbolt,* of London, who, in one voyage (as I remember), had her mast cleft with a thunderbolt, upon the coast of Barbary. After in Dartmouth, going for admirall of the Whaftage,[2] and guard of the fleete for the river of Bourdieux, had also her poope blown up with fire sodainly, and unto this day, never could be knowne the cause, or manner how : and lastly, shee was burned with her whole companie in the river of Bourdieux, and Master Edward Wilson, generall in her, slaine by his enemies, having escaped the fire.

The *Jesus* of Lubeck.
The *Repentance.*

The successe of the *Jesus* of Lubecke, in Saint John de Vlua, in the Nova Spania, infamous to the Spaniardes ;[3] with my *Repentance,* in the South Sea, taken by force, hath utterly impoverished, and overthrowne our house.

The *Journey* of Spaine.

The *Journey* of Spaine, pretended for England, anno 1587, called the *Journey of Revenge,* left the principall of their men and ships on the rocks of Cape Finister, and the rest made a lamentable end, for the most part in the Groyne.[4] No more for this poynt, but to our purpose.

---

[1] The brave defence of Sir Richard Greenfeild, or Greenville, against nearly the whole Spanish fleet, merits being here recorded : himself severely wounded and his ship a complete wreck, he ordered her to be sunk, but to this his officers would not consent, so she surrendered on terms. Out of one hundred men fit to bear arms, near sixty survived this glorious action ; but hardly a man but carried off some wounds as memorials of their courage.

[2] Convoy ? Whafter. A term applied to ships of war,—probably from their carrying flags or whafts.

[3] This alludes to a base attack made on Sir John Hawkins, after he had entered into a friendly agreement with the Viceroy.

[4] Corogne (F.) Coruña (S.).

SECTION II.

THE *Repentance* being put in perfection, and riding at Detford, the queenes majestie passing by her, to her pallace of Greenwych, commanded her bargemen to row round about her, and viewing her from post to stemme, disliked nothing but her name, and said, that shee would christen her anew, and that henceforth shee should be called the *Daintie*; which name she brooked as well for her proportion and grace, as for the many happie voyages shee made in her majesties service; having taken (for her majestie) a great Bysten,[1] of five hundred tunnes, loaden with iron and other commodities, under the conduct of Sir Martin Furbusher; a caracke bound for the East Indies, under my fathers charge, and the principall cause of taking the great caracke, brought to Dartmouth by Sir John Borrow, and the Earl of Cumberlands shippes, anno 1592, with others of moment in her other voyages.[2] To us, shee never brought but cost, trouble, and care. Therefore

[1] Probably an abbreviation or misprint for Biscayan. Lediard relates, that in 1592, an expedition, fitted out against the Spaniards, took a great Biscayan shipp of six hundred tunnes, laden with all sorts of small iron-work.

[2] This great caracke was taken, after a sharp engagement, by six ships, part of the expedition alluded to in note 1; which was dispatched expressly to the Azores, to lie in wait for the East India cabrackes. This expedition left under the command of Sir Walter Raleigh and Sir John Borrough. Sir Walter was, however, superseded by Sir Martin Forbisher. She was called the "*Madre de Dios*," a seven-decked ship of one hundred and sixty-five feet from stem to stern, manned with six hundred men. The burthen of this caracke was sixteen hundred tons, and she carried thirty-two brass guns. Her cargo, besides jewels, *which never came to light*, was as follows : spices, drugs, silks, and calicoes, besides other wares, many in number, but less in value, as elephant's teeth, china, cocoa-nuts, hides, ebony, and cloth made from rinds of trees. All which being appraised, was reckoned to amount to at least one hundred and fifty thousand pounds. The caracke, or Carraca, was a large vessel of two masts, used in the India and Brazilian trade.

my father resolved to sell her, though with some losse, which he imparted with me : and for that I had ever a particular love unto her, and a desire shee should continue ours, I offered to ease him of the charge and care of her, and to take her, with all her furniture at the price he had before taken her of me ; with resolution to put in execution the voyage for which shee was first builded ; although it lay six months and more in suspence, partly, upon the pretended voyage for Nombrededios and Panama, which then was fresh a foote ; and partly, upon the caracke at Dartmouth, in which I was imployed as a commissioner ; but this businesse being ended, and the other pretence waxing colde, the fift of March I resolved, and beganne to goe forward with the journey, so often talked of, and so much desired.

And having made an estimate of the charge of victualls, munition, imprests,[1] sea-store, and necessaries for the sayd ship ; consorting another of an hundred tunnes, which I waited for daily from the Straites of Giberalter, with a pynace of sixtie tunnes, all mine owne : and for a competent number of men for them ; as also of all sorts of marchandises for trade and traffique in all places where wee should come ; I began to wage men, to buy all manner of victualls and provisions, and to lade her with them, and with all sorts of commodities (which I could call to minde) fitting ; and dispatched order to my servant in Plimouth, to put in a readinesse my pynace ;[2] as also to take

up certaine provisions, which are better cheape in those parts then in London, as beefe, porke, bisket, and sider. And with the diligence I used, and my fathers furtherance, at the end of one moneth, I was ready to set sayle for Plimouth, to joyne with the rest of my shippes and provisions.   But the expecting of the coming of the lord high

[1] Bounty ? or perhaps wages paid in advance.
[2] A small vessel fitted with sails and oars.

admirall, Sir Robert Cecill, principall secretary to her majestie, and Sir Walter Rawley, with others, to honour my shippe and me with their presence and farewell, detayned me some dayes; and the rayne and untemperate weather deprived me of the favour, which I was in hope to have received at their hands. Whereupon, being loath to loose more time, and the winde serving according to my wish, the eight of April, 1593, I caused the pilot to set sayle from Blackwall, and to vayle[1] down to Gravesend, whether that night I purposed to come.

Having taken my unhappy last leave of my father Sir John Hawkins, I tooke my barge, and rowed down the river, and coming to Barking, wee might see my ship at an anchor in the midst of the channell, where ships are not wont to more themselves : this bred in me some alteration. And coming aboord her, one and other began to recount the perill they had past of losse of ship and goods, which was not little; for the winde being at east northeast, when they set sayle, and vered out southerly, it forced them for the doubling of a point to bring their tacke aboard, and looffing up; the winde freshing, sodenly the shipp began to make a little hele; and for that shee was very deepe loaden, and her ports open, the water began to enter in at them, which no bodie having regard unto, thinking themselves safe in the river, it augmented in such maner as the waight of the water began to presse downe the side, more then the winde : at length when it was seene and the shete flowne, shee could hardly be brought upright. But God was pleased that with the diligence and travell of the company, shee was freed of that danger; which may be a gentle warning[2] to all such as

[1] Drop down.

[2] We ought to profit by the experience of those who precede us. Had this "gentle warning" been attended to, probably the loss of the *Royal George* might have been prevented. She went down at her

take charge of shipping, even before they set sayle, eyther in river or harbour, or other part, to have an eye to their ports, and to see those shut and callked, which may cause danger; for avoyding the many mishaps which dayly chance for the neglect thereof, and have beene most lamentable spectacles and examples unto us: experiments in the *Great Harry*, admirall[1] of England, which was overset and suncke at Portsmouth, with her captaine, Carew, and the most part of his company drowned in a goodly summers day, with a little flawe of winde; for that her ports were all open, and making a small hele, by them entred their destruction; where if they had beene shut, no wind could have hurt her, especially in that place.

In the river of Thames, Master Thomas Candish had a small ship over-set through the same negligence. And one of the fleete of Syr Francis Drake, in Santo Domingo harbour, turned her keele upward likewise, upon the same occasion; with many others, which we never have knowledge of.

And when this commeth to passe, many times negligence is cloaked with the fury of the winde: which is a double fault; for the truth being knowne, others would bee warned to shun the like neglects; for it is a very bad ship whose masts crackt not asunder, whose sayles and tackling flie not in peeces, before she over-set, especially if shee be English built. And that which over-setteth the

anchors while lying at Spithead, the 29th of August, 1782, having been struck by a squall, while her lower ports were open.

[1] The term admirall, appears formerly to have been applied as well to the principal ship in a fleet, as to the superior officer. To cite one among many instances, in an expedition under the Earl of Cumberland, in 1594, we find the *Royal Exchange*, Admiral, two hundred and fifty tons, commanded by Captain George Cave. The *May-flower*, two hundred and fifty tons, Vice-Admiral, commanded by Captain W. Anthony. The *Samson* Rear-Admiral, by Captain Nicholas Downton, together with a caravel and pinnace.

ship is the waight of the water that presseth down the side, which as it entreth more and more, increaseth the waight, and the impossibilitie of the remedie: for, the water not entring, with easing of the sheate, or striking the sayles, or putting the ship before the winde or sea, or other diligences, as occasion is offered (and all expert mariners know) remedie is easily found.[1]

With this mischaunce the mariners were so daunted, that they would not proceede with the ship any further, except shee was lighted, which indeede was needelesse, for many reasons which I gave: but mariners are like to a stiffe necked horse, which taking the bridle betwixt his teeth, forceth his rider to what him list, mauger his will; so they having once concluded, and resolved, are with great difficultie brought to yeelde to the raynes of reason; and to colour their negligence, they added cost, trouble, and delay. In fine, seeing no other remedie, I dispatched that night a servant of mine to give account to my father of that which had past, and to bring mee presently some barke of London, to goe along with me to Plimouth; which not finding, he brought me a hoye, in which I loaded some sixe or eight tunnes, to give content to the company; and so set sayle the 13th of Aprill, and the next day wee put in at Harwich, for that the winde was contrary, and from thence departed the 18th of the sayd moneth in the morning.

When wee were cleere of the sands, the winde veered to the south-west, and so we were forced to put into Margat Roade, whether came presently after us a fleete of Hollanders of above an hundreth sayle, bound for Rochell, to loade salt; and in their companie a dozen shippes of

---

[1] A remarkable instance of carelessness occurred in 1801. The Dutch Frigate *Ambuscade*, went down by the head half an hour after leaving her moorings in Sheerness harbour. This arose from the hawse holes being unusually large, and the plugs not in.

warre; their wafters very good ships and well appointed in all respects.   All which came alongst by our ship, and saluted us, as is the custome of the sea, some with three, others with five, others with more peeces of ordinance.

The next morning the winde vering easterly, I set sayle, and the Hollanders with me, and they with the flood in hand, went out at the North-sands-head, and I through the Gulls to shorten my way, and to set my pilate ashore.

Comming neere the South-fore-land, the winde began to vere to the south-east and by south, so as we could not double the point of the land, and being close abourd the shore, and puting our ship to stay, what with the chapping sea, and what with the tide upon the bowe, shee mist staying, and put us in some danger, before we could flatt

Note.

about; therefore for doubling the point of any land better is ever a short bourd, then to put all in perill.[1]

Being tacked about, wee thought to anchor in the Downes, but the sayles set, we made a small bourd, and after casting about agayne, doubled the foreland, and ran alongst the coast till we came to the Isle of Wight : where being becalmed, wee sent ashore Master Thomson, of Harwich, our pilot, not being able before to set him on shore for the perversnes of the winde.

Being cleere of the Wight, the winde vered southerly, and before we came to Port-land, to the west, south-west, but with the helpe of the ebbe wee recovered Port-land-roade, where we anchored all that night; and the next morning with the ebbe, wee set sayle againe, the winde at west south-west; purposing to beare it up, all the ebbe, and to stop the flood being under sayle.

---

[1] This is sound advice and good seamanship.   In turning to windward, it is wise to keep in the fair way, so that in case of missing stays, you have not a danger under your lee.

SECTION III.

THE fleete of Flemings which had beene in our company Sec. III.
before, came towring into the road, which certainly was a The providence of the
thing worth the noting, to behold the good order the Dutch.
masters observed in guard of their fleete.

The admirall headmost, and the rest of the men of
warre, spread alongst to wind-ward, all saving the vice-
admirall and her consort, which were lee-most and stern-
most of all; and except the admirall, which was the first,
that came to an anchor, none of the other men of warre
anchored, before all the fleete was in safetie; and then
they placed themselves round about the fleete; the vice-
admirall seamost and leemost; which we have taught unto
most nations, and they observe it now a dayes better then
we, to our shame, that being the authors and reformers of The English
authors of
the best discipline and lawes in sea causes, are become sea discipline.
those which doe now worst execute them.

And I cannot gather whence this contempt hath growne,
except of the neglect of discipline, or rather in giving By them
againe ne-
commands for favour to those, which want experience of glected.
what is committed to their charge : or that there hath
beene little curiositie in our countrey in writing of the
discipline of the sea; which is not lesse necessary for us,
then that of the law; and I am of opinion, that the want
of experience is much more tollerable in a generall by
land, then in a governour by sea: for in the field, the
lieutenant generall, the sergeant major, and the coronels
supply what is wanting in the generall, for that they all
command, and ever there is place for counsell, which in
the sea by many accidents is denied; and the head is he
that manageth all, in whom alone if there be defect, all
is badly governed, for, by ignorance how can errors be
judged or reformed? And therefore I wish all to take

B

Sect. IV. upon them that which they understand, and refuse the
contrary.

The modesty of Sir Henry Palmer.
As Sir Henry Palmer, a wise and valiant gentleman, a
great commander, and of much experience in sea causes,
being appoynted by the queens majesties counsell, to goe
for generall of a fleete for the coast of Spaine, anno 1583,
submitting himselfe to their lordships pleasure, excused
the charge, saying, that his trayning up had beene in the
narrow seas; and that of the other he had little experience:
and therefore was in dutie bound to intreate their honours
to make choice of some other person, that was better ac-
quainted and experimented in those seas; that her majestie
and their lordships might be the better served. His
modestie and discretion is doubtlesse to be had in remembrance and great estimation; for the ambition of
many which covet the command of fleetes, and places of
government (not knowing their compasse, nor how, nor
what to command) doe purchase to themselves shame;
and losse to those that employ them: being required in a
Parts required in a commander at sea.
commander at sea, a sharpe wit, a good understanding,
experience in shipping, practise in management of sea
business, knowledge in navigation, and in command. I
hold it much better to deserve it, and not to have it, then
to have it not deserving it.

SECTION IV.

THE fruits and inconveniences of the latter we daily partake of, to our losse and dishonor. As in the fleete that
The losse of the Burdieux fleete anno 1592.
went for Burdieux, anno 1592, which had six gallant ships
for wafters. At their going out of Plimouth, the vice-
admirall, that should have beene starnmost of all, was the
headmost, and the admirall the last, and he that did exe-

cute the office of the vice-admirall, lanching off into the
sea, drew after him the greater part of the fleete, and night
comming on, and both bearing lights, caused a separation: so that the head had a quarter of the bodie, and
the fleete three quarters, and he that should goe before,
came behinde. Whereof ensued, that the three parts
meeting with a few Spanish men of warre, wanting their
head, were a prey unto them. For the vice-admirall, and
other wafters, that should be the shepheards to guard
and keepe their flocke, and to carry them in safetie before
them, were headmost, and they the men who made most
hast to flie from the wolfe. Whereas if they had done as The cause.
they ought, in place of losse and infamie, they had gained
honor and reward.

This I have beene enformed of by the Spanish and
English, which were present in the occasion. And a ship
of mine, being one of the starnmost, freed her selfe, for
that shee was in warlike manner, with her false netting,
many pendents and streamers, and at least sixteen or eight-
teen peeces of artillery; the enemie thinking her to be a
wafter, or ship of warre, not one of them durst lay her
aboord: and this the master and company vaunted of at
their returne.

In the same voyage, in the river of Burdieux (as is
credibly reported), if the six wafters had kept together,
they had not onely not received domage, but gotten much
honour and reputation. For the admirall of the Spanish The weak-
armado, was a Flemish shippe of not above 130 tunnes, enemy.
and the rest flie-boates[1] and small shipping, for the most
part.

And although there were twenty-two sayle in all, what
manner of ships they were, and how furnished and appoynted, is well knowne, with the difference.

---

[1] Boats built for speed (?) or perhaps from the Dutch *Filibote.*

Sect. IV.

The voyage
of Sir John
Hawkins
anno 1590.

In the fleete of her majestie, under the charge of my father Sir John Hawkins, anno 1590, upon the coast of Spaine, the vice-admirall being a head one morning, where his place was to be a sterne, lost us the taking of eight men of warre loaden with munition, victuals, and provisions, for the supplie of the souldiers in Brittaine : and although they were seven or eight leagues from the shore, when our vice-admirall began to fight with them, yet for that the rest of our fleete were some four, some five leagues, and some more distant from them, when we beganne to give chase, the Spaniards recovered into the harbour of Monge, before our admirall could come up to give direction; yet well beaten, with losse of above two hundreth men, as they themselves confessed to me after.

And doubtlesse, if the wind had not over-blowne, and that to follow them I was forced to shut all my lower ports, the ship I undertooke doubtles had never endured to come to the port; but being doubble fli-boates, and all of good sayle, they bare for their lives, and we what we could to follow and fetch them up.

Sir Richard
Greenfield
at Flores.

In this poynt, at the Ile of Flores, Sir Richard Greenfield got eternall honour and reputation of great valour, and of an experimented souldier, chusing rather to sacrifice his life, and to passe all danger whatsoever, then to fayle in his obligation, by gathering together those which had remained a shore in that place, though with the hazard of his ship and companie; and rather we ought to imbrace an honourable death, then to live with infamie and dishonour, by fayling in dutie; and I account, that he and his country got much honor in that occasion; for one ship, and of the second sort of her majesties, sustained the force of all the fleete of Spain, and gave them to understand, that they be impregnible, for having bought deerely the boording of her, divers and sundry times, and with many

joyntly, and with a continuall fight of fourteen or sixteen
houres, at length leaving her without any mast standing, and
like a logge in the seas, shee made, notwithstanding, a most
honourable composition of life and libertie for above two
hundreth and sixtie men, as by the pay-booke appeareth :
which her majestie of her free grace, commanded, in recompence of their service, to be given to every one his six
moneths wages. All which may worthily be written in our
chronicles in letters of gold, in memory for all posterities,
some to beware, and others, by their example in the like
occasions, to imitate the true valour of our nation in these
ages.

In poynt of Providence, which captaine Vavisor, in the
Foresight,[1] gave also good proofe of his valour, in casting
about upon the whole fleete, notwithstanding the greatnesse and multitude of the Spanish armado, to yeeld that
succour which he was able; although some doe say, and I
consent with them, that the best valour is to obey, and to
follow the head, seeme that good or bad which is commanded. For God himselfe telleth us, that obedience is
better than sacrifice. Yet in some occasions, where there
is difficultie or impossibilitie to know what is commanded,

---

[1] In the list of seven ships composing Lord Thomas Howard's fleet,
we find the *Foresight*, Captain Vavasour. He deserves great credit for
attempting to yield what succour he was able to the gallant Sir R.
Greenville, whose brave defence has been already alluded to in page 10.
One other vessel followed, or perhaps set, the example : the *George
Noble*, of London, falling under the lee of the *Revenge*, asked Sir
Richard if he had anything to command him ; but as he was one of the
victuallers and but of small force, Sir Richard bid him shift for himself, and leave him to his fortune. Lediard adds in a note, that it is
more than probable had all the other vessels behaved with the same
vigour and resolution as Sir Richard and his company, they might
have given a good account of the Spanish fleet. It is to be regretted
the name of the commander of the *George Noble* is not recorded. We
know not which to admire most, his bravery in fully acting up to the
principle of " succouring a known friend in view," or the magnanimity
of Sir Richard in dismissing him from an unequal contest.

many times it is great discretion and obligation, judiciously to take hold of the occasion to yeeld succour to his associats, without putting himselfe in manifest danger. But to our voyage.

SECTION V.

BEING cleare of the race of Portland, the wind began to suffle[1] with fogge and misling rayne, and forced us to a short sayle, which continued with us three dayes; the wind never veering one poynt, nor the fogge suffering us to see the coast.

The third day in the fogge, we met with a barke of Dartmouth, which came from Rochell, and demanding of them if they had made any land, answered, that they had onely seene the Edie stone that morning, which lyeth thwart of the sound of Plimouth, and that Dartmouth (as they thought) bare off us north north-east: which seemed strange unto us; for we made account that we were thwart of Exmouth. Within two houres after, the weather beganne to cleare up, and we found ourselves thwart of the Berry, and might see the small barke bearing into Torbay, having over-shot her port; which error often happeneth to those that make the land in foggie weather, and use not good diligence by sound, by lying off the land, and other circumstances, to search the truth; and is cause of the losse of many a ship, and the sweet lives of multitudes of men.[2]

That evening we anchored in the range of Dartmouth, till the floud was spent; and the ebbe come, wee set sayle

---

[1] *Souffler*—to blow.

[2] It is still unfortunately too much the custom to risk the loss of ship and "sweet lives," by neglecting the use of the lead.

againe. And the next morning early, being the 26th of
Aprill, wee harboured our selves in Plimouth.

My ship at an anchor, and I ashore, I presently dispatched a messenger to London, to advise my father, Sir
John Hawkins, what had past: which, not onely to him,
but to all others, that understood what it was, seemed
strange; that the wind contrary, and the weather such as
it had beene, wee could be able to gaine Plimouth; but
doubtlesse, the *Daintie* was a very good sea ship, and excellent by the winde; which with the neap streames, and
our diligence to benefit our selves of all advantages, made
fezible that which almost was not to be beleeved.

And in this occasion, I found by experience, that one of
the principall parts required in a mariner that frequenteth
our coastes of England, is to cast his tydes, and to know
how they set from poynt to poynt, with the difference of
those in the channell from those of the shore.[1]

SECTION VI.

Now presently I began to prepare for my dispatch, and to
hasten my departure; and finding that my ship which I
expected from the Straites, came not, and that shee was
to goe to London to discharge, and uncertaine how long
shee might stay, I resolved to take another of mine owne
in her place, though lesser, called the *Hawke*, onely for a
victualler; purposing in the coast of Brasill, or in the
Straites,[2] to take out her men and victualls, and to cast her
off.

---

[1] The tide runs two or three hours later in the offing than in shore;
by attending to this, a vessel working down channel may gain great
advantage.

[2] Of Magellan.

SECTION VII.

WITH my continuall travell, the helpe of my good friends, and excessive charge (which none can easily beleeve, but those which have prooved it), towardes the end of May, I was readie to set sayle with my three ships, drawne out into the sound, and began to gather my company aboord.

The 28th of May (as I remember) began a storme of winde, westerly; the two lesser shippes presently harboured themselves, and I gave order to the master of the *Daintie* (called Hugh Cornish), one of the most sufficientest men of his coate, to bring her also into Catt-water, which he laboured to doe; but being neere the mouth of the harbour, and doubting least the anchor being weighed, the ship might cast the contrary way, and so run on some perill, entertained himselfe a while in laying out a warpe, and in the meane time, the wind freshing, and the ship riding by one anchor, brake the flooke of it, and so forced them to let fall another; by which, and by the warpe they had layd out, they rydd. The storme was such, as being within hearing of those upon the shore, we were not able by any meanes to send them succour, and the second day of the storme, desiring much to goe aboord, there joined with me captaine William Anthony, captaine John Ellis, and master Henry Courton, in a light horsman[1] which I had: all men exercised in charge, and of valour and sufficiencie, and from their youth bred up in businesse of the sea: which notwithstanding, and that wee laboured what we could, for the space of two houres against waves and wind, we could finde no possibilitie to accomplish our desire; which seene, we went aboord the other shippes,

A cruell storme.

And therein the effects of courage and advice.

---

[1] Probably what is now called a " gig"; a fast-pulling boat.

and put them in the best securitie wee could. Thus busied,
we might see come driving by us the mayne mast of the
Daintie, which made me to feare the worst, and so hasted
a shore, to satisfie my longing.

And comming upon Catt-downe, wee might see the ship
heave and sett, which manifestly shewed the losse of the
mast onely, which was well imployed; for it saved the ship,
men, and goods. For had shee driven a ships length
more, shee had (no doubt) beene cast away; and the men
in that place could not chuse but run into danger.

Comming to my house to shift me (for that we were all
wett to the skinne), I had not well changed my clothes,
when a servant of mine, who was in the pynace at my
comming ashore, enters almost out of breath, with newes,
that shee was beating upon the rocks, which though I
knew to be remedilesse, I put my selfe in place where I
might see her, and in a little time after shee sunk downe
right. These losses and mischances troubled and grieved,
but nothing daunted me; for common experience taught
me, that all honourable enterprises are accompanied with
difficulties and daungers; *Si fortuna me tormenta; Esperança me contenta :*[2] of hard beginnings, many times
come prosperous and happy events. And although, a well-
willing friend wisely foretold me them to be presages of
future bad successe, and so disswaded me what lay in him
with effectual reasons, from my pretence, yet the hazard
of my credite, and danger of disreputation, to take in hand
that which I should not prosecute by all meanes possible,
was more powerfull to cause me to goe forwardes, then his
grave good counsell to make me desist. And so the
storme ceasing, I beganne to get in the *Daintie,* to mast
her a-new, and to recover the *Fancy,* my pynace, which,

---

[2] Obviously a phrase of the period. Ancient Pistol is made to say·
" Si fortuna me contenta, spero me contenta."

with the helpe and furtherance of my wives father, who supplyed all my wants, together with my credit (which I thanke God was unspotted), in ten dayes put all in his former estate, or better. And so once againe, in Gods name, I brought my shippes out into the sound, the wind being easterly, and beganne to take my leave of my friends, and of my dearest friend, my second selfe, whose unfeyned teares had wrought me into irresolution, and sent some other in my roome, had I not considered that he that is in the daunce, must needs daunce on, though he doe but hopp, except he will be a laughing stocke to all the lookers on : so remembering that many had their eyes set upon me, with diverse affections, as also the hope of good successe (my intention being honest and good), I shut the doore to all impediments, and mine eare to all contrary counsell, and gave place to voluntary banishment from all that I loved and esteemed in this life, with hope thereby better to serve my God, my prince, and countrie, then to encrease my tallent any way.[1]

And so began to gather my companie aboord, which occupied my good friends and the justices of the towne two dayes, and forced us to search all lodgings, tavernes, and ale-houses. (For some would be ever taking their leave and never depart):[3] some drinke themselves so drunke, that except they were carried aboord, they of themselves were not able to goe one steppe : others, knowing the necessity of the time, fayned themselves sicke : others, to be indebted to their hostes, and forced me to ransome them ; one, his chest ; another, his sword ; another, his

---

[2] Familiar as we are with the present resources of the dockyard at Plymouth, we can hardly estimate the firmness that could bear up against such mischances ; of this stuff were the founders of the British naval power composed.

[3] Now fitted the halter, now traversed the cart,
And often took leave yet was loath to depart.
The Thief and the Cordelier.—Prior.

shirts; another, his carde[4] and instruments for sea: and others, to benefit themselves of the imprest given them, absented themselves, making a lewd living in deceiving all, whose money they could lay hold of; which is a scandall too rife amongst our sea-men; by it they committing three great offences: 1, Robbery of the goods of another person; 2, breach of their faith and promise; 3, and hinderance (with losse of time) unto the voyage; all being a common injury to the owners, victuallers, and company; which many times hath beene an utter overthrow and undoing to all in generall. An abuse in our common-wealth necessarily to be reformed; and as a person that hath both seene, and felt by experience, these inconveniences, I wish it to be remedied; for, I can but wonder, that the late lord high admirall of England, the late Earle of Cumberland; and the Lord Thomas Howard, now Earle of Suffolke, being of so great authoritie, having to their cost and losse so often made experience of the inconveniences of these lewd proceedings, have not united their goodnesses and wisedomes to redress this dis-loyall and base absurditie of the vulgar.[5]

Master Thomas Candish,[6] in his last voyage, in the sound of Plimmouth, being readie to set sayle, complained unto me, that persons which had absented themselves in

---

[4] Chart, or perhaps card for reducing the courses and distances:—

> *Second Witch.* I will give thee a wind.
> *First Witch.* Thou art kind.
> *Third Witch.* And I another.
> *First Witch.* I myself have all the other,
>   And the very ports they blow,
>   All the quarters that they know;
>   I' the shipman's card.   —*Macbeth.*

[5] The seaman of 1600 appears to have differed very little from the seaman of 1800. Let us hope that the present race will discountenance such "lewd proceedings."

[6] Thomas Cavendish, one of the early circumnavigators.

imprests, had cost him above a thousand and five hundred pounds: these varlets, within a few dayes after his departure, I saw walking the streets of Plimouth, whom the justice had before sought for with great diligence; and without punishment. And therefore it is no wonder that others presume to doe the like. *Impunitas peccandi illecebra.*

Master George Reymond.   The like complaint made master George Reymond; and in what sort they dealt with me is notorious, and was such, that if I had not beene provident to have had a third part more of men then I had need of, I had beene forced to goe to the sea unmanned; or to give over my voyage. And many of my company, at sea, vaunted how they had cosoned the Earle of Cumberland, master Candish, master Reymond, and others; some of five poundes, some of ten, some of more, and some of lesse. And truely, I thinke, my voyage prospered the worse, for theirs and other lewd persons company, which were in my ship; which, I thinke, might be redressed by some extraordinary, severe, and present justice, to be executed on the offenders by the justice in that place where they should be found. And for finding them, it were good that all captaines, and masters of shippes, at their departure out of the port, should give unto the head justice, the names and signes of all their runnawayes, and they presently to dispatch to the nigher ports the advise agreeable, where meeting with them, without further delay or processe, to use martial law upon them. Without doubt, seeing the law once put in execution, they and all others would be terrified from such villanies.

The inconvenience of imprests.   It might be remedied also by utter taking away of all imprests, which is a thing lately crept into our commonwealth, and in my opinion, of much more hurt then good unto all; and although my opinion seeme harsh, it being a deed of charitie to helpe the needy (which I wish ever to

be exercised, and by no meanes will contradict), yet for Sect. vii.
that such as goe to the sea (for the most part) consume
that money lewdly before they depart (as common experience teacheth us) : and when they come from sea, many
times come more beggerly home then when they went
forth, having received and spent their portion before they
imbarked themselves; and having neither rent nor main-
tenance more then their travell, to sustaine themselves,
are forced to theeve, to cozen, or to runne away in debt.
Besides, many times it is an occasion to some to lye upon
a voyage a long time ; whereas, if they had not that imprest, they might perhaps have gayned more in another
imployment, and have beene at home agayne, to save that
which they waite for. For these, and many more weightie
reasons, I am still bold, to maintaine my former assertions.

Those onely used in his majesties shippes I comprehend The true use of imprests.
not in this my opinion : neither the imprests made to
married men, which would be given to their wives monethly
in their absence, for their reliefe. For that is well
knowne, that all which goe to the sea now a-dayes, are
provided of foode, and house-roome, and all things
necessary, during the time of their voyage; and, in all
long voyages, of apparell also : so that nothing is to be
spent during the voyage. That money which is wont
to be cast away in imprestes, might be imployed in
apparell, and necessaries at the sea, and given to those
that have need, at the price it was bought, to be deducted
out of their shares or wages at their returne, which is
reasonable and charitable. This course taken, if any
would runne away, in Gods name fare him well.

Some have a more colourable kinde of cunning to abuse
men, and to sustaine themselves. Such will goe to sea
with all men, and goe never from the shore. For as long
as boord wages last, they are of the company, but those
taking end, or the ship in readinesse, they have one ex-

cuse or other, and thinke themselves no longer bound, but whilst they receive money, and then plucke their heads out of the coller.   An abuse also worthie to be reformed.[7]

SECTION VIII.

THE greater part of my companie gathered aboord, I set sayle the 12th of June 1593, about three of the clocke in the afternoon, and made a bourd or two off and in, wayting the returne of my boat, which I had sent a-shore, for dispatch of some businesse : which being come aboord, and all put in order, I looft[1] near the shore, to give my farewell to all the inhabitants of the towne, whereof the most part were gathered together upon the Howe, to shew their gratefull correspondency, to the love and zeale which I, my father, and predecessors, have ever borne to that place, as to our naturall and mother towne.   And first with my noyse of trumpets, after with my waytes,[2] and then with my other musicke, and lastly, with the artillery of my shippes, I made the best signification I could of a kinde farewell.   This they answered with the waytes of the towne, and the ordinance on the shore, and with shouting of voyces; which with the fayre evening and silence of the night, were heard a great distance off.   All which taking The conse- end, I sent instructions and directions to my other ships. quence of instructions Which is a poynt of speciall importance; for that I have at departure seene commanders of great name and reputation, by neglect and omission of such solemnities, to have runne into

---

[7] Some such long-shore fellows are still to be met with.
[1] From the Dutch word *loeven*, to ply to windward.
[2] The " waytes" seem to have been either music played during the setting of the watch, or occasionally, to show that a look-out was kept. *Guetter* (?)

many inconveniences, and thereby have learnt the necessitie of it. Whereby I cannot but advise all such as shall
have charge committed unto them, ever before they depart
out of the port, to give unto their whole fleete, not onely
directions for civill government, but also where, when, and
how to meete, if they should chance to loose company, and
the signes how to know one another a-far off, with other
poynts and circumstances, as the occasions shall minister
matter different, at the discretion of the wise commander.[3]

But some may say unto me, that in all occasions it is
not convenient to give directions: for that if the enemy
happen upon any of the fleete, or that there be any treacherous person in the company, their designments may be
discovered, and so prevented.

To this I answere, that the prudent governour, by good
consideration may avoyde this, by publication of that
which is good and necessarie for the guide of his fleete
and people; by all secret instructions, to give them sealed,
and not to be opened, but comming to a place appoynted
(after the manner of the Turkish direction to the Bashawes,
who are their generalls); and in any eminent perill to cast
them by the boord, or otherwise to make away with them.
For he that setteth sayle, not giving directions in writing
to his fleete, knoweth not, if the night or day following, he
may be separated from his company; which happeneth
sometimes: and then, if a place of meeting be not knowne,
he runneth in danger not to joyne them together agayne.

And for places of meeting, when seperation happeneth,
I am of opinion, to appoynt the place of meeting in such a
height, twentie, or thirtie, or fortie leagues off the land, or
iland. East or west is not so fitting, if the place affoord
it, as some sound betwixt ilands, or some iland, or harbour.

---

[3] The use of private signals and the appointment of a place of ren-
dezvous, may perhaps date from this period.

It may be alleged in contradiction, and with probable reason, that it is not fit for a fleete to stay in a harbour for one ship, nor at an anchor at an iland, for being discovered, or for hinderance of their voyage.

Answered.
Yet it is the best; for when the want is but for one or two ships, a pynace or ship may wayte the time appoynted and remaine with direction for them. But commonly one ship, though but a bad sayler, maketh more haste then a whole fleete, and is at the meeting place first, if the accident be not very important.

The place of meeting, if it might be, would be able to give, at the least, refreshing of water and wood.

SECTION IX.

LANCHING out into the channell, the wind being at east and by south, and east south-east, which blowing hard, and a flood in hand, caused a chapping sea, and my viceadmirall bearing a good sayle made some water, and shooting off a peece of ordinance, I edged towardes her, to know the cause; who answered me, that they had sprung a great leake, and that of force they must returne into the sound; which seeing to be necessary, I cast about, where anchoring, and going aboord, presently found, that betwixt wind and water, the calkers had left a seame uncalked, which being filled up with pitch only, the sea labouring that out, had been sufficient to have sunk her in short space, if it had not beene discovered in time.

False calking.

And truely there is little care used now adaies amongst our countrimen in this profession, in respect of that which was used in times past, and is accustomed in France, in Spaine, and in other parts. Which necessitie will cause to be reformed in time, by assigning the portion that every workeman is to calke; that if there be damage through his default, he may be forced to contribute towards the losse occasioned through his negligence.

And for more securitie I hold it for a good custome used For prevention thereof. in some parts, in making an end of calking and pitching the ship, the next tide to fill her with water, which will undoubtedly discover the defect, for no pitcht place without calking, can suffer the force and peaze[1] of the water. In neglect whereof, I have seene great damage and danger to ensue. The *Arke Royall* of his majesties, may serve Example. for an example : which put all in daunger at her first going to the sea, by a trivuell hole left open in the post,[2] and covered only with pitch. In this point no man can be too circumspect, for it is the security of ship, men and goods.[3]

SECTION X.

THIS being remedied, I set sayle in the morning, and ran south-west, till we were cleere of Ushent; and then south south-west, till we were some hundred leagues off, where wee met with a great hulke, of some five or six hundred tunnes, well appointed, the which my company (as is naturall to all mariners), presently would make a prize, and loaden with Spaniard's goods; and without speaking to her, wished that the gunner might shoote at her, to cause her to amaine.[1] Which is a bad custome received and used of Advise for shooting at sea. many ignorant persons, presently to gun at all whatsoever they discover, before they speake with them; being con-

[1] Weight—*peso*. (Spanish.) [2] Stern-post.

[3] A trivial hole left open, or a treenail not driven by a careless workman, may cause the failure of an important expedition ; or at least cause great mischief and discomfort : which neglect still occasionally happens.

[1] *Amener le pavillon*—to haul down the ensign.

trary to all discipline, and many times is cause of dissention betwixt friends, and the breach of amitie betwixt princes; the death of many, and sometimes losse of shippes and all, making many obstinate, if not desperate; whereas in using common courtesie, they would better bethinke themselves, and so with ordinarie proceeding (justified by reason, and the custome of all well disciplined people) might perhaps many times breede an increase of amitie, a succour to necessity, and excuse divers inconveniencies and sutes, which have impoverished many : for it hath chanced

Sundry mis-
chances for
neglect
thereof.
by this errour, that two English ships, neither carrying flag for their perticular respects, to change each with other a dozen payre of shott, with hurt to both, being after too late to repent their follie. Yea a person of credit hath told mee, that two English men of warre in the night, have layed each other aboord willingly, with losse of many men and dammage to both, onely for the fault of not speaking one to the other; which might seeme to carrie with it some excuse, if they had beene neere the shore, or that the one had beene a hull,[2] and the other under sayle, in feare shee should have escaped, not knowing what shee was (though in the night it is no wisedome to bourd with any ship), but in the maine sea, and both desiring to joyne, was a sufficient declaration that both were seekers : and therefore by day or night, he that can speake with the ship hee seeth, is bound, upon payne to bee reputed voyd of good govern-

Object.
ment, to hayle her before hee shoote at her. Some man may say, that in the meanetime, shee might gaine the

Answer.
winde : in such causes, and many others, necessity giveth exception to all lawes; and experience teacheth what is fit to be done.

Master
Thomas
Hampton.
Master Thomas Hampton, once generall of a fleete of wafters, sent to Rochell, anno 1585, with secret instructions, considering (and as a man of experience), wisely

[2] Under bare poles.

understanding his place and affaires, in like case shut his
eare to the instigations and provocations of the common
sort, preferring the publique good of both kingdomes before his owne reputation with the vulgar people: and as
another Fabius Maximus, *cunctando restituit rem, non po-
nendo rumores ante salutem.* The French kings fleete The French
comming where he was, and to winde-ward of him, all his fleete salute
company were in an uproare; for that hee would not one another.
shoote presently at them, before they saw their intention:
wherein had beene committed three great faults: the first
and principall, the breach of amitie betwixt the princes and
kingdomes: the second, the neglect of common curtesie, in
shooting before hee had spoken with them: and the third,
in shooting first, being to lee-wards of the other.

Besides, there was no losse of reputation, because the
French kings fleete was in his owne sea; and therefore for
it to come to winde-ward, or the other to go to lee-ward,
was but that which in reason was required, the kingdomes
being in peace and amitie. For every prince is to be acknowledged and respected in his jurisdiction, and where
hee pretendeth it to be his.

The French generall likewise seemed well to understand
what he had in hand; for though he were farre superiour
in forces, yet used hee the termes which were required;
and comming within speech, hayled them, and asked if
there were peace or warre betwixt England and France:
whereunto answere being made that they knew of no other
but peace, they saluted each other after the maner of the
sea, and then came to an anchor all together, and as friends
visited each other in their ships.

One thing the French suffered (upon what occasion or The English
ground I know not), that the English alwayes carried their their flag in
flag displayed; which in all other partes and kingdomes is seas.
not permitted: at least, in our seas, if a stranger fleete
meete with any of his majesties ships, the forraigners are

c 2

bound to take in their flags, or his majesties ships to force them to it, though thereof follow the breach of peace or whatsoever discommodity. And whosoever should not be jealous in this point, hee is not worthy to have the commaund of a cock-boat committed unto him : yea no stranger ought to open his flag in any port of England, where there is any shipp or fort of his majesties, upon penaltie to loose his flagg, and to pay for the powder and shott spend upon him. Yea, such is the respect to his majesties shippes in all places of his dominions, that no English ship displayeth the flagge in their presence, but runneth the like daunger, except they be in his majesties service; and then they are in predicament of the kings ships. Which good discipline in other kingdomes is not in that regard as it ought, but sometimes through ignorance, sometimes of malice, neglect is made of that dutie and acknowledgement which is required, to the cost and shame of the ignorant and malicious.

The honour of his majesties ships.

Practised at the comming in of King Philip into England.
In queen Maries raigne, king Philip of Spaine, comming to marry with the queene, and meeting with the royall navie of England, the lord William Haward, high admirall of England, would not consent, that the king in the narrow seas should carrie his flagge displayed, untill he came into the harbour of Plimouth.

And in the passage of Dona Anna de Austria.
I being of tender yeares, there came a fleete of Spaniards of above fiftie sayle of shippes, bound for Flaunders, to fetch the queen, Donna Anna de Austria, last wife to Philip the second of Spaine, which entred betwixt the iland and the maine, without vayling their top-sayles, or taking in of their flags : which my father, Sir John Hawkins, (admirall of a fleete of her majesties shippes, then ryding in Cattwater), perceiving, commanded his gunner to shoot at the flagge of the admirall, that they might thereby see their error : which, notwithstanding, they persevered arrogantly to keepe displayed; whereupon the gunner at the next

shott, lact[3] the admirall through and through, whereby the
Spaniards finding that the matter beganne to grow to
earnest, tooke in their flags and top-sayles, and so ranne
to an anchor.

The generall presently sent his boat, with a principall
personage to expostulate the cause and reason of that proceeding; but my father would not permit him to come
into his ship, nor to heare his message; but by another
gentleman commanded him to returne, and to tell his
generall, that in as much as in the queenes port and
chamber, he had neglected to doe the acknowledgment
and reverence which all owe unto her majestie (especially
her ships being present), and comming with so great a
navie, he could not but give suspition by such proceeding
of malicious intention, and therefore required him, that
within twelve houres he should depart the port, upon paine
to be held as a common enemy, and to proceed against him
with force.

Which answere the generall understanding, presently
imbarked himselfe in the same boat, and came to the
Jesus of Lubecke, and craved licence to speake with my
father; which at the first was denyed him, but upon the
second intreatie was admitted to enter the ship, and to
parley. The Spanish generall began to demand if there
were warres betwixt England and Spaine; who was answered, that his arrogant manner of proceeding, usurp-
ing the queene his mistresses right, as much as in him lay,
had given sufficient cause for breach of the peace, and that
he purposed presently to give notice thereof to the queene
and her counsell, and in the meane time, that he might
depart. Whereunto the Spanish generall replyed, that he
knew not any offence he had committed, and that he
would be glad to know wherein he had misbehaved him-

---

[3] Probably derived from *lâcher un coup :* to fire a shot.

Sect. XI.   selfe.   My father seeing he pretended to escape by ignorance, beganne to put him in mind of the custome of
Spaine and Fraunce, and many other parts, and that he
could by no meanes be ignorant of that, which was common
right to all princes in their kingdomes; demanding, if a
fleete of England should come into any port of Spaine (the
kings majesties ships being present), if the English should
carry their flags in the toppe, whether the Spanish would
not shoot them downe; and if they persevered, if they
would not beate them out of their port.   The Spanish
generall confessed his fault, pleaded ignorance not malice,
and submitted himselfe to the penaltie my father would
impose: but intreated, that their princes (through them)
might not come to have any jarre.   My father a while
(as though offended), made himselfe hard to be intreated,
but in the end, all was shut up by his acknowledgement,
and the auncient amitie renewed, by feasting each other
aboord and ashore.

As also in   The self same fleete, at their returne from Flaunders,
her re-
passage.   meeting with her majesties shippes in the Channell, though
sent to accompany the aforesaid queene, was constrained
during the time that they were with the English, to vayle
their flagges, and to acknowledge that which all must doe
that passe through the English seas.[4]   But to our voyage.

SECTION XI.

COMMING within the hayling of the hulke, wee demanded
whence shee was?   Whether shee was bound?   And what
her loading?   Shee answered, that shee was of Denmarke,

------

[4] In those days the principle of "mare clausum" was acted upon;
now it is "mare liberum" everywhere.

comming from Spaine, loaden with salt; we willed her to strike her top-sayles, which shee did, and shewed us her charter-parties, and billes of loading, and then saluted us, as is the manner of the sea, and so departed.

SECTION XII.

THE next day the wind became southerly, and somewhat too much, and my shipps being all deepe loaden, beganne to feel the tempest, so that wee not able to lye by it, neither a hull nor a try, and so with an easie sayle bare up before the wind, with intent to put into Falmouth; but God was pleased that comming within tenne leagues of Sylly, the wind vered to the north-east, and so we went on in our voyage.

Thwart of the Flees of Bayon,[1] wee met with a small ship of master Wattes, of London, called the *Elizabeth*, which came out of Plimouth some eyght dayes after us; of whom wee enformed ourselves of some particularities, and wrote certaine letters to our friends, making relation of what had past till that day, and so tooke our farewell each of the other. The like we did with a small carvell[2] of Plimouth, which wee mett in the height of the rocke in Portingall.[3]

From thence wee directed our course to the ilands of Madera; and about the end of June, in the sight of the ilands, we descryed a sayle some three leagues to the east-wards, and a league to windward of us, which by her manner of working, and making, gave us to understand,

---

[1] Probably the islands that lie off Bayona, near Vigo.
[2] *Carabela*, (Spanish) a small vessel so called.
[3] Still well known as the rock of Lisbon.

Sect. xii.   that shee was one of the kings frigatts; for shee was long
and snugg, and spread a large clewe, and standing to the
west-wards, and wee to the east-wards to recover her wake,
when we cast about, shee beganne to vere shete, and to
goe away lasking;[4] and within two glasses, it was plainely
seene that shee went from us, and so we followed on our
course, and shee seeing that, presently stroke her top-
sayles, which our pynace perceiving, and being within shot
continued the chase, till I shot off a peece and called her
away; which fault many runne into, thinking to get
thereby, and sometimes loose themselves by being too bold
to venture from their fleete; for it was impossible for us,
being too leeward, to take her, or to succour our owne,
shee being a ship of about two hundreth tunnes.

The dutie of   And pynaces to meddle with ships, is to buy repentance
pynaces.   at too deare a rate. For their office is, to wayte upon their
fleete, in calmes (with their oares) to follow a chase, and in
occasions to anchor neere the shore, when the greater
ships cannot, without perill; above all, to be readie and
obedient at every call.   Yet will I not, that any wrest my
meaning; neither say I, that a pynace, or small ship
armed, may not take a great ship unarmed; for daily
experience teacheth us the contrary.[5]

The Madera   The Madera Ilands are two : the greater, called La
Ilands.   Madera, and the other, Porto Santo; of great fertilitie,
and rich in sugar, conserves, wine, and sweet wood, whereof
they take their name.   Other commodities they yeeld, but
these are the principall.   The chiefe towne and port is on
the souther side of the Madera, well fortified; they are
subject to the kingdome of Portingall; the inhabitants
and garrison all Portingalles.

----

[4] With the wind abeam.

[5] Although Sir Richard thinks it necessary to hold such prudent
language, we have little doubt he was just the man to attempt to take
a large ship armed or unarmed, in a " pynace."

The third of July, we past along the Ilands of Canaria, which have the name of a kingdome, and containe these seaven ilands: Grand Canaria, Tenerifa, Palma, Gomera, Lancerota, Forteventura, and Fierro. These ilands have abundance of wine, sugar, conserves, orcall,[6] pitch, iron, and other commodities, and store of cattell, and corne, but that a certaine worme, called *gorgosho*, breedeth in it, which eateth out the substance, leaving the huske in manner whole. The head iland, where the justice, which they call *Audiencia,* is resident, and whither all sutes have their appealation and finall sentence, is the grand Canaria, although the Tenerifa is held for the better and richer iland, and to have the best sugar; and the wine of the Palma is reputed for the best. The pitch of these ilands melteth not with the sunne, and therefore is proper for the higher works of shipping. Betwixt Forteventura and Lancerota is a goodly sound, fit for a meeting place for any fleete; where is good anchoring and aboundance of many sorts of fish. There is water to be had in most of these ilands, but with great vigilance. For the naturalls of them are venturous and hardie, and many times clime up and downe the steepe rockes and broken hills, which seeme impossible, which I would hardly have beleeved, had I not seene it, and that with the greatest art and agilitie that may be. Their armes, for the most part, are launces of nine or ten foote, with a head of a foote and halfe long, like unto boare-spears, save that the head is somewhat more broad.

Two things are famous in these ilands, the Pike of Tenerifa, which is the highest land in my judgement that I have seene, and men of credit have told they have seene it more than fortie leagues off.[7] It is like unto a sugar loafe, and continually covered with snow, and

---

[6] *Orchilla*—a lichen yielding a purple dye.

[7] The latest measurement, by Captain Vidal, R.N., makes the height of the Peak 12,370 feet.

placed in the middest of a goodly vallie, most fertile, and temperate round about it. Out of which, going up to the Pike, the colde is so great, that it is insufferable, and going downe to the townes of the iland, the heate seemeth most extreame, till they approach neere the coast. The other is a tree in the iland of Fierro, which some write and affirme, with the dropping of his leaves, to give water for the sustenance of the whole iland, which I have not seene, although I have beene on shoare on the iland;[8] but those which have seene it, have recounted this mysterie differently to that which is written; in this manner: that this tree is placed in the bottome of a valley, ever florishing with broad leaves, and that round about it are a multitude of goodly high pynes, which over-top it, and as it seemeth were planted by the divine providence to preserve it from sunne and wind. Out of this valley ordinarily rise every day great vapours and exhalations, which by reason that the sunne is hindered to worke his operation, with the heighte of the mountaines towards the south-east, convert themselves into moysture, and so bedewe all the trees of the valley, and from those which over-top this tree, drops down the dewe upon his leaves, and so from his leaves into a round well of stone, which the naturalls of the land have made to receive the water, of which the people and cattle have great reliefe; but sometimes it raineth, and then the inhabitants doe reserve water for many days to come, in their cisternes and tynaxes,[9] which is that they drinke of, and wherewith they principally sustaine themselves.

The citty of the Grand Canaria, and chiefe port, is on the west side of the iland; the head towne and port of Tenerifa is towards the south part, and the port and towne of the Palma and Gomera, on the east side.

[8] The old voyagers were fond of dealing in the marvellous; our author is singularly free from this defect.

[9] We cannot trace the meaning of this word, unless it be a closed vessel, derived from the Anglo-Saxon *tynan*—to close. At Bermuda all the drinking water is preserved in tanks.

In Gomera, some three leagues south-ward from the towne, is a great river of water, but all these ilands are perilous to land in, for the seege[10] caused by the ocean sea, which always is forcible, and requireth great circumspection; whosoever hath not urgent cause, is either to goe to the east-wards, or the west-wards of all these ilands, as well to avoyd the calmes, which hinder sometimes eight or ten dayes sayling, as the contagion which their distemperature is wont to cause, and with it to breed calenturas, which wee call burning fevers. These ilands are sayd to be first discovered by a Frenchman, called John de Betancourt, about the year 1405.[11] They are now a kingdome subject to Spaine.

The first discoverers of these Ilands.

SECTION XIII.

BEING cleare of the ilands, wee directed our course for Cape Black,[1] and two howres before sunne set, we had sight of a carvell some league in the winde of us, which seemed to come from Gynea, or the ilands of Cape de Verde, and for that hee, which had the sery-watch,[2] neglected to look out, being to lee-ward of the ilands, and so out of hope of sight of any shipp, for the little trade and contrariety of the winde, that though a man will, from few places hee can recover the ilands. Comming from the south-wards, wee had the winde of her, and perhaps the possession also, whereof men of warre are to have particular care; for in an houre and place unlookt for, many times chance acci-

Note.

10 Further on written "sedge," surf (?)

11 The Fortunate islands were known before they were conquered by MM. Bethencourt, in the sixteenth century.

1 Although the difference between *black* and *white* be great, we think Cape Blanco is meant.

2 Probably the evening watch.

dents contrary to the ordinary course and custome; and to have younkers in the top continually, is most convenient and necessary, not onely for descrying of sayles and land, but also for any sudden gust or occasion that may be offered.[3]

Seeing my selfe past hope of returning backe, without some extraordinary accident, I beganne to set in order my companie and victuals. And for that to the south-wards of the Canaries is for the most part an idle navigation, I devised to keepe my people occupied, as well to continue them in health (for that too much ease in hott countries is neither profitable nor healthfull), as also to divert them from remembrance of their home, and from play, which breedeth many inconveniences, and other bad thoughts and workes which idleness is cause of;[4] and so shifting my companie, as the custome is, into starboord and larboord men, the halfe to watch and worke whilest the others slept and take rest; I limited the three dayes of the weeke, which appertayned to each, to be imploied in this manner; the one for the use and clensing of their armes, the other for roomeging, making of sayles, nettings, decking,[5] and defences for our shippes; and the third, for clensing their bodies, mending and making their apparell, and necessaries, which though it came to be practised but once in seaven dayes, for that the Sabboth is ever to be reserved for God alone, with the ordinary obligation which each person had besides, was many times of force to be omitted. And thus wee entertained our time with a fayre wind, and in few

---

[3] This has become a standing order in the service. Many a good prize has been made by sending a mast head man up before daylight.

[4] Most of us are familiar with Dr. Watts' lines,—

" For Satan finds some mischief still
For idle hands to do."

[5] Covering—the deck so called because it covers in the ship—
cubierta (Spanish).

dayes had sight of the land of Barbary, some dozen leagues to the northwards of Cape Blacke.

Before wee came to the Cape, wee tooke in our sayles, and made preparation of hookes and lines to fish. For in all that coast is great abundance of sundry kinds of fish, but especially of porgus, which we call breames; many Portingalls and Spaniards goe yearely thither to fish, as our country-men to the New-found-land, and within Cape Blacke have good harbour for reasonable shipping, where they dry their fish, paying a certaine easie tribute to the kings collector. In two houres wee tooke store of fish for that day and the next, but longer it would not keepe goode: and with this refreshing set sayle again, and directed our course betwixt the ilands of Cape de Verd and the Maine. These ilands are held to be scituate in one of the most unhealthiest climates of the world, and therefore it is wisedome to shunne the sight of them, how much more to make abode in them.

In two times that I have beene in them, either cost us the one halfe of our people, with fevers and fluxes of sundry kinds; some shaking, some burning, some partaking of both; some possesst with frensie, others with sloath, and in one of them it cost me six moneths sicknesse, with no small hazard of life; which I attribute to the distemperature of the ayre, for being within fourteene degrees of the equinoctiall lyne, the sunne hath great force all the yeare, and the more for that often they passe, two, three, and four yeares without rayne; and many times the earth burneth in that manner as a man well shodd, cannot endure to goe where the sunne shineth.

With which extreame heate the bodie fatigated, greedily desireth refreshing, and longeth the comming of the breze, which is the north-east winde, that seldome fayleth in the after-noone at foure of the clocke, or sooner; which comming cold and fresh, and finding the poores of the body open, and (for the most part) naked, penetrateth the very bones, and so causeth sudden distemperature, and sundry manners of sicknesse, as the subjects are divers whereupon they worke.

Departing out of the calmes of the ilands, and comming into the fresh breeze, it causeth the like, and I have seene within two dayes after that we have partaked of the fresh ayre, of two thousand men, above a hundred and fiftie have beene crazed in their health.

The remedie. The inhabitants of these ilands use a remedie for this, which at my first being amongst them, seemed unto me ridiculous; but since, time and experience hath taught to be grounded upon reason. And is, that upon their heads they weare a night-capp, upon it a montero,[6] and a hat over that, and on their bodies a sute of thicke cloth, and upon it a gowne, furred or lyned with cotton, or bayes, to defend them from the heate in that manner, as the inhabitants of cold countries, to guard themselves from the extreamitie of the colde. Which doubtlesse, is the best diligence that any man can use, and whosoever prooveth it, shall find himselfe lesse annoyed with the heate, then if he were thinly cloathed, for that where the cold ayre commeth, it peirceth not so subtilly.

The influence of the moone in hot countries. The moone also in this climate, as in the coast of Guyne, and in all hott countries, hath forcible operation in the body of man; and therefore, as the plannet most prejudiciall to his health, is to be shunned; as also not to sleepe in the open ayre, or with any scuttle or window open, whereby the one or the other may enter to hurt.

For a person of credit told me, that one night, in a river of Guyne, leaving his window open in the side of his cabin, the moone shining upon his shoulder, left him with such an extraordinary paine and furious burning in it, as

[6] *Montera*—a species of hat worn in Spain.

in above twentie houres, he was like to runne madde, but in fine, with force of medicines and cures, after long torment, he was eased.

Some I have heard say, and others write, that there is a starre which never seperateth it self from the moone, but a small distance; which is of all starres the most beneficiall to man.[7] For where this starre entreth with the moone, it maketh voyde her hurtfull enfluence, and where not, it is most perilous. Which, if it be so, is a notable secret of the divine Providence, and a speciall cause amongst infinite others, to move us to continuall thankesgiving; for that he hath so extraordinarily compassed and fenced us from infinite miseries, his most unworthie and ungratefull creatures.

Of these ilands are two pyles:[8] the one of them lyeth out of the way of trade, more westerly, and so little frequented; the other lyeth some fourscore leagues from the mayne, and containeth six in number, to wit: Saint Iago, Fuego, Mayo, Bonavisto, Sal, and Bravo.

They are belonging to the kingdome of Portingall, and inhabited by people of that nation, and are of great trade, by reason of the neighbour-hood they have with Guyne and Bynne;[9] but the principall is the buying and selling of negroes. They have store of sugar, salt, rice, cotton wool, and cotton-cloth, amber-greece, cyvit, oliphants teeth, brimstone, pummy stone, spunge, and some gold, but little, and that from the mayne.

Saint Iago is the head iland, and hath one citie and two townes, with their ports. The cittie called Saint Iago, whereof the iland hath his name, hath a garrison, and two fortes, scituated in the bottome of a pleasant valley, with a running streame of water passing through the middest of

---

[7] We apprehend the whole of this story to be "moonshine."
[8] Groups.   [9] Coast of Guinea and Bight of Benin.

it, whether the rest of the ilands come for justice, being the seat of the Audiencia, with his bishop.

The other townes are Playa, some three leagues to the eastwards of Saint Iago, placed on high, with a goodly bay, whereof it hath his name; and Saint Domingo, a small towne within the land. They are on the souther part of the iland, and have beene sacked sundry times in anno 1582, by Manuel Serades, a Portingall, with a fleete of French-men; in anno 1585, they were both burnt to the ground by the English, Sir Francis Drake being generall; and in anno 1596, Saint Iago was taken and sacked by the English, Sir Anthony Shyrley being generall.[10]

Sacked by Manuel Serades, Sir Francis Drake, and Sir Anthony Shyrley.

Fuego. The second iland is Fuego; so called, for that day and night there burneth in it a vulcan, whose flames in the night are seene twentie leagues off in the sea. It is by nature fortified in that sort, as but by one way is any accesse, or entrance into it, and there cannot goe up above two men a brest. The bread which they spend in these ilands, is brought from Portingall and Spaine, saving that which they make of rice, or of mayes, which wee call Guynne-wheate.

Bravo. The best watering is in the ile of Bravo, on the west part of the iland, where is a great river, but foule anchoring, as is in all these ilands, for the most part. The fruits are few, but substantiall, as palmitos, plantanos, patatos, and coco-nutts.

The Palmito The palmito is like to the date tree, and as I thinke a

[10] From the account in Lediard, it appears that Sir A. Shyrley failed in his object; but he deserves credit for effecting a safe retreat to his ships in the face of a superior force. The expedition under Sir F. Drake was successful. It is curious to notice how the titles of military rank have changed since those days. The troops were commanded by Christopher Carlisle, an experienced officer; under him Captain A. Powel, *Sergeant Major;* Captain M. Morgan, and Captain J. Sampson, *Corporals of the field.* (See p. 17, line 26.)

kinde of it, but wilde. In all parts of Afrique and
America they are found, and in some parts of Europe, and
in divers parts different. In Afrique, and in the West
Indies they are small, that a man may cut them with a
knife, and the lesser the better : but in Brazill, they are
so great, that with difficultie a man can fell them with an
axe, and the greater the better; one foote within the top
is profitable, the rest is of no value; and that which is to
be eaten is the pith, which in some is better, in some
worse.[12]

The plantane is a tree found in most parts of Afrique The
plantane. and America, of which two leaves are sufficient to cover a
man from top to toe. It beareth fruit but once, and then
dryeth away, and out of his roote sprouteth up others, new.
In the top of the tree is his fruit, which groweth in a great
bunch, in the forme and fashion of puddings, in some
more, in some lesse. I have seene in one bunch above
foure hundred plantanes, which have weighed above fourescore pound waight. They are of divers proportions, some
great, some lesser, some round, some square, some triangle,
most ordinarily of a spanne long, with a thicke skinne,
that peeleth easily from the meate; which is either white
or yellow, and very tender like butter, but no conserve is
better, nor of a more pleasing taste. For I never have
seene any man to whom they have bred mis-like, or done
hurt with eating much of them, as of other fruites.[13]

The best are those which ripen naturally on the tree, but
in most partes they cut them off in braunches, and hange
them up in their houses, and eate them as they ripe. For

[12] The terminal bud of the areca or cabbage palm, when boiled, makes
a delicate dish.
[13] This is a most valuable production : we believe it bears, on the
same area, a greater weight of food than any other vegetable. The
fruit of the plantain, *Musa sapientum*, is chiefly eaten cooked. The
banana, *Musa paradisiaca*, is eaten raw. There are many species,
almost all excellent.

the birds and vermine presently in ripning on the tree, are feeding on them. The best that I have seene are in Brasill, in an iland called Placentia, which are small, and round, and greene when they are ripe; whereas the others in ripning become yellow. Those of the West Indies and Guynne are great, and one of them sufficient to satisfie a man; the onely fault they have is, that they are windie. In some places they eate them in stead of bread, as in Panama, and other parts of Tierra Firme. They grow and prosper best when their rootes are ever covered with water; they are excellent in conserve, and good sodden in different manners, and dried on the tree, not inferior to suckett.[14]

The coco nutt is a fruit of the fashion of a hassell nutt, but that it is as bigge as an ordinary bowle, and some are greater. It hath two shells, the uttermost framed (as it were) of a multitude of threeds, one layd upon another, with a greene skinne over-lapping them, which is soft and thicke; the innermost is like to the shell of a hassell nutt in all proportion, saving that it is greater and thicker, and some more blacker. In the toppe of it is the forme of a munkies face, with two eyes, his nose, and a mouth. It containeth in it both meate and drinke; the meate white as milke, and like to that of the kernell of a nutt, and as good as almonds blancht, and of great quantitie: the water is cleare, as of the fountaine, and pleasing in taste, and somewhat answereth that of the water distilled of milke. Some say it hath a singular propertie in nature for conserving the smoothnesse of the skinne; and therefore in Spaine and Portingall, the curious dames doe ordinarily wash their faces and necks with it. If the holes of the shell be kept close, they keepe foure or six moneths good, and more; but if it be opened, and the water kept in the shell, in few dayes it turneth to vineger.

---

[14] *Succade*—preserved citron.

They grow upon high trees, which have no boughes; onely in the top they have a great cap of leaves, and under them groweth the fruite upon certaine twigs. And some affirme that they beare not fruite before they be above fortie yeares old, they are in all things like to the palme trees, and grow in many parts of Asia, Afrique, and America.[15] The shels of these nuts are much esteemed for drinking cups, and much cost and labour is bestowed upon them in carving, graving, and garnishing them, with silver, gold, and precious stones.

In the kingdome of Chile, and in Brasill, is another kinde of these, which they call coquillos, (as wee may interpret, little cocos) and are as big as wal-nuts; but round and smooth, and grow in great clusters; the trees in forme are all one, and the meate in the nut better, but they have no water.

Another kinde of great cocos groweth in the Andes of Peru, which have not the delicate meate nor drinke, which the others have, but within are full of almonds, which are placed as the graines in the pomegrannet, being three times bigger then those of Europe, and are much like them in tast.

In these ilands are cyvet-cats, which are also found in parts of Asia, and Afrique; esteemed for the civet they yeelde, and carry about them in a cod in their hinder parts, which is taken from them by force.

In them also are store of monkies, and the best pro- portioned that I have seene; and parrots, but of colour different to those of the West Indies; for they are of a russet or gray colour, and great speakers.

---

15 The cocoa nut palm is too well known to need description. All its parts are applied by the natives to innumerable uses. Few visitors to tropical countries but have been refreshed by a draught of cocoa nut water; always preserved cool by the thick husk.

SECTION XIV.

WITH a faire and large winde we continued our course, till we came within five degrees of the equinoctiall lyne, where the winde tooke us contrary by the south-west, about the twentie of Julie, but a fayre gale of wind and a smooth sea, so that wee might beare all a taunt:[1] and to advantage ourselves what wee might, wee stoode to the east-wards, being able to lye south-east and by south. The next day about nine of the clocke, my companie being gathered together to serve God, which wee accustomed to doe every morning and evening, it seemed unto me that the coulour of the sea was different to that of the daies past, and which is ordinarily where is deepe water; and so calling the captaine, and master of my ship, I told them that to my seeming the water was become very whitish, and that it made shewe of sholde water. Whereunto they made answere, that all the lynes in our shippes could not fetch ground: for wee could not be lesse then threescore and tenne leagues off the coast, which all that kept reckoning in the ship agreed upon, and my selfe was of the same opinion. And so wee applyed ourselves to serve God, but all the time that the service endured, my heart could not be at rest, and still me thought the water beganne to waxe whiter and whiter. Our prayers ended, I commanded a lead and a lyne to be brought, and heaving the lead in fourteene fathoms, wee had ground, which put us all into a maze, and sending men into the toppe, presently discovered the land of Guynne, some five leagues from us, very low land. I commanded a peece to be shott, and lay by the lee, till my other shippes came up. Which hayling us, wee demanded of them how farre they found them-

---

[1] *All sail set*—at present its signification is confined to a vessel rigged and ready for sea.

selves off the land; who answered, some threescore and
tenne, or fourescore leagues : when wee told them wee
had sounded and found but foureteene fathomes, and that
we were in sight of land, they began to wonder. But
having consulted what was best to be done, I caused
my shalop to be manned, which I towed at the sterne of
my ship continually, and sent her and my pynace a head to
sound, and followed them with an easie sayle, till we came
in seaven and six fathome water, and some two leagues
from the shore anchored, in hope by the sea, or by the
land to find some refreshing. The sea we found to be
barren of fish, and my boates could not discover any landing place, though a whole day they had rowed alongst the
coast, with great desire to set foote on shore, for that the
sedge was exceeding great and dangerous. Which experienced, wee set sayle, notwithstanding the contrarietie
of the winde, sometimes standing to the west-wards, some-
time to the east-wards, according to the shifting of the
wind.

SECTION XV.

HERE is to be noted, that the error which we fell into in
our accompts, was such as all men fall into where are currants that set east or west, and are not knowne; for that
there is no certaine rule yet practised for triall of the
longitude, as there is of the latitude, though some curious
and experimented of our nation, with whom I have had
conference about this poynt, have shewed me two or three
manner of wayes how to know it.[1]

1 It is still the custom to attribute all similar discordancies to the
effect of current. This is a simple if not very philosophical mode of
making the reckoning agree with observation. In this case, probably
both the reckoning of the ship and the position of the land on the chart
were faulty.

This, some years before, was the losse of the *Edward Cotton,* bound for the coast of Brasill, which taken with the winde contrary neere the lyne, standing to the eastwards, and making accompt to be fiftie or sixtie leagues off the coast, with all her sayles standing, came suddenly a ground upon the sholes of Madre-bomba, and so was cast away, though the most part of their company saved themselves upon raffes; but with the contagion of the countrie, and bad entreatie which the negros gave them, they died; so that there returned not to their country above three or foure of them.

But God Almightie dealt more mercifully with us, in shewing us our error in the day, and in time that wee might remedie it; to him be evermore glory for all.

This currant from the line equinoctiall, to twentie degrees northerly, hath great force, and setteth next of any thing east, directly upon the shore; which we found by this meanes: standing to the westwards, the wind southerly, when we lay with our ships head west, and by south, we gayned in our heith[2] more then if wee had made our way good west south-west; for that, the currant tooke us under the bow; but lying west, or west and by north, we lost more in twelve houres then the other way we could get in foure and twentie. By which plainly we saw, that the currant did set east next of any thing. Whether this currant runneth ever one way, or doth alter, and how, we could by no meanes understand, but tract of time and observation will discover this, as it hath done of many others in sundry seas.

The currant that setteth betwixt New-found-land and Spaine, runneth also east and west, and long time deceived many, and made some to count the way longer, and others shorter, according as the passage was speedie or slowe; not

---

[2] The term height is used for latitude; probably because the pole star was the principal object used to determine position.

knowing that the furtherance or hinderance of the currant was cause of the speeding or flowing of the way. And in sea cardes I have seene difference of above thirtie leagues betwixt the iland Tercera, and the mayne. And others have recounted unto me, that comming from the India's, and looking out for the ilands of Azores, they have had sight of Spaine. And some have looked out for Spaine, and have discovered the ilands.

The selfe same currant is in the Levant sea, but runneth trade betwixt the maynes, and changeable sometimes to the east-wards, sometimes to the west-wards.

In Brasill and the South sea, the currant likewise is changeable, but it runneth ever alongst the coast, accompanying the winde : and it is an infallible rule, that twelve or twentie foure houres before the winde alters, the currant begins to change.

In the West Indies onely the currant runneth continually one way, and setteth alongst the coast from the equinoctiall lyne towards the north. No man hath yet found that these courrants keepe any certaine time, or run so many dayes, or moneths, one way as another, as doth the course of ebbing and flowing, well knowne in all seas ; only neere the shore they have small force ; partly, because of the reflux which the coast causeth, and partly for the ebbing and flowing, which more or lesse is generall in most seas.[3]

When the currant runneth north or south, it is easily discovered by augmenting or diminishing the height ; but how to know the setting of the currant from east to west in the mayne sea, is difficult ; and as yet I have not knowne any man, or read any authour, that hath prescribed any certaine meane or way to discover it.[4] But experience

[3] The current in the West Indies, known as the Gulf stream, still runs to the northward through the Gulf of Florida, and then trending to the eastward, expends its force in the Atlantic.

[4] At the present day, by the general use of chronometers, the longitude can be determined with almost as great facility as the latitude.

Sect. XVI. teacheth that in the mayne sea, for the most part, it is variable; and therefore the best and safest rule to prevent the danger (which the uncertainty and ignorance heereof may cause), is carefull and continuall watch by day and night, and upon the east and west course ever to bee before the shipp, and to use the meanes possible to know the errour, by the rules which newe authours may teach; beating off and on, somtimes to the west-wards, sometimes to the east-wards, with a fayre gale of winde.

SECTION XVI.

The scurvey. BEING betwixt three or foure degrees of the equinoctiall line, my company within a fewe dayes began to fall sicke, of a disease which sea-men are wont to call the scurvey: and seemeth to bee a kind of dropsie, and raigneth most in this climate of any that I have heard or read of in the world; though in all seas it is wont to helpe and increase the miserie of man; it possesseth all those of which it taketh hold, with a loathsome sloathfulnesse, even to eate: they would be content to change their sleepe and rest, which is the most pernicious enemie in this sicknesse, that is knowne. It bringeth with it a great desire to drinke, and causeth a generall swelling of all parts of the body, especially of the legs and gums, and many times the teeth fall out of the jawes without paine.

The signes. The signes to know this disease in the beginning are divers: by the swelling of the gummes, by denting of the flesh of the leggs with a mans finger, the pit remayning without filling up in a good space. Others show it with their lasinesse: others complaine of the cricke of the backe, etc., all which are, for the most part, certaine tokens of infection.

The cause of this sicknes some attribute to sloath; some to conceite; and divers men speake diversly: that which I have observed is, that our nation is more subject unto it then any other; because being bred in a temperate clymate, where the naturall heate restrayned, giveth strength to the stomacke, sustayning it with meates of good nourishment, and that in a wholesome ayre; whereas comming into the hot countries (where that naturall heate is dispersed through the whole body, which was wont to be proper to the stomache; and the meates for the most part preserved with salt, and its substance thereby diminished, and many times corrupted), greater force for digestion is now required then in times past; but the stomache finding less virtue to doe his office, in reparting to each member his due proportion in perfection, which either giveth it rawe, or remayneth with it indigested by his hardnes or cruditie, infeebleth the body, and maketh it unlusty and unfit for any thing; for the stomache being strong (though all parts els be weake), there is ever a desire to feede, and aptnes to perform whatsoever can be required of a man; but though all other members be strong and sound, if the stomache be opprest, or squemish, all the body is unlustie, and unfit for any thing, and yeeldeth to nothing so readily as sloathfulnes, which is confirmed by the common answere to all questions: as, will you eate? will you sleepe? will you walke? will you play? The answere is, I have no stomache: which is as much as to say, no, not willingly: thereby confirming, that without a sound and whole stomache, nothing can bee well accomplished, nor any sustenance well digested.[1]

[1] The cause of scurvy is now known to be, the use for a long period of one diet, and that unwholesome. Since greater attention has been paid to the proper admixture of articles of food, and also to the cleanliness and ventilation of the vessel, this disease has nearly disappeared.

Sect. XVI.

Seething of meat in salt water.

Corruption of victuall.

Vapours of the sea.

Azores.

The remedies.

The seething of the meate in salt water, helpeth to cause this infirmitie, which in long voyages can hardly be avoyded: but if it may be, it is to be shunned; for the water of the sea to man's body is very unwholesome. The corruption of the victuals, and especially of the bread, is very pernicious; the vapours and ayre of the sea also is nothing profitable, especially in these hot countries, where are many calmes. And were it not for the moving of the sea by the force of windes, tydes, and currants, it would corrupt all the world.

The experience I saw in anno 1590, lying with a fleete of her majesties ships about the ilands of the Azores, almost six moneths; the greatest part of the time we were becalmed: with which all the sea became so replenished with several sorts of gellyes, and formes of serpents, adders, and snakes, as seemed wonderfull: some greene, some blacke, some yellow, some white, some of divers coulours; and many of them had life, and some there were a yard and halfe, and two yards long; which had I not seene, I could hardly have beleeved. And hereof are witnesses all the companies of the ships which were then present; so that hardly a man could draw a buckett of water cleere of some corruption.[2] In which voyage, towards the end thereof, many of every ship (saving of the *Nonpereil*, which was under my charge, and had onely one man sicke in all the voyage), fell sicke of this disease, and began to die apace, but that the speedie passage into our country was remedie to the crazed, and a preservative for those that were not touched. The best prevention for this disease (in my judgement) is to keepe cleane the shippe; to besprinkle her

---

[2] "The very deep did rot!
That ever this should be!
Yea slimy things did crawl with legs
Upon the slimy sea." *Ancient Mariner.—Coleridge.*

ordinarily with vineger, or to burne tarre, and some sweet _{Sect. xvi.}
savours; to feed upon as few salt meats in the hot country as
may be; and especially to shunne all kindes of salt fish, and _{By dyet.}
to reserve them for the cold climates; and not to dresse
any meate with salt water, nor to suffer the companie to
wash their shirts nor cloathes in it, nor to sleepe in their
cloaths when they are wett. For this cause it is necessarily
required, that provision be made of apparell for the com-
pany, that they may have wherewith to shift themselves; _{By shift.}
being a common calamitie amongst the ordinary sort of
mariners, to spend their thrift on the shore, and to bring
to sea no more cloaths then they have backes. For the
bodie of man is not refreshed with any thing more then
with shifting cleane cloaths; a great preservative of health
in hott countries.

The second antidote is, to keepe the companie occupied
in some bodily exercise of worke, of agilitie, of pastimes, of _{By labour.}
daunicing, of use of armes; these helpeth much to banish
this infirmitie. Thirdly, in the morning, at discharge of _{By early eating and}
the watch, to give every man a bit of bread, and a draught _{drinking.}
of drinke, either beere or wine mingled with water (at the
least, the one halfe), or a quantitie mingled with beere, that
the pores of the bodie may be full, when the vapours of the
sea ascend up.[3]

The morning draught should be ever of the best and
choysest of that in the ship. Pure wine I hold to be more
hurtfull then the other is profitable. In this, others will
be of a contrary opinion, but I thinke partiall. If not,
then leave I the remedies thereof to those physitions and
surgeons who have experience; and I wish that some
learned man would write of it, for it is the plague of the
sea, and the spoyle of mariners. Doubtlesse, it would be a

---

[3] It forms part of a naval surgeon's instructions, that in tropical
countries, when the crew are likely to be employed on shore, each is to
take a morning draught of spirits or wine, with bark infused.

meritorious worke with God and man, and most beneficiall for our countrie; for in twentie yeares, since that I have used the sea, I dare take upon me to give accompt of ten thousand men consumed with this disease.

By sower orranges and lemons.

That which I have seene most fruitfull for this sicknesse, is sower oranges and lemmons,[4] and a water which amongst others (for my particular provision) I carried to the sea,

By Doctor Stevens water.

called Dr. Stevens his water, of which, for that his vertue was not then well knowne unto me, I carried but little, and it tooke end quickly, but gave health to those that used it.

By oyle of vitry.

The oyle of vitry[5] is beneficiall for this disease; taking two drops of it, and mingled in a draught of water, with a little sugar. It taketh away the thirst, and helpeth to clense and comfort the stomache. But the principall of

By the ayre of the land.

all, is the ayre of the land; for the sea is naturall for fishes, and the land for men. And the oftener a man can have his people to land, not hindering his voyage, the better it is, and the profitablest course that he can take to refresh them.[6]

[4] The scurvy is not peculiar to seamen. It raged with great violence during the siege of Gibralter. Oranges and lemons were found of great benefit in arresting the disease. Lime juice has been long a fixed article of diet in men-of-war, and lately merchant vessels are compelled to carry it as an article of provision.

[5] Oil of vitriol or sulphuric acid.

[6] In the year 1776, the Royal Society awarded their gold medal to Captain James Cook, for a paper on " Preserving the health of the crew of her majesty's *Resolution*, &c." Captain Cook considers that much was owing to the extraordinary care taken by the admiralty in causing such articles to be put on board, as by experience or conjecture were judged to be useful. But he adds, that the introduction of the most salutary articles will prove unsuccessful, unless supported by certain rules. The men being at three watches, except on emergency, were consequently less exposed to the weather, and generally had dry clothes to shift themselves. Care was taken to keep their persons and clothes clean and dry. A fire was often burned in the well. The coppers were kept clean, and no fat allowed to be given to the people. Fresh water was obtained at every opportunity. Few places but what offered some refreshment, and example and authority were not wanting to induce

SECTION XVII.

HAVING stood to the westwards some hundreth leagues and
more, and the wind continuing with us contrarie, and the
sicknesse so fervent, that every day there dyed more or
lesse,—my companie in generall began to dismay, and to
desire to returne homewards, which I laboured to hinder
by good reasons and perswasions; as that to the West
Indies we had not above eight hundreth leagues, to the
ilands of Azores little lesse, and before we came to the
ilands of Cape de Verde, that we should meete with the
breze; for every night we might see the reach goe contrary
to the winde which wee sayled by; verifying the old
proverbe amongst mariners,—that he hath need of a long
mast, that will sayle by the reach: and that the neerest
land and speediest refreshing we could look for, was the
coast of Brasill; and that standing towards it with the wind
we had, we shortned our way for the Indies; and that to put
all the sicke men together in one shippe, and to send her
home, was to make her their grave. For we could spare
but few sound men, who were also subject to fall sicke,
and the misery, notwithstanding, remedilesse. With which
they were convinced, and remayned satisfied. So leaving
all to their choyse, with the consideration of what I perswaded, they resolved, with me, to continue our course, till
that God was pleased to looke upon us with his Fatherly
eyes of mercie.

As we approached neerer and neerer the coast of Brasill,
the wind began to vere to the east-wardes; and about the

their being employed. These methods, under Divine Providence, en-
abled the *Resolution* to complete a voyage of three years and eighteen
days with the loss of only *one man* by disease.

We may remark that our author seems to have been fully alive to
the importance of caring for the health of his company, and it is not
improbable that Cook benefited by some of his suggestions.

Sect. XVII.
Cape S.
Augustine.
Farnambuca
Todos
Santos.
Pura de
Vitoria.
Dangers of
fire.
By heating
of pitch.

middle of October, to be large and good for us; and about the 18th of October, we were thwart of Cape Saint Augustine, which lyeth in six degrees to the southwards of the lyne; and the twenty-one in the height of Farnambuca, but some fourscore leagues from the coast; the twentie foure in the height of Bayea de Todos Santos; neere the end of October, betwixt seventeen and eighteen degrees, we were in sixteen fathomes, sounding of the great sholes, which lye alongst the coast, betwixt the bay of Todos Santos, and the port of Santos, alias Pura Senora de Vitoria; which are very perilous.[7]

But the divine Providence hath ordayned great flockes of small birds, like snytes,[8] to live upon the rockes and broken lands of these sholes, and are met with ordinarily twentie leagues before a man come in danger of them.

It shall not be amisse here to recount the accidents which befell us during this contrary winde, and the curiosities to be observed in all this time. Day and night we had continually a fayre gale of winde, and a smooth sea, without any alteration; one day, the carpenters having calked the decke of our shippe, which the sunne with his extreame heate had opened, craved licence to heate a little pitch in the cook-roome; which I would not consent unto by any meanes; for that my cooke-roomes were under the decke, knowing the danger; until the master undertooke that no danger should come thereof. But he recommended the charge to another, who had a better name then experience. He suffered the pitch to rise, and to runne into the fire, which caused so furious a flame as amazed him, and forced all to flie his heate. One of my company, with a double payre of gloves, tooke off the pitch-pot, but the fire forced him to let slip his hold-fast, before he could set it on the hearth, and so overturned it, and as the pitch

<hr>

[7] Shoals called the Abrolhos.   [8] Snyte for snipe.

began to runne, so the fire to enlarge it selfe, that in a moment a great part of the shippe was on a light fire. I being in my cabin, presently imagined what the matter was, and for all the hast I could make, before I came the fire was above the decke : for remedie whereof, I commanded all my companie to cast their rugge-gownes into the sea, with ropes fastened unto them. These I had provided for my people to watch in; for in many hott countries the nights are fresh and colde; and devided one gowne to two men, a starboord and a larboord man; so that he which watched had ever the gowne : for they which watched not, were either in their cabins, or under the decke, and so needed them not. The gownes being well soked, every man that could, tooke one, and assaulted the fire; and although some were singed, others scalded, and many burned, God was pleased that the fire was quenched, which I thought impossible; and doubtlesse, I never saw my selfe in greater perill in all the dayes of my life. Let all men take example by us, not to suffer, in any case, pitch to be heate in the ship, except it be with a shotte heate in the fire, which cannot breed daunger; nor to permit fire to be kindled, but upon meere necessitie; for the inconvenience thereof is for the most part remedilesse.[9]

With drinking of tobacco it is said, that the *Roebucke* was burned in the range of Dartmouth.

The *Primrose*, of London, was fired with a candle, at Tilbery-hope, and nothing saved but her kele.

And another ship bound for Barbary, at Wapping.

The *Jesus of Lubecke* had her gunner-roome set on fire with a match, and had beene burnt without redemption, if that my father, Sir John Hawkins, knight, then generall

---

[9] Heating pitch, and drawing off spirits in the hold, using a light, are the most common causes that lead to fire. Excluding the air is the best remedy, and no better device could have been hit upon than wetting the rug gowns.

in her, had not commaunded her sloppers[10] to be stopt, and the men to come to the pumpes, wherof shee had two which went with chaynes; and plying them, in a moment there was three or foure inches of water upon the decke, which with scoopes, swabbles,[11] and platters, they threw upon the fire, and so quenched it, and delivered both ship and men out of no small danger.

Great care is to be had also in cleaving of wood, in hooping or scuttling[12] of caske, and in any businesse where violence is to be used with instruments of iron, steele, or stone : and especially in opening of powder, these are not to be used, but mallets of wood; for many mischances happen beyond all expectation.

I have beene credibly enformed by divers persons, that comming out of the Indies, with scuttling a butt of water, the water hath taken fire, and flamed up, and put all in hazard. And a servant of mine, Thomas Gray, told me, that in the shippe wherein he came out of the Indies, anno 1600, there happened the like; and that if with mantles they had not smothered the fire, they had bin all burned with a pipe of water, which in scutling tooke fire.

Master John Hazlelocke reported, that in the arsenall of Venice happened the like, he being present. For mine own part, I am of opinion, that some waters have this propertie, and especially such as have their passage by mines of brimstone, or other mineralls, which, as all men know, give extraordinary properties unto the waters by which they runne. Or it may be that the water being in

[10] Holes in the ship's side to carry off the water. The term now in use is *scupper :* slopper appears to be as good a word.

[11] Swabs are a species of mop, made of a collection of rope yarns, used to dry the deck. *Swebban* — (Anglo-Saxon) to sweep.

[12] *To scuttle*—to make openings. *Escotilla* (Spanish), is applied to the openings in the deck, called by us hatch-ways. The term scuttle is also applied to the small openings made in the ship's side, to admit light and air.

wine caske, and kept close, may retayne an extraordinary propertie of the wine.[13] Yea, I have drunke fountaine and river waters many times, which have had a savour as that of brimstone.

Three leagues from Bayon, in France, I have proved of a fountaine that hath this savour, and is medicinable for many diseases. In the South sea, in a river some five leagues from Cape Saint Francisco, in one degree and a halfe to the northwardes of the lyne, in the bay of Atacames, is a river of fresh water, which hath the like savour. Of this I shall have occasion to speake in another place, treating of the divers properties of fountaines and rivers; and therefore to our purpose.

SECTION XVIII.

WE had no small cause to give God thankes and prayse for our deliverance; and so, all our ships once come together, wee magnified his glorious Name for his mercie towards us, and tooke an occasion hereby to banish swearing out of our shippes, which amongst the common sort of mariners and sea-faring men, is too ordinarily abused. So with a generall consent of all our companie, it was ordayned that in every ship there should be a palmer or ferula, which should be in the keeping of him who was taken with an oath; and that he who had the palmer should give to every other that he tooke swearing, in the palme of the hand, a palmada with it, and the ferula. And whosoever at the time of evening, or morning prayer, was found to have the palmer, should have three blowes given him by the captaine or master; and that he should be still bound to free him-

---

[13] If impure water be confined in a close cask, gas will be generated, and the effect described happen.

selfe, by taking another, or else to runne in daunger of
continuing the penaltie: which executed, few dayes reformed the vice; so that in three dayes together, was not
one oath heard to be sworne.   This brought both ferulas
and swearing out of use.[1]

And certainly, in vices, custome is the principall sustenance; and for their reformation, it little availeth to give
good counsell, or to make good lawes and ordenances except they be executed.

SECTION XIX.

IN this time of contrary wind, those of my company
which were in health, recreated themselves with fishing,
and beholding the hunting and hawking of the sea, and
the battell betwixt the whale and his enemies, which truly
are of no small pleasure.   And therefore for the curious,
I will spend some time in declaration of them.

Ordinarily such ships as navigate betweene the tropiques,
are accompanied with three sorts of fish: the dolphin,
which the Spaniards call *dozado;* the *bonito,* or Spanish
makerell; and the sharke, alias *tiberune.*

The dolphin.   The dolphin I hold to be one of the swiftest fishes in the
sea.   He is like unto a breame, but that he is longer and
thinner, and his scales very small.   He is of the colour
of the rayn-bow, and his head different to other fishes;

------

[1] In the instructions given by the Lords Generals, the Earl of Essex
and Charles Lord Howard, Lord High Admiral of England, to the
captains of the ships composing the expedition to Cadiz, in 1596, the
second article runs thus : Item—You shall forbid swearing, brawling,
dicing, and such like disorders, as may breed contention and disorder
in your ship, wherein you shall also avoid God's displeasure and win
his favour.

for, from his mouth halfe a spanne, it goeth straight upright, as the head of a wherry, or the cut-water of a ship.[1] He is very good meate if he be in season, but the best part of him is his head, which is great. They are some bigger, some lesser; the greatest that I have seene, might be some foure foote long.

I hold it not without some ground, that the auncient philosophers write, that they be enamoured of a man; for in meeting with shipping, they accompany them till they approach to colde climates; this I have noted divers times. For disembarking out of the West Indies, anno 1583, within three or foure dayes after, we mett a scole[2] of them, which left us not till we came to the ilands of Azores, nere a thousand leagues. At other times I have noted the like.

But some may say, that in the sea are many scoles[2] of this kinde of fish, and how can a man know if they were the same?

Who may be thus satisfied, that every day in the morning, which is the time that they approach neerest the ship, we should see foure, five, and more, which had, as it were, our eare-marke; one hurt upon the backe, another neere the tayle, another about the fynnes; which is a sufficient proofe that they were the same; for if those which had received so bad entertainment of us would not forsake us, much less those which we had not hurt. Yet that which makes them most in love with ships and men, are the scrappes and refreshing they gather from them.

The bonito, or Spanish makerell, is altogether like unto a makerell, but that it is somewhat more growne; he is   The bonito.

---

[1] The early painters and sculptors, and others who deal in "naval attributes," have treated the dolphin very ill; Sir Richard's description, if studied, might have amended the monsters given out to the public as dolphins.

[2] A shoal or scull of fish; that is, separated from the main body. This is Horne Tooke's derivation. We think the term is more commonly applied to the main body itself.

reasonable foode, but dryer then a makerell. Of them there are two sorts : the one is this which I have described ; the other, so great as hardly one man can lift him. At such times as wee have taken of these, one sufficed for a meale for all my company. These, from the fynne of the tayle forwards, have upon the chyne seven small yellow hillocks, close one to another.

The dolphins and bonitos are taken with certaine instruments of iron which we call vysgeis,[3] in forme of an eel speare, but that the blades are round, and the poynts like unto the head of a broad arrow : these are fastened to long staves of ten or twelve foote long, with lynes tied unto them, and so shott to the fish from the beake-head, the poope, or other parts of the shippe, as occasion is ministered. They are also caught with hookes and lynes, the hooke being bayted with a redd cloth, or with a white cloth made into the forme of a fish, and sowed upon the hooke.

The sharke.   The shark, or tiberune, is a fish like unto those which wee call dogge-fishes, but that he is farre greater. I have seene of them eight or nine foote long ; his head is flatt and broad, and his mouth in the middle, underneath, as that of the scate ; and he cannot byte of the bayte before him, but by making a halfe turne ; and then he helpeth himselfe with his tayle, which serveth him in stead of a rudder.   His skinne is rough (like to the fish which we call a rough hound), and russet, with reddish spottes, saving that under the belly he is all white : he is much hated of sea-faring men, who have a certaine foolish superstition with them, and say, that the ship hath seldome good successe, that is much accompanied with them.

It is the most ravenous fish knowne in the sea ; for he swalloweth all that he findeth. In the puch[4] of them hath

---

[3] *Fisgig* or *grains*—a small trident used for striking fish.   From the Spanish *fisga*.

[4] Pouch or stomach.

beene found hatts, cappes, shooes, shirts, leggs and armes
of men, ends of ropes, and many other things ; whatsoever
is hanged by the shippes side, hee sheereth it, as though
it were with a razor ; ·for he hath three rowes of teeth on
either side, as sharpe as nailes ; some say they are good for
pick-tooths. It hath chanced that a yonker casting himselfe into the sea to swimme, hath had his legge bitten off
above the knee by one of them. And I have beene enformed, that in the *Tyger*, when Sir Richard Greenfield
went to people Virginia, a sharke cut off the legge of one
of the companie, sitting in the chaines and washing himselfe. They spawne not as the greatest part of fishes doe,
but whelpe, as the dogge or wolfe ; and for many dayes
after that shee hath whelped, every night, and towards any
storme, or any danger which may threaten them hurt, the
damme receiveth her whelpes in at her mouth, and preserveth them, till they be able to shift for themselves. I
have seene them goe in and out, being more then a foote
and halfe long ; and after taking the damme, we have
found her young ones in her belly.[5]

Every day my company tooke more or lesse of them, not
for that they did eat of them (for they are not held wholesome ; although the Spaniards, as I have seene, doe eate
them), but to recreate themselves, and in revenge of the
injuries received by them ; for they live long, and suffer
much after they bee taken, before they dye.[6]

At the tayle of one they tyed a great logge of wood, at
another, an empty batizia,[7] well stopped ; one they yoaked
like a hogge ; from another, they plucked out his eyes, and
so threw them into the sea. In catching two together,
they bound them tayle to tayle, and so set them swimming ;
another with his belly slit, and his bowels hanging out,

[5] One species produces its young alive : others in a hard membraneous
pouch.

[6] This enmity betwixt sailors and sharks still exists, and the interest
attending their capture is great.

[7] Probably a small cask.

which his fellowes would have every one a snatch at; with other infinite inventions to entertayne the time, and to avenge themselves; for that they deprived them of swimming, and fed on their flesh being dead. They are taken with harping irons, and with great hookes made of purpose, with swyvels and chaines; for no lyne nor small rope can hold them, which they share not asunder.

There doth accompany this fish divers little fishes, which are callet pilats fishes, and are ever upon his fynnes, his head, or his backe, and feede of the scraps and superfluities of his prayes. They are in forme of a trought, and streked like a makerell, but that the strekes are white and blacke, and the blacke greater then the white.

The manner of hunting and hawking representeth that which we reasonable creatures use, saving onely in the disposing of the game. For by our industry and abilitie the hound and hawke is brought to that obedience, that whatsoever they seize is for their master; but here it is otherwise: for the game is for him that seizeth it. The dolphins and bonitoes are the houndes, and the alcatraces the hawkes, and the flying fishes the game; whose wonderfull making magnifieth the Creator, who for their safetie and helpe, hath given them extraordinary manner of fynnes, which serve in stead of wings, like those of the batt or rere-mouse; of such a delicate skinne, interlaced with small bones so curiously, as may well cause admiration in the beholders. They are like unto pilchards in colour, and making; saving that they are somewhat rounder, and (for the most part) bigger. They flie best with a side wind, but longer then their wings be wett they cannot sustaine the waight of their bodies; and so the greatest flight that I have seene them make, hath not beene above a quarter of a myle. They commonly goe in scoles, and serve for food for the greater fishes, or for the foules. The dolphins and bonitoes doe continually hunt after them, and the alcatraces lye soaring in the ayre, to

Flying fishes

see when they spring, or take their flight; and ordinarily, he that escapeth the mouth of the dolphin or bonito, helping himselfe by his wings, falleth prisoner into the hands of the alcatrace, and helpeth to fill his gorge.

The alcatrace[8] is a sea-fowle, different to all that I have seene, either on the land or in the sea. His head like unto the head of a gull, but his bill like unto a snytes bill, somewhat shorter, and in all places alike. He is almost like to a heronshaw; his leggs a good spanne long, his wings very long, and sharpe towards the poynts, with a long tayle like to a pheasant, but with three or foure feathers onely, and these narrower. He is all blacke, of the colour of a crow, and of little flesh; for he is almost all skinne and bones. He soareth the highest of any fowle that I have seene, and I have not heard of any, that have seene them rest in the sea.

Now of the fight betwixt the whale and his contraries; which are the sword-fish and the thresher. The whale is of the greatest fishes in the sea; and to count but the truth, unlesse dayly experience did witnesse the relation, it might seeme incredible; hee is a huge unwildlie fish, and to those which have not seene of them, it might seeme strange, that other fishes should master him; but certaine it is, that many times the thresher and sword-fish, meeting him joyntly, doe make an end of him.

The sword fish[9] is not great, but strongly made; and in the top of his chine, as a man may say, betwixt the necke and shoulders, he hath a manner of sword in substance, like unto a bone, of foure or five inches broad, and above three foote long, full of prickles of either side: it is but thin, for the greatest that I have seene, hath not beene above a finger thicke.

[8] The man-of-war bird, or cormorant—*Pelecanidœ.* On the coast of Brazil, in latitude twenty-four, are the Alcatrasse islands.

[9] *Xiphias*—the sword or snout is about three-tenths of his whole length.

The thresher is a greater fish, whose tayle is very broad and thicke, and very waightie. They fight in this maner; the sword fish placeth himselfe under the belly of the whale, and the thresher upon the ryme[10] of the water, and with his tayle thresheth upon the head of the whale, till hee force him to give way; which the sword fish perceiving, receiveth him upon his sword, and wounding him in the belly forceth him to mount up againe (besides that he cannot abide long under water, but must of force rise upp to breath): and when in such manner they torment him, that the fight is sometimes heard above three leagues distance, and I dare affirme, that I have heard the blowes of the thresher two leagues off, as the report of a peece of ordinance; the whales roaring being heard much farther. It also happeneth sundry times that a great part of the water of the sea round about them, with the blood of the whale, changeth his colour. The best remedy the whale hath in this extremitie to helpe himselfe, is to get him to land, which hee procureth as soone as hee discovereth his adversaries; and getting the shore, there can fight but one with him, and for either of them, hand to hand, he is too good.[11] The whale is a fish not good to be eaten, hee is almost all fat,[12] but esteemed for his trayne; and many goe to the New-found-land, Greene-land, and other parts onely to fish for them; which is in this maner: when they which seeke the whale discover him, they compasse him round about with pynaces or shalops. In the head of every boat is placed a man, with a harping iron, and a long lyne, the one end of it fastned to the harping iron, and the other

[10] *The surface*—from cream or ream, what rises to the surface—or perhaps from rim, brim.

[11] This story seems to be founded on the fact that the snout of the sword fish is often found driven through parts of vessels' bottoms; whence it has been inferred, the fish mistook them for whales. We imagine the account of the thresher to be fabulous.

[12] In the thirteenth century the tongue of the whale was esteemed as an article of food; and whale beef, as it is called, is eaten at Bermuda, and probably elsewhere.

end to the head of the boat, in which it lyeth finely coiled; and for that he cannot keepe long under water, he sheweth which way he goeth, when rising neere any of the boats, within reach, he that is neerest, darteth his harping iron at him. The whale finding himself to be wounded, swimmeth to the bottome, and draweth the pynace after him; which the fisher-men presently forsake, casting themselves into the sea; for that many times he draweth the boat under water: those that are next, procure to take them up. For this cause all such as goe for that kind of fishing, are experimented in swimming. When one harping iron is fastned in the whale, it is easily discerned which way he directeth his course: and so ere long they fasten another, and another in him. When he hath three or foure boats dragging after him, with their waight, his bleeding, and fury, he becommeth so over-mastred, that the rest of the pynaces with their presence and terror, drive him to the place where they would have him, nature instigating him to covet the shore.

Being once hurt, there is little need to force him to land. Once on the shore, they presently cut great peeces of him, and in great cauldrons seeth them.[13] The uppermost in the cauldrons is the fatt, which they skimme off, and put it into hogsheads and pipes. This is that they call whales oyle, or traine oyle, accompted the best sort of traine oyle. It is hard to be beleeved, what quantitie is gathered of one whale; of the tongue, I have beene enformed, have many pipes beene filled. The fynnes are also esteemed for many and sundry uses; as is his spawne for divers purposes: this wee corruptly call *parmacittie;* of the Latine word, *spermaceti.*[14]

[13] In the early days of the whale fishery, when the fish were plentiful, the oil was boiled out on shore, near the place of capture. At present the blubber is imported from the northern fishery.

[14] "And telling me the sovereign'st thing on earth
Was parmaceti for an inward bruise."—*Henry IV*, Part i.
Spermaceti is obtained from the brain of the sperm whale,—*physeter monocephalus*—not from the spawn.

And the precious amber-greece some thinke also to be found in his bowells, or voyded by him: but not in all seas: yea, they maintaine for certaine, that the same is ingendred by eating an hearbe which groweth in the sea. This hearbe is not in all seas, say they, and therefore, where it wanteth, the whales give not this fruit. In the coast of the East Indies in many partes is great quantitie. In the coastes of Guyne, of Barbary, of the Florida, in the islands of Cape de Verde, and the Canaries, amber-greece hath beene many times found, and sometimes on the coast of Spaine and England. Whereupon it is presumed, that all these seas have not the hearbe growing in them. The cause why the whale should eate this hearbe, I have not heard, nor read. It may be surmised, that it is as that of the becunia, and other beasts, which breed the beazer stone;[15] who feeding in the valleyes and mountaines, where are many venemous serpents, and hearbes; when they find themselves touched with any poyson, forthwith they runne for remedie to an hearbe, which the Spaniards call *contra-yerva*, that is to say, contrary to poyson: which having eaten, they are presently cured: but the substance of the hearbe converteth it selfe into a medicinable stone; so it may be, that the whale feeding of many sortes of fishes, and some of them, as is knowne, venemous, when he findeth himselfe touched, with this hearbe he cureth himselfe; and not being able to digest it, nature converteth it into this substance, provoketh it out, or dyeth with it in his belly; and being light, the sea bringeth it to the coast.

All these are imaginations, yet instruments to moove us to the glorifying of the great and universal Creatour of all, whose secret wisedome, and wonderfull workes, are incomprehensible.

[15] *Bezoar*—name applied to a concretion found in the stomach of various animals. Many extraordinary virtues were formerly ascribed to it, without much foundation.

But the more approved generation of the amber-greece,
and which carrieth likliest probabilitie is, that it is a liquor
which issueth out of certaine fountaines, in sundry seas,
and being of a light and thicke substance, participating of
the ayre, suddenly becommeth hard, as the yellow amber,
of which they make beads;[16] which is also a liquor of a
fountayne in the Germayne sea. In the bottome it is soft
and white, and partaking of the ayre becommeth hard and
stonie : also the corrall in the sea is soft, but comming into
the ayre, becommeth a stone.

Those who are of this former opinion, thinke the reason
why the amber greece is sometimes found in the whale,
to be, for that he swalloweth it, as other things which he
findeth swimming upon the water ; and not able to digest
it, it remaineth with him till his death.

Another manner of fishing and catching the whale I
cannot omit, used by the Indians, in Florida ; worthy to
be considered, in as much as the barbarous people have
found out so great a secret, by the industry and diligence
of one man, to kill so great and huge a monster : it is in
this manner.

The Indian discovering a whale, procureth two round
billets of wood, sharpneth both at one end, and so binding
them together with a cord, casteth himselfe with them into
the sea, and swimmeth towards the whale : if he come to
him, the whale escapeth not ; for he placeth himselfe upon
his necke, and although the whale goeth to the bottome,
he must of force rise presently to breath (for which nature
hath given him two great holes in the toppe of his head,
by which, every time that he breatheth, he spouteth out a
great quantitie of water); the Indian forsaketh not his
holde, but riseth with him, and thrusteth in a logg into
one of his spowters, and with the other knocketh it in so

[16] Ambergris is still considered to be a concretion formed in the
stomach of the sperm whale.

fast, that by no meanes the whale can get it out. That
fastned, at another opportunitie, he thrusteth in the second
logg into the other spowter, and with all the force he can,
keepeth it in.

The whale not being able to breath, swimmeth presently
ashore, and the Indian a cock-horse upon him, which his
fellowes discovering, approach to helpe him, and to make
an end of him : it serveth them for their foode many dayes
after.[17]

Since the Spaniards have taught them the estimation of
amber greece, they seeke curiously for it, sell it to them,
and others, for such things as they best fancie, and most
esteeme ; which are, as I have beene enformed, all sortes
of edge tooles, copper, glasses, glasse-beads, red caps, shirts,
and pedlery ware. Upon this subject, divers Spaniards
have discoursed unto mee, who have beene eye witnesses
thereof, declaring them to be valorous, ventrous, and industrious : otherwise they durst not undertake an enterprise
so difficult and full of danger.

SECTION XX.

FROM the tropike of Cancer to three or foure degrees of
the equinoctiall, the breze, which is the north-east winde,
doth raigne in our ocean sea the most part of the yeare,
except it be neere the shore, and then the wind is variable,
In three or foure degrees of eyther side the line, the winde
hangeth southerly, in the moneths of July, August, September, and October ; all the rest of the yeare, from the
Cape Bona Esperança to the ilands of Azores, the breze

Best times
to passe the
lyne from
the north-
wards to the
southward.

[17] In Waterton's *Wanderings* will be found a parallel story, of a
gentleman riding on a cayman.

raygneth continually ; and some yeares in the other moneths also, or calmes; but he that purposeth to crosse the lyne from the north-wards to the south-wards, the best and surest passage is, in the moneths of January, February, and March. In the moneths of September, October, and November, is also good passage, but not so sure as in the former.[1]

SECTION XXI.

BETWIXT nineteene and twenty degrees to the south-wards of the lyne, the winde tooke us contrary, which together with the sicknes of my people made mee to seeke the shore; and about the end of October, we had sight of the land, which presently by our height and the making of it, discovered it selfe to be the port of Santos, alias Nostra Senora de Victoria, and is easie to be knowne, for it hath a great high hill over the port, which (howsoever a man commeth with the land) riseth like a bell, and comming neere the shore, presently is discovered a white tower or fort, which standeth upon the top of a hill over the harbour, and upon the seamost land. It is the first land a man must compasse before he enter the port. Comming within two leagues of the shore, we anchored; and the captaynes and masters of my other ships being come aboord, it was thought convenient (the weaknes of our men considered, for wee had not in our three ships twenty foure men sound), and the winde uncertaine when it might change, we thought with pollicie to procure that which wee could not by force ; and so to offer traffique to the people of the

[1] According to Horsburgh, the least favorable season for getting to the southward, is the period from June to September inclusive.

shore; by that meanes to prove if wee could attayne some refreshing for our sicke company.

In execution whereof, I wrote a letter to the governour in Latine, and sent him with it a peece of crymson velvet, a bolt of fine holland, with divers other things, as a present; and with it, the captaine of my ship, who spake a little broken Spanish, giving the governour to understand that I was bound to the East Indies, to traffique in those parts, and that contrary windes had forced me upon that coast : if that hee were pleased to like of it, for the commodities the country yeelded in aboundance, I would exchange that which they wanted. With these instructions my captaine departed about nine of the clocke in the morning, carrying a flagge of truce in the head of the boate, and sixteene men well armed, and provided; guided by one of my company which two yeares before had beene captaine in that place, and so was a reasonable pilot.

Entering the port, within a quarter of a mile is a small village, and three leagues higher up is the chief towne; where they have two forts, one on eyther side of the harbour, and within them ride the ships which come thither to discharge, or loade. In the small village is ever a garrison of one hundreth souldiers, whereof part assist there continually, and in the white tower upon the top of the hill, which commaundeth it.

Heere my captaine had good entertainment, and those of the shore received his message and letter, dispatching it presently to the governour, who was some three leagues off in another place : at least they beare us so in hand. In the time that they expected the post, my captaine with one other entertained himselfe with the souldiers a shore, who after the common custome of their profession (except when they be *besonios*),[1] sought to pleasure him, and finding

---

[1] Bisoño — (Spanish) raw, undisciplined :—
  Pistol. Under which king, Bezonian ? speak or die.
  Henry IV, Part II.

that he craved but oranges, lemmons, and matters of smal moment for refreshing for his generall, they suffered the women and children to bring him what hee would, which hee gratified with double pistolets,[2] that I had given him for that purpose. So got hee us two or three hundreth oranges and lemmons, and some fewe hennes.

All that day and night, and the next day, till nine of the clocke, wee waited the returne of our boate; which not appearing, bred in me some suspition; and for my satisfaction, I manned a light horseman which I had, and the *Fancie*, the best I could, shewing strength where was weaknesse and infirmity, and so set sayle towardes the port; our gunner taking upon him to bee pilot, for that he had beene there some yeares before.

Thus, with them we entred the harbour. My captaine having notice of our being within the barre, came aboord with the boat, which was no small joy to me; and more, to see him bring us store of oranges and lemmons, which was that we principally sought for, as the remedie of our diseased company. He made relation of that had past, and how they expected present answere from the governour. We anchored right against the village; and within two houres, by a flagge of truce, which they on the shore shewed us, we understood that the messenger was come: our boat went for the answere of the governour, who said, he was sorry that he could not accomplish our desire, being so reasonable and good; for that in consideration of the warre betwixt Spaine and England, he had expresse order from his king, not to suffer any English to trade within his jurisdiction, no, nor to land, or to take any refreshing upon the shore. And therefore craved pardon, and that wee should take this for a resolute answere: and further required us to depart the port within three dayes, which he said he

---

[2] The double pistole was a coin of about the value of thirty or thirty-five shillings.

gave us for our courteous manner of proceeding. If any
of my people from that time forwards, should approach to
the shore, that he would doe his best to hinder and annoy
them. With this answere wee resolved to depart; and before it came, with the first faire wind we determined to be
packing : but the wind suffered us not all that night, nor
the next day. In which time, I lived in a great perplexitie,
for that I knew our own weaknesse, and what they might
doe unto us, if that they had knowne so much. For any
man that putteth himself into the enemies port, had need
of Argus eyes, and the wind in a bagge,[3] especially where
the enemie is strong, and the tydes of any force. For with
either ebbe or flood, those who are on the shore may
thrust upon him inventions of fire : and with swimming or
other devises, may cut his cables. A common practise in
all hot countries. The like may be effected with raffes,
cannoas, boates, or pynaces, to annoy and assault him :
and if this had beene practised against us, or taken effect,
our shippes must of force have yeelded themselves ; for
they had no other people in them but sicke men; but
many times opinion and feare preserveth the shippes, and
not the people in them.

For preven-
tion of an-
noyances,
etc , in
harbours.
Wherefore it is the part of a provident governour, to
consider well the daungers that may befall him, before he
put himselfe into such places; so shall he ever be provided
for prevention.

In Saint John de Vlua, in the New Spaine, when the
Spanyards dishonoured their nation with that foule act of
perjury, and breach of faith, given to my father, Sir John
Hawkins (notorious to the whole world), the Spanyards
fired two great shippes, with intention to burne my fathers
Admirall, which he prevented by towing them with his
boates another way.

---

[3] So that he may get away when it pleases him.

The great armado of Spaine, sent to conquer England, anno 1588, was with that selfe same industry overthrowne; for the setting on fire of six or seaven shippes (whereof two were mine), and letting them drive with the flood, forced them to cut their cables, and to put to sea, to seeke a new way to Spaine.[4] In which the greatest part of their best shippes and men were lost and perished.

For that my people should not be dismayed, I dispatched presently my light horsman, with onely foure men, and part of the refreshing, advising them that with the first calme or slent[5] of wind, they should come off.

The next night, the wind comming off the shore, wee set sayle, and with our boates and barkes sounded as we went.

It flowed upon the barre not above foure foote water, and once in foure and twentie houres, as in some parts of the West Indies ; at full sea, there is not upon the barre above seventeen or eighteen foote water. The harbour runneth to the south-westwards. He that will come into it, is to open the harbour's mouth a good quarter of a league before he beare with it, and be bolder of the wester side ; for of the easterland[6] lyeth a great ledge of rocks, for the most part, under water, which sometimes break not ; but with small shipping, a man may goe betwixt them and the poynt.

Comming aboord of our shippes, there was great joy amongst my company ; and many, with the sight of the oranges and lemmons, seemed to recover heart. This is a

[4] Alluding to the attempt the fleet made to return northabout. In the British Museum is preserved a curious old pack of playing cards, on which are depicted subjects relating to the defeat of the " Spanish Armada". On the ten of spades is shewn a consultation about returning by the North Ocean.

[5] Such a wind as would enable them to lie aslant or obliquely near the desired course. It is commonly said that " a calm is half a fair wind"; it is more than this, as out of thirty-two points, twenty would be fair.

[6] Easterhand ?

F

wonderfull secret of the power and wisedome of God, that hath hidden so great and unknowne vertue in this fruit, to be a certaine remedie for this infirmitie; I presently caused them all to be reparted[7] amongst our sicke men, which were so many, that there came not above three or foure to a share : but God was pleased to send us a prosperous winde the next day, so much to our comfort, that not any one dyed before we came to the ilands, where we pretended to refresh ourselves; and although our fresh water had fayled us many dayes before we saw the shore, by reason of our long navigation, without touching any land, and the excessive drinking of the sicke and diseased, which could not be excused, yet with an invention I had in my shippe, Distilling of salt water. I easily drew out of the water of the sea, sufficient quantitie of fresh water to sustaine my people with little expence of fewell; for with foure billets I stilled a hogshead of water, and therewith dressed the meat for the sicke and whole. The water so distilled, we found to be wholesome and nourishing.[8]

SECTION XXII.

THE coast from Santos to Cape Frio, lyeth west and by south, southerly. So we directed our course west southwest. The night comming on, and directions given to our other shippes, we sett the watch, having a fayre fresh gale of wind and large. My selfe with the master of our ship, having watched the night past, thought now

---

[7] *Répartir*—(French) to divide.

[8] Various schemes have been tried to distil fresh water at sea from salt water ; but none apparently have succeeded in producing an equivalent for the expense of fuel. In steam vessels a considerable supply is obtained from the condensation of the steam.

to give nature that which shee had beene deprived of, and so recommended the care of steeridge to one of his mates ;[1] who with the like travell past being drowsie, or with the confidence which he had of him at the helme, had not that watchfull care which was required ; he at the helme steered west, and west and by south, and brought us in a little time close upon the shore ;[2] doubtlesse he had cast us all away, had not God extraordinarily delivered us; for the master being in his dead sleepe, was suddenly awaked, and with such a fright that he could not be in quiet : whereupon waking his youth, which ordinarily slept in his cabin by him, asked him how the watch went on ; who answered, that it could not be above an houre since he layd himselfe to rest. He replyed, that his heart was so unquiet that he could not by any meanes sleepe, and so taking his gowne, came forth upon the deck, and presently discovered the land hard by us. And for that it was sandie and low, those who had their eyes continually fixed on it, were dazeled with the reflection of the starres, being a fayre night, and so were hindered from the true discovery thereof. But he comming out of the darke, had his sight more forcible, to discerne the difference of the sea, and the shore. So that forthwith he commaunded him at the helme, to put it close a starbourd, and tacking our ship, wee edged off; and sounding, found scant three fathome water, whereby we saw evidently the miraculous mercie of our God; that if he had not watched over us, as hee doth continually over his, doubtlesse we had perished without remedie. To whom be all glory, and prayse everlastingly, world without end.

[1] The term mate, as used at present, implies some one under the master. The real meaning implies persons co-equal. Thus we still speak of ship-mates, etc., without reference to rank.

[2] The coast lies nearer south and by west, than west and by south, so they would certainly have run on shore without any blame attaching to the helmsman.

Immediatly we shot off a peece, to give warning to our other shippes; who having kept their direct course, and far to wind-wards and sea-wards, because we carried no light, for that we were within sight of the shore, could not heare the report; and the next morning were out of sight.

SECTION XXIII.

Care of steeridge,

In this poynt of steeridge, the Spaniards and Portingalls doe exceede all that I haue seene, I mean for their care, which is chiefest in navigation. And I wish in this, and in all their workes of discipline, wee should follow their examples; as also those of any other nation.

exquisit in the Spanyards and Portingalls.

In every ship of moment, upon the halfe decke, or quarter decke,[1] they have a chayre or seat; out of which whilst they navigate, the pilot, or his adjutants[2] (which are the same officers which in our shippes we terme the master and his mates), never depart, day nor night, from the sight of the compasse; and have another before them, whereby they see what they doe, and are ever witnesses of the good or bad steeridge of all men that take the helme. This I have seene neglected in our best shippes, yet nothing more necessary to be reformed. For a good helme-man may be overcome with an imagination, and so mis-take one poynt for another;[3] or the compasse may erre, which by another

[1] The quarter deck may be defined as the space betwixt the main-mast and the after-hatchway; it seems also to have been called the half deck. Both terms arising from the fact that before the main-mast, the skids or beams were not planked. We still speak of being *on* the quarter deck, but *under* the half deck. The quarter deck is set apart for purposes of parade, and there the officer of the watch should always be sought.

[2] *Adjutare*—(Latin) to assist.

[3] On a still night, unless the attention of the helmsman be continually excited, it is quite possible that he get into a dreamy state

is discerned. The inconveniences which hereof may ensue, all experimented sea-men may easily conceive, and by us take warning to avoyd the like.

SECTION XXIV.

THE next day about tenne of the clocke, wee were thwart CapeBlanco. of Cape Blanco,[4] which is low sandie land, and perilous; for foure leagues into the sea (thwart it), lye banks of sand, which have little water on them; on a sudden we found our selves amongst them, in lesse then three fathome water; but with our boat and shalope we went sounding, and so got cleare of them.

The next day following, we discovered the ilands where Saint James wee purposed to refresh ourselves. They are two, and some ilands, alias call them Saint James, his ilands, and others, Saint Annes.[5] They lie in two and twenty degrees and a halfe to the south-wards of the lyne; and towards the evening (being the fifth of November) we anchored betwixt them and the mayne, in six fathome water, where wee found our other shippes.

All which being well moored, we presently began to set up tents and booths for our sicke men, to carry them a shore, and to use our best diligence to cure them. For which intent our three surgeons, with their servants and adherents, had two boates to wayte continually upon them, to fetch whatsoever was needfull from the shippes, to procure refreshing, and to fish, either with netts, or hookes

and, if at the same time, the officer of the watch is thinking of "those far away," the ship may be run for a time some points off her course. In the preceding section, Sir Richard well describes the difficulty of distinguishing betwixt a sandy shore and the water, on a calm bright night.

₄ Cape Saint Thomé?   ₅ Now called Saint Anna.

and lynes. Of these implements wee had in aboundance, and it yeelded us some refreshing. For the first dayes, the most of those which had health, occupied themselves in romeging our ship; in bringing ashore of emptie caske; in filling of them, and in felling and cutting of wood: which being many workes, and few hands, went slowly forwards.

Neere these ilands, are two great rockes, or small ilands adjoyning. In them we found great store of young gan-
Gannets. netts in their nests, which we reserved for the sicke, and being boyled with pickled porke well watered,[6] and mingled with oatmeale, made reasonable pottage, and was good refreshing and sustenance for them. This provision fayled us not, till our departure from them.

Upon one of these rockes also, we found great store of
Purslane. the hearbe purslane,[7] which boyled and made into sallets, with oyle and vineger, refreshed the sicke stomaches, and gave appetite.

With the ayre of the shore, and good cherishing, many recovered speedily. Some died away quickly, and others continued at a stand. We found here some store of fruits;
Cherries. a kind of cherry that groweth upon a tree like a plum-tree, red of colour, with a stone in it, but different in making to ours, for it is not altogether round, and dented about: they have a pleasing taste.

Palmitos. In one of the ilands, we found palmito trees, great and high, and in the toppe a certaine fruit like cocos, but no bigger then a wall-nut. We found also a fruit growing upon trees in codds, like beanes, both in the codd and the fruit. Some of my company proved of them,[8] and they

[6] Well soaked in water to remove the salt.

[7] *Portulaca sativa*—a fleshy-leaved plant, much esteemed in hot countries for its cooling properties.

[8] Great caution should be used in tasting unknown fruits; perhaps this tree was the *croton tiglium*, every part of which possesses powerful drastic properties.

caused vomits and purging, as any medicine taken out of
the apothecaries shop, according to the quantitie received.
They have hudds, as our beanes, which shaled off; the kernell parteth itselfe in two, and in the middle is a thin
skinne, like that of an onion, said to be hurtfull, and to
cause exceeding vomits, and therefore to be cast away.

Monardus writing of the nature and propertie of this
fruit, as of others of the Indies, for that it is found in other
parts, also calleth them *kavas purgativas*, and sayth, that
they are to be prepared by peeling them first, and then
taking away the skinne in the middle, and after beaten into
powder, to take the quantitie of five or six, either with wine
or sugar. Thus they are good against fevers, and to purge
grosse humors; against the collicke, and payne of the
joynts; in taking them a man may not sleepe, but is to use
the dyet usuall, as in a day of purging.

One other fruit we found, very pleasant in taste, in
fashion of an artechoque, but lesse; on the outside of
colour redd, within white, and compassed about with
prickles; our people called them pricke-pears;[9] no conserve
is better. They grow upon the leaves of a certaine roote,
that is like unto that which we call *semper viva* [9] and many
are wont to hang them up in their houses; but their leaves
are longer and narrower, and full of prickes on either side.
The fruit groweth upon the side of the leafe, and is one of
the best fruites that I have eaten in the Indies. In ripen-
ing, presently the birds or vermine are feeding on them;
a generall rule to know what fruit is wholesome and good
in the Indies, and other parts. Finding them to be eaten
of the beastes or fowles, a man may boldly eate of them.

The water of these ilands is not good: the one, for being
a standing water, and full of venemous wormes and ser-

[9] A species of cactus; the fruit is eaten in Sicily and elsewhere. We cannot join Sir Richard in its praise: perhaps as he had been long at sea, he found it grateful. The cochineal insect feeds on one species of this plant.

pents, which is neare a butt-shot from the sea shore; where we found a great tree fallen, and in the roote of it the names of sundry ·Portingalls, Frenchmen, and others, and amongst them, Abraham Cockes; with the time of their being in this island.

Contagious
water.

The other, though a running water, yet passing by the rootes of certaine trees, which have a smell as that of gar-lique, taketh a certaine contagious sent of them. Here two of our men dyed with swelling of their bellies. The accident we could not attribute to any other cause, then to this suspitious water. It is little, and falleth into the sand, and soketh through it into the sea; and therefore we made a well of a pipe, and placeth it under the rocke from which it falleth, and out of it filled our caske: but we could not fill above two tunnes in a night and day.

SECTION XXV.

So after our people began to gather their strength, wee manned our boates, and went over to the mayne, where presently we found a great ryver of fresh and sweete water, and a mightie marish countrie; which in the winter[1] seemeth to be continually over-flowne with this river, and others, which fall from the mountaynous country adjacent.

We rowed some leagues up the ryver, and found that the further up we went, the deeper was the river, but no fruit, more then the sweate of our bodies for the labour of our handes.

At our returne, wee loaded our boate ·with water, and afterwardes from hence wee made our store.

[1] This river is now called the Maccahe : probably it floods in the rainy season.

SECTION XXVI.

THE sicknesse having wasted more then the one halfe of
my people, we determined to take out the victualls of the
Hawke, and to burne her; which wee put in execution.
And being occupied in this worke, we saw a shippe turning
to windwards, to succour her selfe of the ilands;[1] but having
discryed us, put off to sea-wards.

Two dayes after, the wind changing, we saw her againe
running alongst the coast, and the *Daintie* not being in
case to goe after her, for many reasons, we manned the
Fancie, and sent her after her; who about the setting of
the sunne fetched her up, and spake with her; when finding her to be a great fly-boat, of at least three or foure
hundreth tunnes, with eighteen peeces of artillery, would
have returned, but the wind freshing in, put her to lee-
wards; and standing in to succour her selfe of the land,
had sight of another small barke, which after a short chase
shee tooke, but had nothing of moment in her, for that she
had bin upon the great sholes of Abreoios,[2] in eighteen
degrees, and there throwne all they had by the board, to
save their lives.

This and the other chase were the cause that the *Fancie*
could not beat it up in many dayes: but before we had
put all in a readinesse, the wind changing, shee came unto
us, and made relation of that which had past; and how
they had given the small barke to the Portingalls, and
brought with them onely her pilot, and a marchant called
Pedro de Escalante of Potosi.

1 By working up under their lee.
2 These shoals, already alluded to at page 62, are now called the
Abrolhos: there is a channel betwixt the islets and the main: the
soundings extend to the eastward eighty or ninety miles.

SECTION XXVII.

Sect. XXVII. In this coast, the Portingalls, by industrie of the Indians,

Industry of the Indians. have wrought many feats. At Cape Frio they tooke a

They surprise the French. great French ship in the night, the most of her company being on the shore, with cannoas,[1] which they have in this coast so great, that they carry seventie and eightie men in one of them. And in Isla Grand, I saw one that was above threescore foote long, of one tree, as are all that I have seen in Brasill, with provisions in them for twentie or

San Sebastian. thirtie days. At the iland of San-Sebastian, neere Saint Vincent, the Indians killed about eightie of Master Can-

Kill the English, dish his men, and tooke his boat, which was the overthrow of his voyage.

There commeth not any ship upon this coast, whereof these cannoas give not notice presently to every place. And wee were certified in Isla Grand, that they had sent

and discover us. an Indian from the river of Ienero, through all the mountaines and marishes, to take a view of us, and accordingly made a relation of our shippes, boates, and the number of men which we might have. But to prevent the like danger that might come upon us being carelesse and negligent, I determined one night, in the darkest and quietest of it, to see what watch our company kept on the shore; manned our light horsman, and boat, armed them with bowes and targetts, and got a shore some good distance from the places where were our boothes, and sought to come upon them undiscovered: we used all our best endevours to take them at unawares, yet comming within fortie paces, we were discovered; the whole and the sicke came forth to oppose themselves against us. Which we seeing, gave them the hubbub, after the manner of the Indians, and assaulted them, and they us; but being a close darke night, they could not discerne us presently upon the hubbub.[2]

---

[1] Boats hollowed from the trunk of a tree.

[2] Whoop! whoop! Cotgrave gives us the meaning of *hootings* and

From our shippe the gunner shott a peece of ordinance
over our heads, according to the order given him, and
thereof we tooke occasion to retyre unto our boates, and
within a little space came to the boothes and landing places,
as though wee came from our shippes to ayd them.   They
began to recount unto us, how that at the wester poynt of The events
the iland, out of certaine cannoas, had landed a multitude of a good
watch.
of Indians, which with a great out-cry came upon them,
and assaulted them fiercely; but finding better resistance
then they looked for, and seeing themselves discovered by
the shippes, tooke themselves to their heeles and returned
to their cannoas, in which they imbarked themselves, and
departed.   One affirmed, he saw the cannoas; another,
their long hayre; a third, their bowes; a fourth, that it
could not be, but that some of them had their payments.
And it was worth the sight, to behold those which had not
moved out of their beds in many moneths, unlesse by the
helpe of others, gotten some a bow-shoot off into the woods,
others into the toppes of trees, and those which had any
strength, joyned together to fight for their lives.   In fine,
the boothes and tents were left desolate.[3]

To colour our businesse the better, after we had spent
some houres in seeking out and joyning the companie together, in comforting, animating, and commending them,
I left them an extraordinary guard for that night, and so
departed to our shippes, with such an opinion of the assault
given by the Indians, that many so possessed, through all
the voyage, would not be perswaded to the contrary.

whoopings : noises wherewith swine are scared, or infamous old women
disgraced.

[3] A sudden sensation, be it from fear or otherwise, has a surprising
effect upon persons sick or bed-ridden.   Lediard relates that in a sharp
engagement with a combined squadron of French and Dutch ships, off
Sir Christopher, in 1667, Sir John Harman, the English commander,
who had been lame and in great pain from the gout, upon discovering
the enemy's fleet, got up, walked about, and gave orders as well as
ever, till the fight was over, and then became as lame as before.

Which impression wrought such effect in most of my companie, that in all places where the Indians might annoy us, they were ever after most carefull and vigilant, as was convenient.[4]

In these ilands it heigheth and falleth some five or six foot water, and but once in two and twentie houres; as in all this coast, and in many parts of the West Indies; as also in the coast of Perew and Chely, saving where are great bayes or indraughts, and there the tydes keep their ordinary course of twice in foure and twentie houres.

Palmito iland. In the lesser of these ilands, is a cave for a small ship to ryde in, land-lockt, and shee may moore her sele to the trees of either side. This we called Palmito iland, for the aboundance it hath of the greater sort of palmito trees; the other hath none at all. A man may goe betwixt the ilands with his ship, but the better course is out at one end.

In these ilands are many scorpions, snakes, and adders, with other venemous vermine. They have parrots, and a certaine kinde of fowle like unto pheasants, somewhat bigger, and seeme to be of their nature. Here we spent above a moneth in curing of our sicke men, supplying our wants of wood and water, and in other necessary workes. And the tenth of December, all things put in order, we set sayle for Cape Frio, having onely six men sicke, with purpose there to set ashore our two prisoners before named; and anchoring under the Cape, we sent our boat a shore, but they could not finde any convenient place to land them in, and so returned.[5] The wind being southerly, and not good to goe on our voyage, we succoured our selves within

---

[4] We do not approve of such means of exciting vigilance; some might have got their payments. According to Æsop, *wolf* may be called too often.

[5] Cape Frio has since become remarkable as the point on which her majesty's ship *Thetis* was wrecked in December 1830, the night after she had left Rio Janeiro. A landing was effected, and nearly the whole crew saved. A snug cove north of the cape, with a boat entrance to

Isla Grand, which lyeth some dozen or fourteene leagues ^{Sect. xxvii.} from the cape, betwixt the west, and by south and west south-west; the rather to set our prisoners a shore.

In the mid-way betwixt the Cape and this iland, lyeth the river Ienero, a very good harbour, fortified with a ^{Ienero.} garrison, and a place well peopled. The Isla Grand is some eight or ten leagues long, and causeth a goodly harbour for shipping. It is full of great sandie bayes, and in the most of them is store of good water; within this iland are many other smaller ilands, which cause divers sounds and creekes; and amongst these little ilands, one, for the ^{Little iland.} pleasant scituation and fertilitie thereof, called Placentia. This is peopled, all the rest desert: on this island our prisoners desired to be put a shore, and promised to send us some refreshing. Whereto we condescended, and sent them ashore, with two boates well man'd and armed, who found few inhabitants in the iland; for our people saw not above foure or five houses, notwithstanding our boats returned loaden with plantynes, pinias,[6] potatoes, sugarcanes, and some hennes. Amongst which they brought a kind of little plantyne, greene, and round, which were the best of any that I have seene.

With our people came a Portingall, who said, that the island was his; he seemed to be a Mistecho, who are those that are of a Spanish and an Indian brood, poorely apparelled and miserable; we feasted him, and gave him some trifles, and he, according to his abilitie, answered our courtesie with such as he had.

The wind continuing contrary, we emptied all the water wee could come by, which we had filled in Saint James his iland, and filled our caske with the water of this Isla ^{Isla Grand.} Grand. It is a wildernesse, covered with trees and shrubs

the southward, was much used during the operations afterwards carried on to attempt to recover the treasure embarked in her.

[6] Pine apples, *ananassa sativa*.

so thicke, as it hath no passage through, except a man make it by force. And it was strange to heare the howling and cryes of wilde beastes in these woods day and night, which we could not come at to see by any meanes; some like lyons, others like beares, others like hoggs, and of such and so many diversities, as was admirable.

Heere our nets profited us much; for in the sandy bayes they tooke us store of fish. Upon the shore, at full sea-mark, we found in many places certaine shels, like those of mother of pearles, which are brought out of the East Indies, to make standing cups, called *caracoles;* of so great curiositie as might move all the beholders to magnifie the maker of them: and were it not for the brittlenes of them, by reason of their exceeding thinnes, doubtles they were to bee esteemed farre above the others; for, more excellent workemanship I have not seene in shels.[7]

The eighteenth of December, we set sayle, the wind at north-east, and directed our course for the Straites of Magalianes. The twenty two of this moneth, at the going too of the sunne, we descryed a Portingall ship, and gave her chase, and comming within hayling of her, shee rendred her selfe without any resistance; shee was of an hundred tuns, bound for Angola, to load negroes, to be carried and sold in the river of Plate. It is a trade of great profit, and much used, for that the negroes are carried from the head of the river of Plate, to Patosi, to labour in the mynes. It is a bad negro, who is not worth there five or six hundreth peeces, every peece of tenne ryals, which they receive in ryals of plate,[8] for there is no other marchandize in those partes. Some have told me, that of late they have found out the trade and benefit of cochanillia, but the river suffereth not vessels of burthen; for if they drawe above

[7] Probably a species of nautilus.
[8] The ryal of silver, of which ten went to a "piece," is in value about fivepence of our money.

eight or seaven foote water, they cannot goe further then the mouth of the river, and the first habitation is above a hundred and twenty leagues up, whereunto many barkes trade yearely, and carry all kinde of marchandize serving for Patosi and Paraquay ; the money which is thence returned, is distributed in all the coast of Brasill.

The loading of this ship was meale of cassavi, which the _{Cassavi meale.} Portingals call *Farina de Paw.* It serveth for marchandize in Angola, for the Portingals foode in the ship, and to nourish the negroes which they should carry to the river of Plate. This meale is made of a certaine roote which the Indians call *yuca,* much like unto potatoes. Of it are two kindes : the one sweete and good to be eaten (either rosted or sodden) as potatoes, and the other of which they make their bread, called *cassavi*; deadly poyson, if the liquor or juyce bee not thoroughly pressed out. So prepared it is the bread of Brazill, and many parts of the Indies, which they make in this maner : first they pare the roote, and then upon a rough stone they grate it as small as they can, _{The preparing thereof for food.} and after that it is grated small, they put it into a bag or poke, and betwixt two stones, with great waight, they presse out the juyce or poyson, and after keepe it in some bag, till it hath no juyce nor moysture left.[9] Of this they make two sorts of bread, the one finer and the other courser, but bake them after one maner. They place a great broad smooth stone upon other foure, which serve in steede of a trevet, and make a quicke fire under it, and so strawe the flower or meale a foote long, and halfe a foot broad. To make it to incorporate, they sprinkle now and then a little water, and then another rowe of meale, and another sprinkling, till it be to their minde ; that which is

---

[9] Cassava or manioc is of the natural order *euphorbiaceæ.* The root abounds with a poisonous juice, but this after maceration is driven off by heat, and the fecula is obtained in an edible state. Tapioca is a preparation of cassava. *Farina do pao*—flour of wood.

to be spent presently, they make a finger thicke, and some-times more thicke; but that which they make for store, is not above halfe a finger thicke, but so hard, that if it fall on the ground it will not breake easily. Being newly baked, it is reasonable good, but after fewe dayes it is not to be eaten, except it be soaked in water. In some partes they suffer the meale to become fenoed,[10] before they make it into bread, and hold it for the best, saying that it giveth it a better tast; but I am not of that opinion. In other parts they mingle it with a fruite called agnanapes, which are round, and being ripe are grey, and as big as an hazell nut, and grow in a cod like pease, but that it is all curiously wrought: first they parch them upon a stone, and after beate them into powder, and then mingle them with the fine flower of cassavi, and bake them into bread, these are their spice-cakes, which they call *xauxaw*.

The agnanapes are pleasant, give the bread a yellowish coulour, and an aromaticall savour in taste.[11] The finer of this bread, being well baked, keepeth long time, three or foure yeares. In Brazill, since the Portingalls taught the Indians the use of sugar, they eate this meale mingled with remels[12] of sugar, or malasses; and in this manner the Por-tingalls themselves feed of it.

But we found a better manner of dressing this farina, in making pancakes, and frying them with butter or oyle, and sometimes with *manteca de puerco;* when strewing a little sugar upon them, it was meate that our company desired above any that was in the shippe.

The Indians also accustome to make their drinke of this meale, and in three severall manners.

First is chewing it in their mouths, and after mingling

---

[10] *Vinewed*—mouldy.

[11] Probably cacao (*theobroma cacao*), well known from the beverage of the same name, and from which chocolate is manufactured.

[12] In the Devonshire dialect, *remlet* means a remnant.

it with water, after a loathsome manner, yet the common-
est drinke that they have; and that held best which is
chewed by an old woman.[13]

The second manner of their drinke, is baking it till it be
halfe burned, then they beate it into powder; and when
they will drinke, they mingle a small quantitie of it with
water, which giveth a reasonable good taste.

The third, and best, is baking it, as aforesaid, and when
it is beaten into powder, to seeth it in water; after that
it is well boyled, they let it stand some three or foure
dayes, and then drinke it. So, it is much like the ale which
is used in England, and of that colour and taste.

The Indians are very curious in planting and manuring The manner of planting yuca.
of this *yuca*. It is a little shrubb, and carryeth branches
like hazell wands; being growne as bigge as a mans finger,
they breake them off in the middest, and so pricke them
into the ground; it needeth no other art or husbandry,
for out of each branch grow two, three, or foure rootes,
some bigger, some lesser: but first they burne and manure
the ground, the which labour, and whatsoever els is requisite, the men doe not so much as helpe with a finger, but all
lyeth upon their poore women, who are worse then slaves; With the la-bour of the women.
for they labour the ground, they plant, they digge and
delve, they bake, they brew, and dresse their meate, fetch
their water, and doe all drudgerie whatsoever : yea, though
they nurse a childe, they are not exempted from any
labour; their childe they carry in a wallet about their
necke, ordinarily under one arme, because it may sucke
when it will.

The men have care for nothing but for their cannoas, to
passe from place to place, and of their bowes and arrowes
to hunt, and their armes for the warre, which is a sword of
heavie blacke wood, some foure fingers broad, an inch

[13] A similar disagreeable preparation, called *kava*, is prepared and
drunk in the Polynesian islands.

thicke, and an ell long, something broader towards the toppe then at the handle. They call it *macana*, and it is carved and wrought with inlayd works very curiously, but his edges are blunt. If any kill any game in hunting, he bringeth it not with him, but from the next tree to the game, he breaketh a bough (for the trees in the Indies have leaves for the most part all the yeare), and all the way as he goeth streweth little peeces of it, here and there, and comming home giveth a peece to his woman, and so sends her for it.

If they goe to the warre, or in any journey, where it is necessary to carry provision or marchandize, the women serve to carry all, and the men never succour nor ease them ; wherein they shew greater barbarisme then in any thing, in my opinion, that I have noted amongst them, except in eating one another.

Polygamy of the Indians. In Brasill, and in the West Indies, the Indian may have as many wives as he can get, either bought or given by her friends : the men and women, for the most part, goe Their attire. naked, and those which have come to know their shame, cover onely their privie parts with a peece of cloth, the rest of their body is naked. Their houses resemble great barnes, covered over or thatched with plantyne leaves, which reach to the ground, and at either end is the doore.

Their manner of housing. In one house are sometimes ten or twentie households : they have little household stuffe, besides their beds, which they call *hamacas*,[14] and are made of cotton, and stayned with divers colours and workes. Some I have seene white, of great curiositie. They are as a sheete laced at both ends, and at either end of them long strappes, with which they fasten them to two posts, as high as a mans middle,

---

[14] The hammock now in general use at sea, takes its name from this term.

and so sit rocking themselves in them. Sometimes they use them for seates, and sometimes to sleepe in at their pleasures. In one of them I have seene sleepe the man, his wife, and a childe.

SECTION XXVIII.

WE tooke out of this prize, for our provision, some good quantitie of this meale, and the sugar shee had, being not above three or foure chestes : after three dayes we gave the ship to the Portingalls, and to them libertie. In her was a Portingall knight, which went for governour of Angola, of the habit of Christ, with fiftie souldiers, and armes for a hundreth and fiftie, with his wife and daughter. He was old, and complained, that after many yeares service for his king, with sundry mishapps, he was brought to that poore estate, as for the relief of his wife, his daughter, and him-selfe, he had no other substance, but that he had in the ship. It moved compassion, so as nothing of his was di-minished, which though to us was of no great moment, in Angola it was worth good crownes. Onely we disarmed them all, and let them depart, saying that they would re-turne to Saint Vincents.

We continued our course for the Straites, my people much animated with this unlookt for refreshing, and praised God for his bountie, providence, and grace extended towards us. Here it will not be out of the way to speake a word of the particularities of the countrie.

SECTION XXIX.

Sect. XXIX.

The description of
Brasill.

BRASILL is accounted to be that part of America, which lyeth towards our north sea, betwixt the river of the Amazons, neere the lyne to the northwards, untill a man come to the river of Plate in thirty-six degrees to the southwards of the lyne.

This coast generally lyeth next of any thing south and by west; it is a temperate countrie, though in some parts it exceedeth in heat; it is full of good succors for shipping,

Its havens.

and plentifull for rivers and fresh waters; the principal habitations are, Farnambuca, the Bay De todos los Santos, Nostra Senora de Victoria, alias Santos, the river Ienero, Saint Vincents, and Placentia; every of them provided of a good port. The winds are variable, but for the most part trade[1] along the coast.

Its commodities.

The commodities this country yeeldeth, are the wood called Brasill,[2] whereof the best is that of Farnambuc; (so also called, being used in most rich colours) good cotton-wooll, great store of sugar, balsamon, and liquid amber.

Its wants.

They have want of all maner of cloth, lynnen, and woollen, of iron, and edge-tools, of copper, and principally in some places, of wax, of wine, of oyle, and meale (for the country beareth no corne), and of all maner of haberdashery-wares, for the Indians.

The bestiall thereof.

The beasts that naturally breed in this country are, tygers, lyons, hoggs, dogges, deere, monkeyes, mycos, and conies (like unto ratts, but bigger, and of a tawney colour), armadilloes, alagartoes, and store of venemous wormes and serpents, as scorpions, adders, which they call vinoras; and of them, one kind, which the divine Providence hath created with a bell upon his head, that wheresoever he

[1] Blow steadily—in one direction. Whence trade wind.

[2] Before the discovery of America, dye woods were known by this denomination; and Brazil owes its name to the quantity of wood of this nature found among its forests.

goeth, the sound of it might be heard, and so the serpent shunned; for his stinging is without remedie. This they call the vynora with the bell; of them there are many, and great stores of snakes, them of that greatnesse, as to write the truth, might seeme fabulous.

Another worm there is in this country, which killed many of the first inhabitants, before God was pleased to discover a remedie for it, unto a religious person; it is like a magot, but more slender, and longer, and of a greene colour, with a red head; this worme creepeth in at the hinder parts, where is the evacuation of our superfluities, and there, as it were, gleweth himselfe to the gutt, there feedeth of the bloud and humors, and becommeth so great, that stopping the naturall passage, he forceth the principall wheele of the clocke of our bodie to stand still, and with it the accompt of the houres of life to take end, with most cruell torment and paine, which is such, that he who hath beene throughly punished with the collique can quickly decipher or demonstrate. The antidote for this pernicious worme is garlique; and this was discovered by a physitian to a religious person.

The discommodities.

SECTION XXX.

BETWIXT twenty-six and twenty-seven degrees neere the coast lyeth an iland; the Portingalls call it Santa Catalina, which is a reasonable harbour, and hath good refreshing of wood, water, and fruit. It is desolate, and serveth for those who trade from Brasill to the river of Plate, or from the river to Brasill, as an inne, or bayting place.[1]

Santa Catalina.

In our navigation towards the Straites, by our observation wee found, that our compasse varyed a poynt and

Variation of the compasse

[1] Saint Catherine's now ranks as a port after Rio Janeiro and Bahia.

better to the eastwards. And for that divers have written curiously and largely of the variation thereof, I referre them that desire the understanding of it, to the *Discourse* of Master William Aborrawh, and others; for it is a secret, whose causes well understood are of greatest moment in all navigations.[2]

In the height of the river of Plate, we being some fiftie leagues off the coast, a storme took us southerly, which endured fortie-eight houres.[3] In the first day, about the going downe of the sunne, Robert Tharlton, master of the *Fancie*, bare up before the wind, without giving us any token or signe that shee was in distresse.   We seeing her to continue her course, bare up after her, and the night comming on, we carried our light; but shee never answered us; for they kept their course directly for England, which

The over-
throw of
the voyage. was the overthrow of the voyage, as well for that we had no pynace to goe before us, to discover any danger, to seeke out roades and anchoring, to helpe our watering and re-freshing ; as also for the victuals, necessaries, and men which they carryed away with them : which though they were not many, yet with their helpe in our fight, we had taken the Vice-Admirall, the first time shee bourded with us, as shall be hereafter manifested.   For once we cleered her decke, and had we beene able to have spared but a dozen men, doubtlesse we had done with her what we would ; for shee had no close fights.[4]

The cause.   Moreover, if shee had beene with me, I had not beene

[2] The cause of the variation of the compass still remains a secret. But from the close analogy existing between magnetism and electricity, perhaps we are not far from discovering it. The variation at this point in 1820, was $7\frac{1}{2}°$ E.

[3] Sudden squalls are generated on the Pampas or plains lying round Buenos Ayres, called thence Pamperos ; which do great damage. See the account of one in the Voyages of the *Adventure* and *Beagle*.

[4] Probably barricades to retire behind in case of being boarded. The piratical prahus of the Indian Archipelago are fitted with a similar defence.

discovered upon the coast of Perew. But I was worthy to be deceived, that trusted my ship in the hands of an hypo-crite, and a man which had left his generall before in the like occasion, and in the selfe-same place ; for being with Infidelitie. Master Thomas Candish, master of a small ship in the voyage wherein he dyed, this captaine being aboord the Admirall, in the night time forsooke his fleet, his generall and captaine, and returned home.

This bad custome is too much used amongst sea-men, and worthy to be severely punished ; for doubtlesse the not punishing of those offenders hath beene the prime cause of many lamentable events, losses, and overthrowes, to the dishonour of our nation, and frustrating of many good and honourable enterprises.

In this poynt of dicipline, the Spaniards doe farre sur- Dicipline of passe us; for whosoever forsaketh his fleete, or commander, the Spanish. is not onely severely punished, but deprived also of all charge or government for ever after. This in our countrie is many times neglected ; for that there is none to follow the cause, the principalls being either dead with griefe, or drowned in the gulfe of povertie, and so not able to wade through with the burthen of that suite, which in Spaine is prosecuted by the kings atturney, or fiscall ; or at least, a judge appoynted for determining that cause purposely.

Yea, I cannot attribute the good successe the Spaniard The only cause of their hath had in his voyages and peoplings, to any extraordinary prosperities. vertue more in him then in any other man, were not dis-cipline, patience, and justice far superior. For in valour, experience, and travell, he surpasseth us not; in shipping, preparation, and plentie of vitualls, hee commeth not neere us ; in paying and rewarding our people, no nation did goe beyond us : but God, who is a just and bountifull rewarder, regarding obedience farre above sacrifice, doubtlesse, in recompence of their indurance, resolution, and subjection to commandment, bestoweth upon them the blessing due unto it. And this, not for that the Spaniard is of a more tractable disposition, or more docible nature than wee, but that justice halteth with us, and so the old proverbe is verified, *Pittie marreth the whole cittie.*

Thus come we to be deprived of the sweet fruit, which the rod of dicipline bringeth with it, represented unto us in auncient verses, which as a relique of experience I have heard in my youth recorded by a wise man, and a great captaine, thus :

> The rod by power divine, and earthly regall law,
> Makes good men live in peace, and bad to stand in awe :
> For with a severe stroke the bad corrected be,
> Which makes the good to joy such justice for to see ;
> The rod of dicipline breeds feare in every part,
> Reward by due desert doth joy and glad the heart.

The cunning of runna-wayes. These absentings and escapes are made most times onely to pilfer and steale, as well by taking of some prise when they are alone, and without commaund, to hinder or order their bad proceedings, as to appropriate that which is in their intrusted ship; casting the fault, if they be called to account, upon some poore and unknowne mariners, whom they suffer with a little pillage to absent themselves, the cunninglier to colour their greatest disorders, and robberies.

And ignoble captaines. For doubtlesse, if he would, hee might have come unto us with great facilitie; because within sixteene houres the storme ceased, and the winde came fayre, which brought us to the Straites, and dured many days after with us at north-east. This was good for them, though naught for us: if he had perished any mast or yard, sprung any leake, wanted victuals, or instruments for finding us, or had had any other impediment of importance, hee might have had some colour to cloake his lewdnes:[5] but his masts and yards being sound, his shippe staunch and loaden with victuales for two yeares at the least, and having order from place to

---

[5] Misbehaviour. Tooke derives *lewd* from the Anglo-Saxon *lœwan*— to delude or mislead.

place, where to finde us, his intention is easily seene to bee
bad, and his fault such, as worthily deserved to bee made
exemplary unto others. Which he manifested at his returne, by his manner of proceeding, making a spoyle of
the prise hee tooke in the way homewards, as also of that
which was in the ship, putting it into a port fit for his
purpose, where he might have time and commodity to doe
what hee would.

Wee made account that they had beene swallowed up of
the sea, for we never suspected that anything could make
them forsake us; so, we much lamented them. The storme
ceasing, and being out of all hope, we set sayle and went
on our course. During this storme, certaine great
fowles, as big as swannes, soared about us, and the
winde calming, setled themselves in the sea, and fed
upon the sweepings of our ship; which I perceiving,
and desirous to see of them, because they seemed farre
greater then in truth they were, I caused a hooke and
lyne to be brought me; and with a peece of a pilchard
I bayted the hook, and a foot from it, tyed a peece of corke,
that it might not sinke deepe, and threw it into the sea,
which, our ship driving with the sea, in a little time was a
good space from us, and one of the fowles being hungry,
presently seized upon it, and the hooke in his upper
beake. It is like to a faulcons bill, but that the poynt is
more crooked, in that maner, as by no meanes he could
cleare himselfe, except that the lyne brake, or the hooke
righted : plucking him towards the ship, with the waving
of his wings he eased the waight of his body ; and being
brought to the sterne of our ship, two of our company went
downe by the ladder of the poope, and seized on his necke
and wings ; but such were the blowes he gave them with
his pinnions, as both left their hand-fast, being beaten
blacke and blewe ; we cast a snare about his necke, and
so tryced him into the ship.

By the same manner of fishing, we caught so many of them, as refreshed and recreated all my people for that day. Their bodies were great, but of little flesh and tender; in taste answerable to the food whereon they feed.[6]

They were of two colours, some white, some gray; they had three joynts in each wing; and from the poynt of one wing to the poynt of the other, both stretched out, was above two fathomes.

The wind continued good with us, till we came to forty-nine degrees and thirty minutes, where it tooke us westerly, being, as we made our accompt, some fiftie leagues from the shore. Betwixt forty-nine and forty-eight degrees, is Port Saint Julian, a good harbour, and in which a man may grave his ship, though shee draw fifteene or sixteene foote water: but care is to be had of the people called Pentagones. They

are treacherous, and of great stature, so the most give them the name of gyants.[7]

The second of February, about nine of the clocke in the morning, we discryed land, which bare south-west of us, which wee looked not for so timely; and comming neerer and neerer unto it, by the lying, wee could not conjecture what land it should be; for we were next of anything in forty-eight degrees, and no platt nor sea-card which we had made mention of any land which lay in that manner, neere about that height; in fine, wee brought our lar-bord tacke aboord, and stood to the north-east-wardes all that day and night, and the winde continuing westerly and a fayre gale, wee continued our course alongst the coast the day and night following. In which time wee made accompt we dis-

---

[6] This fowl was doubtless the albatross (Diomedea), which seems to be a corruption of the Portuguese word *alcatraz*. The practice of fishing for them still continues, though more for recreation (?) than for refreshment.

[7] The account of the gigantic stature of the Patagonians seems to be fabulous. Magalhaens reported them as giants; but later navigators disputed it: however, Fitzroy states them to average nearly six feet.

coverd well neere threescore leagues of the coast. It is
bold, and made small shew of dangers.

The land is a goodly champion country, and peopled : A description of the
we saw many fires, but could not come to speake with the unknowne land.
people ; for the time of the yeare was farre spent, to shoot
the Straites, and the want of our pynace disabled us for A caveat for comming
finding a port or roade ; not being discretion with a ship suddenly too neere an un-
of charge, and in an unknowne coast, to come neere the knowne land.
shore before it was sounded ; which were causes, together
with the change of winde (good for us to passe the Straite),
that hindered the further discovery of this land, with its
secrets: this I have sorrowed for many times since, for that
it had likelihood to be an excellent country. It hath great
rivers of fresh waters ; for the out-shoot of them colours
the sea in many places, as we ran alongst it. It is not
mountaynous, but much of the disposition of England,
and as temperate. The things we noted principally on the
coast, are these following ; the westermost poynt of the
land, with which we first fell, is the end of the land to the
west-wardes, as we found afterwards. If a man bring this
poynt south-west, it riseth in three mounts, or round hil-
lockes : bringing it more westerly, they shoot themselves
all into one ; and bringing it easterly, it riseth in two
hillocks. This we call poynt Tremountaine. Some twelve Poynt Tre-mountaine.
or foureteene leagues from this poynt to the east-wardes,
fayre by the shore, lyeth a low flat iland of some two
leagues long ; we named it Fayre Iland ; for it was all Fayre Iland.
over as greene and smooth, as any meddow in the spring
of the yeare.

Some three or foure leagues easterly from this iland, is
a goodly opening, as of a great river, or an arme of the
sea, with a goodly low countrie adjacent. And eight or
tenne leagues from this opening, some three leagues from
the shore, lyeth a bigge rocke, which at the first wee had
thought to be a shippe under all her sayles ; but after, as

we came neere, it discovered it selfe to be a rocke, which

we called *Condite-head*; for that howsoever a man commeth with it, it is like to the condite heads about the cittie of London.

All this coast, so farre as wee discovered, lyeth next of any thing east and by north, and west and by south. The land, for that it was discovered in the raigne of Queene Elizabeth, my soveraigne lady and mistres, and a maiden Queene, and at my cost and adventure, in a perpetuall memory of her chastitie, and remembrance of my endea-

vours, I gave it the name of HAWKINS *maiden-land*.[8]

Before a man fall with this land, some twentie or thirtie leagues, he shall meete with bedds of oreweed, driving to and fro in that sea, with white flowers growing upon them, and sometimes farther off; which is a good show and signe the land is neere, whereof the westermost part lyeth some threescore leagues from the neerest land of America.

With our fayre and large wind, we shaped our course

for the Straites; and the tenth of February we had sight of land, and it was the head land of the Straites to the north-wards, which agreed with our height, wherein we found our selves to be, which was in fifty two degrees and fortie minutes.

Within a few houres we had the mouth of the Straites open, which lyeth in fifty-two degrees, and fifty minutes. It riseth like the North Foreland in Kent, and is much like the land of Margates. It is not good to borrow neere the shore, but to give it a fayre birth; within a few houres we entred the mouth of the Straites, which is some six leagues broad, and lyeth in fifty-two degrees, and fifty minutes: doubling the poynt on the

[8] It is generally supposed that this land was the Falkland islands; but as they lie betwixt 51° and 53°, this cannot be reconciled with being "next of anything in 48°." In this parallel, the main land projects to the eastward; and this perhaps was the land he descried. The rock like a sail might be the Bellaco rock.

star-board, which is also flat, of a good birth, we opened a fayre bay, in which we might discry the hull of a ship beaten upon the beach. It was of the Spanish fleete, that went to inhabite there, in anno 1582, under the charge of Pedro Sarmiento,[9] who at his returne was taken prisoner, and brought into England.

In this bay the Spaniards made their principall habita- tion, and called it the cittie of Saint Philip, and left it peopled; but the cold barrennes of the countrie, and the malice of the Indians, with whom they badly agreed, made speedie end of them, as also of those whom they left in the middle of the Straites, three leagues from Cape Froward to the east-wards, in another habitation.

We continued our course alongst this reach (for all the Straites is as a river altering his course, sometimes upon one poynt, sometimes upon another) which is some eight leagues long, and lyeth west north-west. From this we entred into a goodly bay, which runneth up into the land northerly many leagues; and at first entrance a man may see no other thing, but as it were a maine sea. From the end of this first reach, you must direct your course west south-west, and some fourteene or fifteene leagues lyeth one of the narrowest places of all the Straites; this leadeth unto another reach, that lyeth west and by north some six leagues.

[9] The expedition of Drake having excited considerable alarm in Peru, the viceroy despatched Don Pedro Sarmiento with orders to take him dead or alive. Proceeding to the Strait of Magalhaens in pursuit, he took the opportunity to explore its shores. He afterwards pointed out to the King of Spain, Philip II, the importance of fortifying the Straits, to prevent the passage of strangers. Accordingly an expedition was fitted out, which, after some accidents, founded the two settlements of Jesus and San Felipe. The site of the last is now known as Port Famine: so named from the disasters which befell the unhappy colonists, who mostly perished by want. Sarmiento himself having been blown off the coast, appears to have used every effort to obtain and forward supplies from Brazil to his friends, but, proceeding to Europe for further assistance, was captured and taken to England.

Here, in the middle of the reach, the wind tooke us by the north-west, and so we were forced to anchor some two or three dayes.   In which time, we went a shore with our boates, and found neere the middle of this reach, on the star-boord side, a reasonable good place to ground and trimme a small ship, where it higheth some nine or ten foote water.   Here we saw certaine hogges, but they were so farre from us, that wee could not discerne if they were of those of the countrie, or brought by the Spaniards; these were all the beasts which we saw in all the time we were in the Straites.

In two tydes we turned through this reach, and so re-covered the ilands of Pengwins; they lye from this reach

Note. foure leagues southwest and by west.   Till you come to this place, care is to be taken of not comming too neere to any poynt of the land: for being, for the most part, sandie, they have sholding off them, and are somewhat dangerous.

The ilands of Pengwins These ilands have beene set forth by some to be three; we could discover but two : and they are no more, except that part of the mayne, which lyeth over against them, be an iland, which carrieth little likelihood, and I cannot deter-mine it.   A man may sayle betwixt the two ilands, or be-twixt them and the land on the larboord side; from which land to the bigger iland is, at it were, a bridge or ledge, on which is foure or five fathome water; and to him that commeth neere it, not knowing thereof, may justly cause feare; for it showeth to be shold water with his rypling, like unto a race.[10]

Betwixt the former reach, and these ilands, runneth up a goodly bay into the country to the north-wards.   It causeth

[10] The tides run with great velocity in some parts of the straits. The rippling might justly cause fear, ignorant as the parties were of the extent of the rise and fall of tide.   Fitzroy relates that an American captain hardly recovered, being told that it amounted to six or seven fathoms.

a great indraught, and above these ilands runneth a great tide from the mouth of the Straites to these ilands; the land on the larboord side is low land and sandy, for the most part, and without doubt, ilands, for it hath many openings into the sea, and forcible indraughts by them, and that on the starboord side, is all high mountaynous land from end to end; but no wood on eyther side. Before wee passed these 'ilands, under the lee of the bigger iland, we anchored, the wind being at north-east, with intent to refresh ourselves with the fowles of these ilands. They are of divers sorts, and in great plentie, as pengwins, wilde duckes, gulles, and gannets; of the principall we purposed to make provisions, and those were the pengwins; which in Welsh, as I have beene enformed, signifieth a white head. From which derivation, and many other Welsh denominations given by the Indians, or their predecessors, some doe inferre that America was first peopled with Welsh-men; and Motezanna, king, or rather emperour of Mexico, did recount unto the Spaniards, at their first comming, that his auncestors came from a farre countrie, and were white people. Which, conferred with an auncient cronicle, that I have read many yeares since, may be conjectured to bee a prince of Wales, who many hundreth yeares since, with certaine shippes, sayled to the westwards, with intent to make new discoveries. Hee was never after heard of.

The pengwin is in all proportion like unto a goose, and hath no feathers, but a certaine doune upon all parts of his body, and therefore cannot fly, but avayleth himselfe in all occasions with his feete, running as fast as most men. He liveth in the sea, and on the land; feedeth on fish in the sea, and as a goose on the shore upon grasse. They harbour themselves under the ground in burrowes, as the connies, and in them hatch their young. All parts of the iland where they haunted were undermined, save onely one valley, which it seemeth they reserved for their foode; for it was as greene as any medowe in the moneth of Aprill, with a most fine short grasse. The flesh of these pengwins is much of the savour of a certaine fowle taken in the ilands of Lundey and Silley, which wee call puffins : by the tast it is easily discerned that they feede on fish. They are very fatt, and in dressing must be flead as the byter ; they are reasonable meate, rosted, baked, or sodden, but best rosted. We salted some dozen or sixteen hogsheads, which served us, whilest they lasted, in steede of powdred beefe.[11]

The hunting of them, as we may well terme it, was a great recreation to my company, and worth the sight, for in determining to catch them, necessarily was required good store of people, every one with a cudgell in his hand, to compasse them round about, to bring them, as it were, into a ring; if they chanced to breake out, then was the sport ; for the ground being undermined, at unawares it fayled, and as they ran after them, one fell here, another there; another, offering to strike at one, lifting up his hand, sunke upp to the arme-pits in the earth; another, leaping to avoyd one hole, fell into another. And after the first slaughter, in seeing us on the shore, they shunned us, and procured to recover the sea; yea, many times seeing themselves persecuted, they would tumble downe from such high rocks and mountaines, as it seemed impossible to escape with life. Yet as soone as they came to the beach, presently wee should see them runne into the sea, as though they had no hurt. Where one goeth, the other followeth, like sheepe after the bel-wether : but in getting them once within the ring, close together, few escaped, save such as by chance hid themselves in the borrowes; and ordinarily there was no drove which yeelded us not a thousand and

[11] Birds which are strong-flavoured are rendered edible by stripping off their skin.

more : the maner of killing them which the hunters used, being in a cluster together, was with their cudgels to knocke them on the head ; for though a man gave them many blowes on the body, they died not ; besides, the flesh bruised is not good to keepe. The massaker ended, presently they cut off their heads, that they might bleede well : such as we determined to keepe for store, wee saved in this maner. First, we split them, and then washed them well in sea water, then salted them: having layne some sixe howres in salt, wee put them in presse eight howres, and the blood being soaked out, we salted them againe in our other caske, as is the custome to salt beefe ; after this maner they continued good some two moneths, and served us in stead of beefe.

The gulls and gannets were not in so great quantitie, yet we wanted not young gulles to eate all the time of our stay about these ilands. It was one of the delicatest foodes that I have eaten in all my life.

The ducks are different to ours, and nothing so good meate ; yet they may serve for necessitie. They were many, and had a part of the iland to themselves severall, which was the highest hill, and more then a musket shott over.

In all the dayes of my life, I have not seene greater art and curiositie in creatures voyd of reason, then in the placing and making of their nestes ; all the hill being so full of them, that the greatest mathematician of the world could not devise how to place one more then there was upon the hill, leaving onely one path-way for a fowle to passe betwixt.

The hill was all levell, as if it had beene smoothed by art ; the nestes made onely of earth, and seeming to be of the selfe same mould ; for the nests and the soyle is all one, which, with water that they bring in their beakes, they make into clay, or a certaine dawbe, and after fashion them round, as with a compasse. In the bottome they containe the measure of a foote ; in the height about eight inches ; and in the toppe, the same quantitie over; there they are hollowed in, somewhat deepe, wherein they lay their eggs, without other prevention. And I am of opinion that the sunne helpeth them to hatch their young : their nests are for many yeares, and of one proportion, not one exceeding another in bignesse, in height, nor circumference ; and in proportionable distance one from another. In all this hill, nor in any of their nestes, was to be found a blade of grasse, a straw, a sticke, a feather, a moate, no, nor the filing of any fowle, but all the nestes and passages betwixt them, were so smooth and cleane, as if they had beene newly swept and washed.

All which are motives to prayse and magnifie the universall Creator, who so wonderfully manifesteth his wisedome, bountie, and providence in all his creatures, and especially for his particular love to ingratefull mankinde, for whose contemplation and service he hath made them all.

SECTION XXXI.

Of seales, or sea-wolves. ONE day, having ended our hunting of pengwins, one of our mariners walking about the iland, discovered a great company of seales, or sea-wolves (so called for that they are in the sea, as the wolves on the land), advising us that he left them sleeping, with their bellies tosting against the sunne. Wee provided our selves with staves, and other weapons, and sought to steale upon them at unawares, to surprise some of them ; and comming down the side of a hill, wee were not discovered, till we were close upon them: notwithstanding, their sentinell, before we could approach, with a great howle waked them : wee got betwixt the sea and some of them, but they shunned us not ; for they came directly upon us ; and though we dealt here and there a blow, yet not a man that withstood them, escaped the overthrow. They reckon not of a musket shott, a sword peirceth not their skinne, and to give a blow with a staffe, is as to smite upon a stone : onely in giving the blow upon his snowt, presently he falleth downe dead.

After they had recovered the water, they did, as it were, scorne us, defie us, and daunced before us, untill we had shot some musket shott through them, and so they appeared no more.

This fish is like unto a calfe, with foure leggs, but not above a spanne long : his skinne is hayrie like a calfe ; but these were different to all that ever I have seene, yet I have seene of them in many parts ; for these were greater, and in their former parts like unto lyons, with shagge hayre, and mostaches.

They live in the sea, and come to sleepe on the land, and they ever have one that watcheth, who adviseth them of any accident.

They are beneficiall to man in their skinnes for many purposes ; in their mostaches for pick-tooths, and in their fatt to make traine-oyle. This may suffice for the seale, for that he is well knowne.

SECTION XXXII.

ONE day, our boates being loaden with pengwins, and comming aboord, a sudden storme tooke them, which together with the fury of the tyde, put them in such great danger, that although they threw all their loading into the sea, yet were they forced to goe before the wind and sea, to save their lives. Which we seeing, and considering that our welfare depended upon their safetie, being impossible to weigh our anchor, fastned an emptie barrell well pitched to the end of our cable, in stead of a boy, and letting it slip, set sayle to succour our boates, which in short space wee recovered, and after returned to the place where we ryd before.

The storme·ceasing, we used our diligence by all meanes to seeke our cable and anchor; but the tyde being forcible, and the weeds (as in many parts of the Straites), so long, that riding in foureteene fathome water, many times they streamed three and foure fathomes upon the ryme of the water ; these did so inrole our cable, that we could never set eye of our boy; and to sweepe for him was but lost labour, because of the weeds, which put us out of hope to recover it.[1]

And so our forcible businesse being ended, leaving instructions for the *Fancie* our pynace, according to appointment, where to find us, we inroled them in many folds of paper, put them into a barrell of an old musket, and stopped it in such manner as no wett could enter; then placing it an end upon one of the highest hills, and the most frequented of all the iland, wee imbarked our selves, and set sayle with the wind at north-west, which could serve us but to the end of that reach, some dozen leagues long, and some three or foure leagues broad. It lyeth next of any thing, till you come to Cape Agreda, south-west; from this Cape to Cape Froward, the coast lyeth west south-west.

The second peopling of the Spaniards. Some foure leagues betwixt them, was the second peopling of the Spaniards : and this Cape lyeth in fiftie five degrees and better.

Thwart Cape Froward, the wind larged with us, and we

[1] *Fucus giganteus.*—In the voyage of the *Adventure* and *Beagle* it was found firmly rooted in twenty fathoms, yet streaming fifty feet upon the surface.

continued our course towards the iland of Elizabeth; which Sect. xxxii.
lyeth from Cape Froward some foureteene leagues west
and by south. This reach is foure or five leagues broad,
and in it are many channells or openings into the sea; for
all the land on the souther part of the Straites are ilands
and broken land; and from the beginning of this reach to
the end of the Straites, high mountaynous land on both
sides, in most parts covered with snow all the yeare long.

Betwixt the iland Elizabeth and the mayne, is the narrowest passage of all the Straites; it may be some two
musket shott from side to side.[2] From this straite to
Elizabeth bay is some foure leagues, and the course lyeth Elizabeth bay.
north-west and by west.

This bay is all sandie and cleane ground on the easter
part; but before you come at it, there lyeth a poynt of the
shore a good byrth off, which is dangerous. And in this
reach, as in many parts of the Straites, runneth a quick
and forcible tyde. In the bay it higheth eight or nine
foote water. The norther part of the bay hath foule ground,
and rockes under water: and therefore it is not wholesome
borrowing of the mayne. One of master Thomas Candish
his pynaces, as I have beene enformed, came a-ground upon
one of them, and he was in hazard to have left her there.

From Elizabeth bay to the river of Ieronimo, is some The river of Ieronimo.
five leagues. The course lyeth west and by north, and
west. Here the wind scanted, and forced us to seek a place
to anchor in. Our boates going alongst the shore, found
a reasonable harbour, which is right against that which
they call river Ieronimo; but it is another channell, by
which a man may disemboake the straite, as by the other
which is accustomed; for with a storme, which tooke us
one night, suddenly we were forced into that opening un-
wittingly; but in the morning, seeing our error, and the

---

[2] The narrowest part is in Crooked Reach, a little to the westward
of St. Jerome point: here the strait is about one mile across.

wind larging, with two or three bourds wee turned out into the old channell, not daring for want of our pynace to attempt any new discoverie.[3]

Blanches bay.

This harbour we called Blanches bay : for that it was found by William Blanch, one of our masters mates. Here having moored our shippe, we began to make our provision of wood and water, whereof was plentie in this bay, and in all other places from Pengwin ilands, till within a dozen leagues of the mouth of the Straites.

Now finding our deckes open, with the long lying under the lyne and on the coast of Brasill, the sunne having beene in our zenith many times, we calked our ship within bourd and without, above the decks. And such was the diligence we used, that at foure dayes end, we had above threescore pipes of water, and twentie boats of wood stowed in our ship ; no man was idle, nor otherwise busied but in necessary workes : some in felling and cleaving of wood : some in carrying of water ; some in romaging ; some in washing ; others in baking ; one in heating of pitch ; another in gathering of mussells ; no man was exempted, but knew at evening whereunto he was to betake himselfe the morning following.

Objection of wast.

Some man might aske me how we came to have so many emptie caske in lesse then two moneths ; for it seemeth much that so few men in such short time, and in so long a voyage, should waste so much ?

Answere.

Whereto I answere, that it came not of excessive expence ; for in health we never exceeded our ordinary ; but of a mischance which befell us unknowne in the iland of Saint James, or Saint Anne, in the coast of Brasill, where we refreshed our selves, and according to the custome layd our caske a shore, to trimme it, and after to fill it, the place being commodious for us. But with the water a

---

[3] This was probably the opening into Otway water, leading to Skyring water, but not disemboguing into the Pacific.

certaine worm, called *broma* by the Spaniard, and by us
arters, entred also, which eat it so full of holes that all the
water soaked out, and made much of our caske of small use.
This we remedied the best wee could, and discovered it
long before we came to this place.

Hereof let others take warning, in no place to have caske
on the shore where it may be avoyded ; for it is one of the
provisions which are with greatest care to be preserved in
long voyages, and hardest to be supplyed. These *arters*
or *broma,* in all hott countries, enter into the plankes of
shippes, and especially where are rivers of fresh water; for
the common opinion is that they are bred in fresh water,
and with the current of the rivers are brought into the sea;
but experience teacheth that they breed in the great seas
in all hott clymates, especially neere the equinoctiall lyne ;
for lying so long under and neere the lyne, and towing a
shalop at our sterne, comming to clense her in Brasill, we
found her all under water covered with these wormes, as
bigge as the little finger of a man, on the outside of the
planke, not fully covered, but halfe the thicknesse of their
bodie, like to a gelly, wrought into the planke as with a
gowdge. And naturall reason, in my judgement, confirmeth this ; for creatures bred and nourished in the sea,
comming into fresh water die ; as those actually bred in
ponds or fresh rivers, die presently, if they come into salt
water.

But some man may say, this fayleth in some fishes and
beasts. Which I must confesse to be true ; but these
eyther are part terrestryall, and part aquatile, as the mare-
maide, sea-horse, and other of that kind, or have their breeding in the fresh, and growth or continuall nourishment in
the salt water, as the salmond, and others of that kinde.

In little time, if the shippe be not sheathed, they put
all in hazard ; for they enter in no bigger then a small
Spanish needle, and by little and little their holes become

Sect. XXXII. ordinarily greater then a mans finger. The thicker the planke is, the greater he groweth ; yea, I have seene many shippes so eaten, that the most of their plankes under water have beene like honey combes, and especially those betwixt wind and water. If they had not beene sheathed, it had bin impossible that they could have swomme. The entring of them is hardly to be discerned, the most of them being small as the head of a pinne.[4] Which, all such as purpose long voyages, are to prevent by sheathing their shippes.

And for that I have seene divers manners of sheathing, for the ignorant I will set them downe which by experience I have found best.

In Spaine and Portingall. In Spaine and Portingall, some sheathe their shippes with lead ; which, besides the cost and waight, although they use the thinnest sheet-lead that I have seene in any place, yet it is nothing durable, but subject to many casualties.

with double plankes. Another manner is used with double plankes, as thicke without as within, after the manner of furring ; which is little better then that with lead ; for, besides his waight, it dureth little, because the worme in small time passeth through the one and the other.

With cauvas. A third manner of sheathing hath beene used amongst some with fine canvas ; which is of small continuance, and so not to be regarded.

With burnt plankes. The fourth prevention, which now is most accompted of, is to burne the utter planke till it come to be in every place like a cole, and after to pitch it ; this is not bad.

In China with varnish In China, as I have beene enformed, they use a certaine betane or varnish, in manner of an artificiall pitch, wherewith they trim the outside of their shippes. It is said to

---

[4] The *teredo navalis* is very destructive. Nothing but metal is proof against its ravages. It is not clear what may be its purpose in boring into any wood that comes in its way, for it is thought not to be nourished by what it destroys.

be durable, and of that vertue, as neither worme nor water peirceth it ; neither hath the sunne power against it.

Some have devised a certaine pitch, mingled with glasse and other ingredients, beaten into powder, with which if the shippe be pitched, it is said, the worme that toucheth it dyeth ; but I have not heard that it hath beene useful.

But the most approved of all, is the manner of sheathing In England. used now adayes in England, with thin bourds, halfe inche thicke; the thinner the better; and elme better then oake; for it ryveth not, it indureth better under water, and yeeldeth better to the shippes side.

The invention of the materialles incorporated betwixt the planke and the sheathing, is that indeed which avayleth ; for without it many plankes were not sufficient to hinder the entrance of this worme ; this manner is thus :

Before the sheathing board is nayled on, upon the inner Best manner side of it they smere it over with tarre halfe a finger thicke of sheathing. and upon the tarre another halfe finger thicke of hayre, such as the whitelymers use, and so nayle it on, the nayles not above a spanne distance one from another ; the thicker they are driven, the better.

Some hold opinion that the tarre killeth the worme ; others, that the worme passing the sheathing, and seeking a way through, the hayre and the tarre so involve him that he is choked therewith ; which me thinkes is most probable ; this manner of sheathing was invented by my father, and experience hath taught it to be the best and of least cost.[5]

[5] These inventions have been improved upon by the use of copper and other metals; of these, copper is the best ; and an approved method of applying it, is over a coating of *felt*. Truly there is nothing new under the sun.

SECTION XXXIII.

SUCH was the diligence we used for our dispatch to shoot the Straites, that at foure dayes end, wee had our water and wood stowed in our shippe, all our copper-worke finished, and our shippe calked from post to stemme; the first day in the morning, the wind being fayre, we brought our selves into the channell, and sayled towards the mouth of the Straites, praising God; and beginning our course with little winde, we descryed a fire upon the shore, made by the Indians for a signe to call us; which seene, I caused a boat to be man'de, and we rowed ashore, to see what their meaning was, and approaching neere the shore, wee saw a cannoa, made fast under a rocke with a wyth, most artificially made with the rindes of trees, and sowed together with the finnes of whales; at both ends sharpe, and turning up, with a greene bough in either end, and ribbes for strengthening it. After a little while, we might discerne on the fall of the mountaine (which was full of trees and shrubbes), two or three Indians naked, which came out of certaine caves or coates. They spake unto us, and made divers signes; now poynting to the harbour, out of which we were come, and then to the mouth of the Straites: but we understood nothing of their meaning. Yet left they us with many imaginations, suspecting it might be to advise us of our pynace, or some other thing of moment; but for that they were under covert, and might worke us some treacherie (for all the people of the Straites, and the land nere them, use all the villany they can towards white people, taking them for Spaniards, in revenge of the deceit that nation hath used towards them upon sundry occasions; as also for that by our stay we could reape nothing but hinderance of our navigation), wee hasted to our shippe, and sayled on our course.

Long Reach.   From Blanches Bay to long reach, which is some foure leagues, the course lyeth west south-west entring into the Sect xxxiii. long reach, which is the last of the Straits, and longest. For it is some thirty-two leagues, and the course lyeth next of any thing north-west.

Before the setting of the sunne, wee had the mouth of the straits open, and were in great hope the next day to be in the South sea; but about seaven of the clocke that night, we saw a great cloud rise out of the north-east, which began to cast forth great flashes of lightnings, and sodainely sayling with a fresh gale of wind at north-east, another more forcible tooke us astayes;[1] which put us in danger; for all our sayles being a taut, it had like to over-set our ship, before we could take in our sayles. And therefore in all such semblances it is great wisedome to carry a short sayle, or to take in all sayles.

Heere we found what the Indians forewarned[2] us of; for Note. they have great insight in the change of weather, and besides have secret dealings with the prince of darknesse, who many times declareth unto them things to come. By this meanes and other witch-crafts, which he teacheth them, hee possesseth them, and causeth them to doe what pleaseth him.

Within halfe an houre it began to thunder and raine, with so much winde as wee were forced to lye a hull, and so darke, that we saw nothing but when the lightning came. This being one of the narrowest reaches of all the straites, wee were forced, every glasse, to open a little of our fore-sayle, to cast about our ships head : any man may conceive if the night seemed long unto us, what desire we had to see the day. In fine, Phœbus with his beautiful

---

[1] *Taken astayes*—another term for taken aback.

[2] It is possible that the natives may have been aware of the coming change. The suspicion entertained of them is an instance of the mistakes often fallen into by misconceiving the motives of those whose language cannot be understood.

face lightned our hemisphere, and rejoyced our heartes (having driven above twenty-foure leagues in twelve houres, lying a hull: whereby is to be imagined the force of the winde and current.)

We set our fore-sayle, and returned to our former harbour; from whence, within three or foure dayes, we set sayle againe with a faire winde, which continued with us till we came within a league of the mouth of the straite; here the winde tooke us againe contrary, and forced us to returne againe to our former port; where being ready to anchor, the wind scanted with us in such maner, as wee were forced to make a bourd. In which time, the winde and tide put us so farre to lee-wards, that we could by no meanes seize it: so we determined to goe to Elizabeth bay, but before we came at it, the night overtooke us; and this reach being dangerous and narrow, wee durst neither hull, nor trye,[3] or turne to and againe with a short sayle, and therefore bare alongst in the middest of the channell, till we were come into the broad reach, then lay a hull till the morning.

When we set sayle and ran alongst the coast, seeking with our boate some place to anchor in. Some foure leagues to the west-wards of Cape Froward, we found a goodly English bay. bay, which wee named English bay; where anchored, we presently went a shore, and found a goodly river of fresh water, and an old cannoa broken to peeces, and some two or three of the houses of the Indians, with peeces of seale stinking ripe. These houses are made in fashion of an oven seven or eight foote broad, with boughes of trees, and covered with other boughes, as our summer houses; and doubtles do serve them but for the summer time, when they come to fish, and profit themselves of the sea. For

---

[3] To hull, is to lie without sail set; to try, with only low sail; whence we have now special storm sails, called try sails. We believe the correct expression is " to try" either a *hull* or *under sail*.

they retyre themselves in the winter into the country,
where it is more temperate, and yceldeth better sustenance : for on the mayne of the Straits, wee neyther saw
beast nor fowle, sea fowle excepted, and a kind of blacke-
bird, and two hoggs towards the beginning of the straites.

Here our ship being well moored, we began to supply
our wood and water that we had spent. Which being a
dayes worke, and the winde during many dayes contrary,
I endevoured to keepe my people occupied, to divert them
from the imagination which some had conceived, that it
behooved we should returne to Brasill, and winter there,
and so shoot the straites in the spring of the yeare.

So one day, we rowed up the river, with our boat and
light horseman, to discover it and the in-land : where
having spent a good part of the day, and finding shold
water, and many trees fallen thwart it, and little fruite of
our labour, nor any thing worth the noting, we returned.

Another day we trayned our people a-shore, being a
goodly sandie bay; another, we had a hurling of batchelers
against married men. This day we were busied in wrest-
ling, the other in shooting ; so we were never idle, neyther
thought we the time long.

SECTION XXXIV.

AFTER we had past here some seven or eight dayes, one
evening, with a flawe from the shore, our ship drove off
into the channell, and before we could get up our anchor,
and set our sayles, we were driven so farre to lee-wards,
that we could not recover into the bay : and night comming
on, with a short sayle, wee beate off and on till the morning. At the break of the day, conferring with the captaine
and master of my ship what was best to be done, we re-

solved to seeke out Tobias Cove, which lyeth over against
Cape Fryo, on the southern part of the straites, because in
all the reaches of the straites, for the most part, the winde
bloweth trade, and therefore little profit to be made by
turning to winde-wards. And from the ilands of the Pengwins to the ende of the straites towards the South sea,
there is no anchoring in the channell; and if we should be
put to lee-wards of this cove, we had no succour till we
came to the ilands of Pengwins : and some of our company
which had bin with master Thomas Candish in the voyage
in which he died, and in the same cove many weekes, undertooke to be our pilots thither. Whereupon we bare up,
being some two leagues thither, having so much winde as
we could scarce lye by it with our course and bonnet of
each; but bearing up before the winde, wee put out our
topsayles and spritsayle, and within a little while the winde
began to fayle us, and immediately our ship gave a mightie
blow upon a rocke, and stucke fast upon it. And had we
had but the fourth part of the wind which we had in all
the night past, but a moment before we strucke the rocke,
our shippe, doubtlesse, with the blow had broken her selfe
all to peeces. But our provident and most gracious God
which commaundeth wind and sea, watched over us, and
delivered us with his powerfull hand from the unknowne
danger and hidden destruction, that so we might prayse
him for his fatherly bountie and protection, and with the
prophet David say, *Except the Lord keepe the cittie, the
watch-men watch in vaine;* for if our God had not kept our
shippe, we had bin all swallowed up alive without helpe or
redemption; and therefore he for his mercies sake grant
that the memoriall of his benefits doe never depart from
before our eyes, and that we may evermore prayse him for
our wonderfull deliverance, and his continuall providence
by day and by night.

My company with this accident were much amazed, and

not without just cause. Immediately we used our endevour
to free our selves, and with our boates sounded round about
our shippe, in the mean time assaying[4] our pumpe to know
if our shippe made more water then her ordinary ; we found
nothing increased, and round about our shippe deepe water,
saving under the mid-shippe, for shee was a floate a head
and a sterne : and bearing some fathome before the mayne
mast, and in no other part, was like to be our destruction;
for being ebbing water, the waight in the head and sterne
by fayling of the water, began to open her plankes in the
middest ; and upon the upper decke, they were gone one
from another some two fingers, some more; which we
sought to ease and remedie by lightning of her burden, and
throwing into the sea all that came to hand ; and laying
out an anchor, we sought to wend her off :[5] and such was
the will and force we put to the capsten and tackles fastned
upon the cable, that we plucked the ring of the anchor out
of the eye, but after recovered it, though not serviceable.

All our labour was fruitlesse, till God was pleased that
the flood came, and then we had her off with great joy and
comfort, when finding the current favourable with us, we
stood over to English bay, and fetching it, we anchored there,
having beene some three houres upon the rocke, and with the
blow, as after we saw when our ship was brought aground
in Perico (which is the port of Panama), a great part of her
sheathing was beaten off on both sides in her bulges,[6] and
some foure foote long and a foote square of her false
stemme, joyning to the keele, wrested a crosse, like unto
a hogges yoake, which hindered her sayling very much.

Here we gave God prayse for our deliverance, and after-

[4] *To assay*—to prove. Ancient mode of writing essay.

[5] *To move her off.*—To wind a ship now means to turn her. The
term is probably derived from to wend.

[6] Now called bilge—that part of the ship's bottom that bulges or
swells out. When a ship takes the ground and heels over, the bilge
bears all the strain, and consequently suffers damage.

ward procured to supply our wood and water, which we had throwne overbourd to ease our shippe, which was not much, : that supplyed, it pleased God (who is not ever angry), to looke upon us with comfort, and to send us a fayre and large wind, and so we set sayle once againe, in hope to disemboke the straite; but some dozen leagues before we came to the mouth of it, the wind changed, and forced us to seeke out some cove or bay, with our boates to ride in neere at hand, that we might not be forced to re-turne farre backe into the straites.

They sounded a cove some sixteene leagues from the Crabby cove mouth of the straite, which after we called Crabby cove. It brooked its name well for two causes; the one for that all the water was full of a small kinde of redd crabbes; the other, for the crabbed mountaines which over-topped it; a third, we might adde, for the crabbed entertainement it gave us.   In this cove we anchored, but the wind freshing in, and three or foure hilles over-topping, like sugar-loaves, altered and straightned the passage of the wind in such manner, as forced it downe with such violence in flawes and furious blusterings, as was like to over-set our shippe at an anchor, and caused her to drive, and us to weigh; but be-fore we could weigh it, shee was so neere the rockes, and the puffes and gusts of wind so sodaine and uncertaine, sometimes scant, sometimes large, that it forced us to cut our cable, and yet dangerous if our shippe did not cast the right way.   Here necessitie, not being subject to any law, forced us to put our selves into the hands of him that was able to deliver us.   We cut our cable and sayle all in one instant; and God, to shew his power and gratious bountie towardes us, was pleased that our shippe cast the contrary way towards the shore, seeming that he with his own hand did wend her about; for in lesse then her length shee flatted,[7] and in all the voyage but at that instant, shee

---

[7] *To flat in*, means so to adjust the sails as to cause them to act with

flatted with difficultie, for that shee was long, the worst Sect. xxxv.
propertie shee had. On either side we might see the rockes
under us, and were not halfe a shippes length from the
shore, and if she had once touched, it had beene impossible
to have escaped.

Magnified ever be our Lord God, which delivered Ionas out
of the whales belly; and his apostle Peter from being over-
whelmed in the waves; and us from so certaine perishing.

SECTION XXXV.

FROM hence we returned to Blanches bay, and there anchored, expecting Gods good will and pleasure. Here
beganne the bitternesse of the time to increase, with blustering and sharpe winds, accompanied with rayne and
sleeting snow, and my people to be dismayde againe, in
manifesting a desire to returne to Brasill, which I would
never consent unto, no, nor so much as to heare of.[1]

And all men are to take care that they go not one foote Voyages overthrowne by pretences.
backe, more then is of mere force; for I have not seene
that any who have yeelded thereunto, but presently they
have returned home. As in the voyage of master Edward Edward Fenton and master Thomas Candish.
Fenton, which the Earle of Cumberland set forth, to his

the greatest effect to turn the ship's head from the wind; this is done
when the ship is nearly taken aback, either by a sudden flaw or by
carelessness at the helm. As applied here, it means that the vessel
came round on her heel. The time vessels take in performing a similar
evolution, bears a certain ratio to their length; long ships requiring
more time than short ones.

[1] Sir Richard does not exaggerate "the bitternesse of the time."
During the survey of these straits in the *Adventure* and *Beagle*,
Captain Stokes, an active, intelligent, and energetic officer, destroyed
himself, in consequence of his excitable mind becoming worn out by
the severe hardships of the cruize, the dreadful weather experienced, and
the dangerous situations in which the *Beagle* was constantly exposed.

I

great charge.   As also in that of master Thomas Candish,
in which he dyed.   Both which pretended to shoote the
Straites of Magelan, and by perswasion of some ignorant
persons, being in good possibilitie, were brought to consent
to returne to Brasill, to winter, and after in the spring to
attempt the passing of the strait againe.   None of them
made any abode in Brasill; for presently as soone as they
looked homeward, one with a little blustering wind taketh
occasion to loose company ; another complaineth that he
wanteth victuals; another, that his ship is leake; another,
that his masts, sayles, or cordidge fayleth him.   So the
willing never want probable reasons to further their pretences.   As I saw once (being but young, and more bold
then experimented), in anno 1582, in a voyage, under the
charge of my uncle, William Hawkins, of Plimouth, Esquire,
in the Indies, at the wester end of the iland of San Iuan
de Portorico.   One of the shippes, called the barke *Bonner*,
being somewhat leake, the captaine complained that she
was not able to endure to England ; whereupon a counsell
was called, and his reasons heard and allowed.   So it was
concluded that the victuall, munition, and what was serviceable, should be taken out of her, and her men devided
amongst our other shippes; the hull remaining to be sunke
or burned.

To which I never spake word till I saw it resolved; being
my part rather to learne then to advise.   But seeing the
fatall sentence given, and suspecting that the captaine made
the matter worse then it was, rather upon pollicy to come
into another ship, which was better of sayle, then for any
danger they might runne into ; with as much reason as
my capacitie could reach unto, I disswaded my unkle pri-
vately ; and urged, that seeing wee had profited the ad-
venturers nothing, wee should endevour to preserve our
principall, especially having men and victualls.   But seeing
I prevayled not, I went further, and offered to finde out in

the same shippe and others, so many men, as with me would be content to carry her home, giving us the third part of the value of the ship, as shee should be valued at, at her returne, by foure indifferent persons ; and to leave the vice-admirall which I had under my charge, and to make her vice-admirall.

Whereupon, it was condescended that we should all goe aboard the shippe, and that there it should be determined. The captaine thought himselfe somewhat touched in reputation, and so would not that further triall should be made of the matter : saying, that if another man was able to carry the shippe into England, he would in no case leave her; neither would he forsake her till shee sunke under him.

The generall commended him for his resolution, and thanked me for my offer, tending to the generall good; my intention being to force those who for gaine could undertake to carry her home, should also do it gratis, according to their obligation. Thus, this leake-ship went well into England; where after shee made many a good voyage in nine yeares, wherein shee was imployed to and fro; and no doubt would have served many more, had shee not beene laid up and not used, falling into the hands of those which knew not the use of shipping. It were large to recount the voyages and worthy enterprises, overthrowne by this pollicie, with the shippes which have thereby gone to wracke.

SECTION XXXVI.

By this and the like experiences, remembring and knowing that if once I consented to turne but one foote backe, I should overthrow my voyage, and loose my reputation, I resolved rather to loose my life, then to give eare to such

Danger to hearken unto reasons of returne.

prejudiciall counsell. And so as the weather gave leave, we entertained our selves the first dayes in necessary workes, and after in making of coale (for wood was plentifull, and no man would commence an action of wast against us), with intent, the wind continuing long contrary, to see if wee could remedie any of our broken anchors ; a forge I had in my shippe, and of five anchors which we brought out of England, there remained but one that was serviceable.

In the ilands of Pengwins we lost one ; in Crabbe cove, another; of a third, upon another occasion we broke an arme ; and the fourth, on the rocke had the eye of his ring broken. This, one day devising with my selfe, I made to serve, without working him a new. Which when I tooke first in hand, all men thought it ridiculous ; but in fine, we made it in that manner so serviceable, as till our ship came to Callaw, which is the port of Lyma, shee scarce used any other anchor ; and when I came from Lyma to Panama, which was three yeares after, I saw it serve the admirall in which I came, (a ship of above five hundreth tunnes), without other art or addition, then what my owne invention contrived.

The mending of an unserviceable anchor. And for that in the like necessitie or occasion, others may profit themselves of the industrie, I will recount the manner of the forging our eye without fire or iron. It was in this sort.

From the eye of the shanke, about the head of the crosse, we gave two turnes with a new strong halser, betwixt three and foure inches, giving a reasonable allowance for that, which should be the eye, and served in stead of the ring ; then we fastned the two ends of the halser, so as in that part it was as strong as in any other, and with our capsten stretched the two byghtes, that every part might bear proportionably ; then armed we all the halser round about with six yarne synnets, and likewise the shanke of the anchor, and the head with a smooth matt made of the same synnet: this done, with an inch rope, wee woolled the two byghtes to the shanke, from the crosse to the eye, and that also which was to serve for the ring, and fitted the stocke accordingly.   This done, those who before derided the invention, were of opinion, that it would serve for a need; onely they put one difficultie, that with the fall or pitch of the anchor in hard ground, with his waight he would cut the halser in sunder on the head; for prevention whereof, we placed a panch, as the mariners terme it, upon the head of the anchor, with whose softnesse this danger was prevented, and the anchor past for serviceable.[1]

Some of our idle time we spent in gathering the barke and fruite of a certaine tree, which we found in all places of the straites, where we found trees.   This tree carrieth his fruite in clusters like a hawthorne, but that it is greene, each berry of the bignesse of a pepper corne, and every of them containing within foure or five graynes, twise as bigge as a musterd-seed, which broken, are white within, as the good pepper, and bite much like it, but hotter. The barke of this tree hath the savour of all kinde of spices together, most comfortable to the stomache, and held to be better then any spice whatsoever.   And for that a learned country-man of ours, Doctor Turner, hath written of it, by the name of *Winters barke*, what I have said may suffice.   The leafe of this tree is of a whitish greene, and is not unlike to the aspen leafe.[2]

Other whiles we entertained our selves in gathering of pearles out of mussels, whereof there are aboundance in all places, from Cape Froward to the end of the straites.

The pearles are but of a bad colour, and small; but it

Side notes: Entertainement of time to avoyd idlenesse, in gathering of Winters barke. Of pearles.

---

[1] Synnet is plait made from rope yarns. Wooling or woolding is performed by passing turns of rope round a spar or rope, either for strength, or, as in this case, to prevent chafe ; if spun yarn is used, it is called serving.

[2] The tree called Winter's bark, *Drimys Winteri*, was discovered by Captain Winter, one of Drake's officers. The bark is agreeably aromatic, and was found useful in cases of scurvy.

maybe that in the great mussels, in deeper water, the pearles are bigger, and of greater value; of the small seed pearle, there was great quantitie, and the mussels were a great refreshing unto us; for they were exceeding good, and in great plentie. And here let me crave pardon if I erre, seeing I disclaime from being a naturalist, by delivering my opinion touching the breeding of these pearles, which I thinke to be of a farre different nature and qualitie to those found in the East and West Indies, which are found in oysters; growing in the shell, under the ruff of the oyster, some say of the dewe, which I hold to be some old philosophers conceit, for that it cannot bee made probable how the dew should come into the oyster; and if this were true, then questionlesse, wee should have them in our oysters as in those of the East and West Indies; but those oysters were, by the Creator, made to bring foorth this rare fruite, all their shels being, to looke to, pearle itselfe. And the other pearles found in our oysters and mussels, in divers partes, are ingendred out of the fatnesse of the fish, in the very substance of the fish; so that in some mussels have beene found twenty, and thirty, in severall partes of the fish, and these not perfect in colour, nor clearenes, as those found in the pearle-oysters, which are ever perfect in colour and clearenes, like the sunne in his rising, and therefore called orientall; and not, as is supposed, because out of the East, for they are as well found in the West, and no way inferior to those of the East Indies.

Other fish, besides seales and crabbes, like shrimpes, and one whale, with two or three porpusses, wee saw not in all the straites. Heere we made also a survay of our victuals; and opening certaine barrels of oaten meale, wee found a great part of some of them, as also of our pipes and fatts[3] of bread, eaten and consumed by the ratts; doubtlesse, a fift part of my company did not eate so much

3 Used for vats.

as these devoured, as wee found dayly in comming to spend Sec. xxxvii. any of our provisions.

When I came to the sea, it was not suspected that I had Prevention of ratts. a ratt in my shippe; but with the bread in caske, which we transported out of the *Hawke*, and the going to and againe of our boates unto our prise, though wee had divers catts and used other preventions, in a small time they multi-plyed in such a maner as is incredible. It is one of the generall calamities of all long voyages, and would bee carefully prevented as much as may bee. For besides that which they consume of the best victuals, they eate the sayles; and neither packe nor chest is free from their surprises. I have knowne them to make a hole in a pipe The calami-ties they bring to a ship. of water, and saying the pumpe, have put all in feare, doubting least some leake had beene sprung upon the ship.

Moreover, I have heard credible persons report, that shippes have beene put in danger by them to be sunke, by a hole made in the bulge.[4] All which is easily remedied at the first, but if once they be somewhat increased, with difficulty they are to be destroyed. And although I pro-pounded a reward for every ratt which was taken, and sought meanes by poyson and other inventions to consume them; yet their increase being so ordinary and many, wee were not able to cleare our selves from them.

SECTION XXXVII.

At the end of foureteene dayes, one evening, being calme, and a goodly cleare in the easter-boord, I willed our anchor

[4] The devastation caused by rats is very great. We have, however, never heard of their gnawing through the bottom. Indeed if there be any truth in the old sailor's superstition that rats always leave a vessel when in a dangerous state, they must be too clever to perform so dan-gerous an experiment.

to be weyed,[1] and determined to goe into the channell, whereof ensued a murmuring amongst my company, who were desirous to see the winde setled before we put out of the harbour : and in part they had reason, considering how wee had beene canvased from place to place ; yet on the other side, if wee went not out before night, wee should loose the whole nights sayling, and all the time which we should spend in warping out; which would be, doubtles, a great part of the fore-noone.   And although the master signified unto mee the disposition of my people, and master Henry Courton (a discreete and vertuous gentlemen, and my good friend, who in all the voyage was ever an especial furtherer of all that ever I ordained or proposed), in this occasion sought to divert me, that all but my selfe were
contrarily inclined to that which I thought fit : and though the common saying be, that it is better to erre with many, then, all contradicting, alone to hit the right way, yet truth told mee this proverbe to bee falsely founded ; for that it was not to bee understood, that for erring it is better, but because it is supposed that by hitting a man shall get emulation of the contradictors : I encountered it with another, that sayth, better to be envied then pittied ; and well considering, that being out of the harbour, if the winde took us contrary, to go to Elizabeth bay was better then to bee in the port ; for a man must of force warpe in and out of it, and in the time that the shippe could be brought foorth into the channell, the winde being good, a man might come from Elizabeth bay to the port, and that there we should have the wind first, being more to the east-wardes, and in an open bay, and moreover might set sayle in the night, if the wind should rise in the evening or in the night ; whereas, in the port, of force, we must waite the light of

---

[1] Much discussion has arisen as to whether this should be written *way*, or *weigh*. We think the correct phraseology is this : when the anchor is *weighed*, the ship is under *way*.

the day. I made my selfe deafe to all murmurings, and
caused my commaund to be put in execution, and, doubtlesse, it was Gods gracious inspiration, as by the event was
seene ; for being gotten into the channell, within an houre,
the winde came good, and we sayled merrily on our voyage ; and by the breake of the day, wee had the mouth of
the straites open, and about foure of the clocke in the
afternoone, wee were thwart of Cape Desire ;[2] which is the
westermost part of the land on the souther side of the
straites.

SECTION XXXVIII.

HERE such as have command may behold the many miseries Advertise-
ments for
that befall them, not onely by unexpected accidents and commanders.
mischances, but also by contradictions and murmurs of
their owne people, of all calamities the greatest which can
befall a man of discretion and valour, and as difficult to be
overcome ; for, to require reason of the common sort, is, as
the philosopher sayth, to seeke counsell of a madd man.
Herein, as I sayd before, they resemble a stiffe necked
horse, who taking the bridle in his teeth, carrieth the rider
whether he pleaseth ; so once possessed with any imagination, no reason is able to convince them. The best remedie
I can propound, is to wish our nation in this poynt to be
well advised, and in especiall, all those that follow the sea,
ever having before their eyes the auncient discipline of our
predecessors ; who in conformitie and obedience to their
chiefes and commanders, have beene a mirror to all other
nations, with patience, silence, and suffering, putting in The advantage of
execution what they have beene commanded, and thereby obedience.

[2] Now called Cape Pillar—on the modern charts Cape Deseado lies
to the south of it.

gained the blessings due to such vertues, and leaving to posteritie perpetuall memories of their glorious victories. A just recompence for all such as conquer themselves, and subject their most specious willes to the will of their superiors.

SECTION XXXIX.

In apprehension whereof at land, I cannot forbeare the discipline thereof, as at this day, and in the dayes of late memory, it hath beene practised in the states of Flaunders, Fraunce, and Brittayne; whereas the Spaniards, Wallons, Switzers, and other nations, are daily full of murmurings and mutenies, upon every sleight occasion.

The like I also wish should be imitated by those who follow the sea; that is, that those who are subject to command, presume no further then to that which belongeth unto them: *Qui nescit parere, nescit imperare.* I speake this, for that I have sometimes seene unexpert and ignorant persons, yea, unable to judge of any poynt appertaining to government, or the guide of a shippe, or company of men, presuming upon their fine witts, and enamoured of their owne conceits, contradict and dispute against grave, wise, and experimented governours: many forward fellowes, thinking themselves better worthie to command, then to be commanded. Such persons I advise not to goe, but where they may command; or els looking before they leape, to consider well under whom they place themselves, seeing, for the most part, it is in their choyce to choose a governour from whom they may expect satisfaction; but choyce being once made, to resolve with the patient wife in history; that, that day wherein shee married herselfe to

Advertise-
ments for
young
servitors.

an husband, that very day shee had no longer any will
more then the will of her husband : and so he that by sea
or land placeth himselfe to serve in any action, must make
reckoning that the time the journey endureth, he hath no
other will, nor dispose of himselfe, then that of his commander ; for in the governors hand is all power, to recompence and reward, to punish or forgive.

Likewise those who have charge and command, must
sometimes with patience or sufferance overcome their fury
and misconceits, according to occasions ; for it is a great
poynt of wisedome, especially in a generall murmuring,
where the cause is just, or that, as often times it happeneth,
any probable accident may divert the minds of the dis-
contented, and give hope of remedie, or future event may
produce repentance, to turne, as they say, the deafe eare,
and to winke at that a man seeth. As it is sayde of
Charles the fifth, emperour of Germany, and king of
Spaine ; who rounding his campe, one night, disguised,
heard some souldiers rayle and speake evil of him : those
which accompanied him were of opinion, that he should use
some exemplary punishment upon them ; not so, sayth he,
for these, now vexed with the miseries they suffer, ease their
hearts with their tongues ; but if occasion present it selfe,
they will not sticke to sacrifice their lives for my safetie.
A resolution worthy so prudent a commander, and so
magnanimous a prince.

The like is written of Fabius Maximus, the famous
Romayne, who endured the attribute of coward, with many
other infamies, rather then he would hazard the safetie of
his countrie by rash and incertaine provocations.

No lesse worthy of perpetuall memory was the prudent The patience of the Earle
pollicie and government of our English navie, in anno 1588, of Notting-ham.
by the worthy Earle of Nottingham,[1] lord high admirall of

---

[1] After the defeat of the Spanish Armada, Lord Charles Howard, of
Effingham, was created Earl of Nottingham.

England ; who, in like case, with mature and experimented knowledge, patiently withstood the instigations of many couragious and noble captaines, who would have perswaded him to have laid them aboord ; but well he foresaw that the enemy had an armie aboord, he none ; that they exceeded him in. number of shipping, and those greater in bulke, stronger built, and higher molded, so that they who with such advantage fought from above, might easily distresse all opposition below ; the slaughter, peradventure, prooving more fatall then the victory profitable : by being overthrowne, he might have hazzarded the kingdome ; whereas by the conquest, at most, he could have boasted of nothing but glorie, and an enemie defeated. But by sufferance, he alwayes advantaged himselfe of winde and tide ; which was the freedome of our countrey, and securitie of our navie, with the destruction of theirs, which in the eye of the ignorant, who judge all things by the externall appearance, seemed invincible ; but truely considered, was much inferior to ours in all things of substance, as the event prooved ; for we sunke, spoyled, and tooke of them many, and they diminished of ours but one small pynace, nor any man of name, save onely captaine Cocke, who dyed with honour amidst his company. The greatest dammage, that, as I remember, they caused to any of our shippes, was to the *Swallow* of her majestie, which I had in that action under my charge, with an arrow of fire shott into her beake-head, which we saw not, because of the sayle, till it had burned a hole in the nose as bigge as a mans head ; the arrow falling out, and driving alongst by the shippes side, made us doubt of it, which after we discovered.

SECTION XL.

In many occasions, notwithstanding, it is most prejudiciall
to dissemble the reprehension and punishment of murmurings and mutterings, when they carry a likelihood to grow
to a mutenie, seeme to leane to a faction, or that a person
of regard or merite favoureth the intention, or contradicteth
the justice, etc., and others of like qualitie. The prudent
governour is to cut off this hydra's head in the beginning,
and by prevention to provide remedie with expedition ; and
this sometimes with absolute authoritie, although the best
be ever to proceed by counsell, if necessitie and occasion
require not the contrary ; for passion many times over-
ruleth, but that which is sentenced and executed by consent, is justified, although sometimes erronious.[1] March
29, 1594.

SECTION XLI.

From Cape Desire, some foure leagues north-west, lye
foure ilands, which are very small, and the middlemost of
them is of the fashion of a sugar-loafe. We were no
sooner cleare of Cape Desire, and his ledge of rockes, which
lie a great way off into the sea, but the wind took us contrary by the north-west ; and so we stood off into the sea
two dayes and two nights to the west-wards.

In all the straites it ebbeth and floweth more or lesse,
and in many places it higheth very little water ; but in
some bayes, where are great indraughts, it higheth eight
or ten foote, and doubtlesse further in, more. If a man be
furnished with wood and water, and the winde good, he

[1] These observations appear to have occurred to our author, in consequence of what had taken place during the voyages of Magalhaens
and Drake. Both these great commanders, while lying at Port Saint
Julian, tried for mutiny, and executed, some of their chief officers ;
doubtless deeming it wise to cut off the hydra's head at an early period.

Sect. XLI. may keepe the mayne sea, and goe round about the straites
to the southwards, and it is the shorter way; for besides
the experience which we made, that all the south part of
the straites is but ilands, many times having the sea open, I
remember that Sir Francis Drake told me, that having shott
the straites, a storme first tooke him at north-west, and after
vered about to the south-west, which continued with him
South part
of the Straites
ilands. many dayes, with that extremitie, that he could not open
any sayle, and that at the end of the storme, he found
himselfe in fiftie degrees;[1] which was sufficient testimony
and proofe, that he was beaten round about the straites :
for the least height of the straites is in fifty two degrees
and fiftie minutes; in which stands the two entrances or
mouths.

And moreover, he said, that standing about, when the
winde changed, he was not well able to double the southermost iland, and so anchored under the lee of it; and going
a-shore, carried a compasse with him, and seeking out
Sir Francis
Drake im-
braceth the
southermost
point of the
world. the southermost part of the iland, cast himselfe downe upon
the uttermost poynt, grovelling, and so reached out his
bodie over it. Presently he imbarked, and then recounted
unto his people that he had beene upon the southermost
knowne land in the world, and more further to the south-
wards upon it then any of them, yea, or any man as yet
knowne. These testimonies may suffice for this truth unto
all, but such as are incredulous, and will beleeve nothing
but what they see : for my part, I am of opinion, that the
straite is navigable all the yeare long, although the best
time be in November, December, and January, and then
the winds more favourable, which other times are variable,
as in all narrow seas.[2]

[1] This must be a misprint; it should be perhaps 56°. Some accounts
state that Drake visited a bay in 57° : this must be erroneous, as Cape
Horn, the most southern part of South America, is in the parallel of 56°.

[2] Much interesting information respecting these straits will be found
in the voyages of the *Adventure* and *Beagle*. Since the days of Anson,
the difficulties experienced in rounding Cape Horn have been such as

Being some fiftie leagues a sea-boord the straites, the
winde vering to the west-wards, we cast about to the
north-wards, and lying the coast along, shaped our course
for the iland Mocha. About the fifteenth of April, we
were thwart of Baldivia, which was then in the hands of
the Spaniards, but since the Indians, in anno 1599, dis-
possessed them of it, and the Conception ; which are two
of the most principall places they had in that kingdome,
and both ports.

Baldivia had its name of a Spanish captaine so called,
whom afterwards the Indians tooke prisoner, and it is said,
they required of him the reason why he came to molest
them and to take their country from them, having no title
nor right thereunto ; he answered, to get gold : which the
barbarous understanding, caused gold to be molten, and
powred down his throat, saying, Gold was thy desire, glut
thee with it.

It standeth in fortie degrees, hath a pleasant river and
navigable, for a ship of good burden may goe as high up
as the cittie; and is a goodly woody country.

Here our beefe beganne to take end, and was then as
good as the day wee departed from England ; it was preserved in pickell, which, though it be more chargeable, yet
the profit payeth the charge, in that it is made more durable,
contrary to the opinion of many, which hold it impossible
that beefe should be kept good passing the equinoctiall
lyne. And of our porke I eate in the house of Don Beltran de Castro, in Lyma, neere foure yeares old, very good,
preserved after the same manner, notwithstanding it had
lost his pickle long before.

Some degrees before a man come to Baldivia to the

to cause navigators to look to the passage through these straits with
great interest, hoping, that if found practicable, adverse gales and a heavy
sea might be avoided. Now that the labours of King and Fitzroy have
provided correct charts, the road is well known ; still it can hardly be
recommended to large vessels to " shoot the straits."

southwards, as Spaniards have told me, lyeth the iland Chule,[3] not easily to be discerned from the mayne; for he that passeth by it, cannot but thinke it to be the mayne. It is said to be inhabited by the Spaniards, but badly, yet rich of gold.

The 19th of April, being Easter-even, we anchored under the iland Mocha. It lyeth in thirty-nine degrees, it may be some foure leagues over, and is a high mountainous hill, but round about the foote thereof, some halfe league from the sea-shore, it is champion ground, well inhabited, and manured.

From the straites to this iland, we found that either the coast is set out more westerly then it is, or that we had a great current, which put us to the west-wards : for we had not sight of land in three dayes after. Our reckoning was to see it, but for that we coasted not the land I cannot determine, whether it was caused by the current, or lying of the land. But Spaniards which have sayled alongst it, have told me that it is a bold and safe coast, and reasonable sounding off it.

In this iland of Mocha we had communication and contratation[4] with the inhabitants, but with great vigilancie and care ; for they and all the people of Chily are mortall enemies to the Spaniards, and held us to be of them ; and so esteemed Sir Francis Drake when he was in this iland, which was the first land also that he touched on this coast. They used him with so fine a trechery, that they possessed themselves of all the oares in his boate, saving two, and in striving to get them also, they slew and hurt all his men : himselfe, who had fewest wounds, had three, and two of them in the head. Two of his company which lived long after, had, the one seaventeene (his name was John Bruer, who afterward was pilot with master Candish), and the other above twentie, a negroe-servant to Sir Francis Drake.

---

[3] Chiloe.   [4] *Contractation*—commerce or dealings with them.

And with me they used a pollicie, which amongst barbarous people was not to be imagined, although I wrought sure; for I suffered none to treate with me nor with my people with armes. We were armed, and met upon a rock compassed with water, whether they came to parley and negotiate. Being in communication with the casiques and others, many of the Indians came to the heads of our boates, and some went into them. Certaine of my people standing to defend the boates with their oares, for that there went a bad sege, were forced to lay downe their musketts; which the Indians perceiving, endevoured to fill the barrells with water, taking it out of the sea in the hollow of their hands. By chance casting mine eye aside, I discovered their slynesse, and with a truncheon, which I had in mine hand, gave the Indians three or foure good lamskinnes:[5] the casiques seeing it, began to give me satisfaction, by using rigor towardes those which had beene in the boates; but I having gotten the refreshing I desired, and all I could hope from them, would have no further conversation with them. At our first comming, two of their casiques, who are their lords or kings, came aboord our shippe (we leaving one of our company ashore as a pledge), whom we feasted in good manner; they eat well of all that was set before them, and dranke better of our wine: one of them became a little giddie headed, and marvayled much at our artillery: I caused a peece to be primed, and after to be shott off, whereat the one started, but the other made no shew of alteration. After putting them ashore, loaden with toyes and trifles, which to them seemed great riches; from all parts of the iland the people came unto us, bringing all such things as they had, to wit, sheepe, cockes, etc. (from hennes they would not part), and divers sorts of fruits and rootes, which they exchanged with

[5] *To lamm* is used by Beaumont and Fletcher in the sense of *beat—bruise.*

Sect. XLI. us for knives, glasses, combes, belles, beades, counters, pinnes, and other trifles. We saw little demonstration of gold or silver amongst them, though some they had; and for that we saw they made estimation of it, we would not make reckoning of it: but they gave us to understand that they had it from the mayne.

Of sheepe.   The sheepe of this iland are great, good, and fatt; I have not tasted better mutton any where. They were as ours, and doubtlesse of the breed of those which the Spaniards brought into the country. Of the sheepe of the country we could by no meanes procure any one, although we saw of them, and used meanes to have had of them; for they esteem them much, as reason willeth, serving them for many uses; as in another place, God willing, I shall declare more at large. They have small store of fish.

This iland is scituate in the province of Arawca,[6] and is held to be peopled with the most valiant nation in all Chily, though generally the inhabitants of that kingdome are very couragious.

Their apparell,   They are clothed after the manner of antiquitie, all of woollen; their cassockes made like a sacke, square, with two holes for the two armes, and one for the head, all open below, without lining or other art: but of them some are most curiously wooven, and in colours, and on both sides alike.

and housing.   Their houses are made round, in fashion like unto our pigeon houses, with a laver[7] in the toppe, to evacuate the smoake when they make fire.

They brought us a strange kinde of tobacco, made into little cakes, like pitch, of a bad smell, with holes through the middle, and so laced many upon a string. They presented us also with two Spanish letters, thinking us to be

---

[6] The Araucanians have been immortalized in the *Araucano*, a poem written by Don Alonzo d'Ercilla y Zuniga; Madrid, 1632.

[7] This word is perhaps derived from *lave, to draw out, to exhaust.*

Spaniards, which were written by a captaine of a frigate, that some dayes before had received courtesie at their hands, and signified the same to the governour; wishing that the people of the iland would become good subjects to the king, and that therefore he would receive them into his favour and protection, and send them some person as governour; but none of them spake Spanish, and so we dealt with them by signes. The people of this iland, as of all Chily,[8] are of good stature, and well made, and of better countenance then those Indians which I have seene in many parts. They are of good understanding, and agilitie, and of great strength. Their weapons are bowes and arrowes, and macanas : their bowes short and strong, and their arrowes of a small reede or cane, three quarters of a yard long, with two feathers, and headed with a flint stone, which is loose, and hurting, the head remaining in the wound; some are headed with bone, and some with hard wood, halfe burnt in the fire. Wee came betwixt the iland and the mayne. On the south-west part of the iland lyeth a great ledge of rockes, which are dangerous; and it is good to bee carefull how to come too neere the iland on all parts.

People of Chily.

Their weapons.

Immediately when they discovered us, both upon the iland and the maine, wee might see them make sundry great fires, which were to give advise to the rest of the people to be in a readinesse : for they have continuall and mortall warre with the Spaniards, and the shippes they see they beleeve to be their enemies. The citie imperiall lyeth over against this iland, but eight or tenne leagues into the countrey : for all the sea coast from Baldivia till thirty-six degrees, the Indians have now, in a manner, in their hands free from any Spaniards.

Their hate to the Spaniards.

[8] Chile.

SECTION XLII.

HAVING refreshed our selves well in this iland, for that little time wee stayed, which was some three dayes, wee set sayle with great joy, and with a fayre winde sayled alongst the coast; and some eight leagues to the north-wards, we anchored againe in a goodly bay, and sent our boates ashore, with desire to speake with some of the Indians of Arawca, and to see if they would be content to entertaine amitie, or to chop and change with us. But all that night and the next morning appeared not one person, and so wee set sayle againe; and towardes the evening the winde began to change, and to blow contrary, and that so much, and the sea to rise so sodainely, that we could not

A cruel storme. take in our boates without spoyling of them. This storme continued with us ten dayes, beyond expectation, for that wee thought our selves out of the climate of fowle weather; but truely it was one of the sharpest stormes that ever I felt to endure so long.

In this storme, one night haling up our boates to free the water out of them, one of our younkers that went into them for that purpose, had not that regard, which reason required, unto our light horseman : for with haling her

The import-ant losse of a small vessell. up to step into her out of the boate, he split her asunder, and so we were forced to cut her off; which was no small heartes grief unto me, for that I knew, and all my company felt, and many times lamented, the losse of her.[1]

The storme tooke end, and wee shaped our course for

Saint Maries. the iland of Saint Maries, which lyeth in thirtie seaven degrees and forty minuts; and before you come unto the iland some two leagues, in the trade way lyeth a rocke, which, a farre off, seemeth to be a shippe under sayle. This iland is little and low, but fertill and well peopled, with Indians and some few Spaniards in it. Some ten leagues

---

[1] A storm is often judged to be severe in inverse proportion to the size of the vessel caught in it. We may form some idea of this sharp storm from the fact that the boats in tow lived through it.

to the north-wards of this iland, lyeth the citty Conception, Sect. XLII.
with a good port; from this we coasted alongst till wee Citty of
Conception.
came in thirty-three degrees and forty minutes. In which
height lay the ilands of Iuan Fernandes, betwixt threescore Iuan
Fernandes.
and fourescore leagues from the shore, plentiful of fish, and
good for refreshing. I purposed for many reasons not to
discover my selfe upon this coast, till wee were past Lyma Good to
avoid
discovery.
(otherwise called Cividad de Los Reyes, for that it was
entered by the Spaniard the day of the three kings); but
my company urged me so farre, that except I should seem
in all things to over-beare them, in not condescending to
that which in the opinion of all, but my selfe, seemed profitable and best, I could not but yeelde unto, though it
carried a false colour, as the ende prooved, for it was our
perdition. This all my company knoweth to be true,
whereof some are yet living and can give testimonie.

But the mariner is ordinarily so carried away with the Wilfulnesse
of mariners
desire of pillage, as sometimes for very appearances of small
moment hee looseth his voyage, and many times himselfe.
And so the greedines of spoyle, onely hoped for in shippes
of trade, which goe too and fro in this coast, blinded them
from forecasting the perill whereinto wee exposed our voyage, in discovering our selves before we past the coast of
Callao, which is the port of Lyma. To be short, wee haled
the coast aboord, and that evening we discovered the port
of Balparizo,[2] which serveth the citty of Saint Iago, standing
some twenty leagues into the countrey; when presently
we descried foure shippes at an anchor: whereupon wee They seize
upon four
ships.
manned and armed our boate, which rowed towards the
shippes: they seeing us turning in, and fearing that which
was, ran a shore with that little they could save, and leaft
us the rest; whereof we were masters in a moment, and
had the rifling of all the storehouses on the shoare.

This night I set a good guard in all the shippes, longing

[2] Val paraiso—vale of Paradise.

to see the light of the next morning to put all things in order; which appearing, I began to survay them, and found nothing of moment, saving five hundred botozios[3] of wine, two or three thousand of hennes, and some refreshing of bread, bacon, dried beefe, waxe, candles, and other necessaries. The rest of their lading was plankes, spares, and timber, for Lyma, and the valleyes, which is a rich trade; for it hath no timber but that which is brought to it from other places. They had also many packes of Indian mantles, but of no value unto us, with much tallow, and manteca de puerco,[4] and aboundance of great new chests, in which wee had thought to be some great masse of wealth, but opening them, found nothing but apples therein; all which was good marchandize in Lyma, but to And the warehouses. us of small accompt. The marchandize on shore in their store-houses was the like, and therefore in the same predicament. The owners of the shippes gave us to understand that at a reasonable price they would redeeme their shippes and loading, which I hearkened unto; and so admitted certaine persons which might treat of the matter, and concluded with them for a small price rather then to burne them, saving for the greatest, which I carryed with me, more to give satisfaction to my people then for any other respect; because they would not be perswaded but that there was much gold hidden in her; otherwise shee would have yeelded us more then the other three.

They seize upon another ship, Being in this treatie, one morning at the breake of day came another shippe touring into the harbour, and standing into the shore, but was becalmed. Against her wee manned a couple of boates, and tooke her before many houres. In this shippe we had some good quantitie of and some gold. gold, which shee had gathered in Baldivia, and the Conception, from whence shee came. Of this shippe was pilot

---

3 *Bota* is Spanish for a wine-skin or vessel: *botija,* a jar used for the same purpose.   4 Lard.

and part owner, Alonso Perezbueno, whom we kept for our pilot on this coast; till moved with compassion (for that he was a man charged with wife and children), we set him ashore betwixt Santa and Truxillo. Out of this shippe we had also store of good bacon, and some provision of bread, hennes, and other victuall. And for that shee had brought us so good a portion, and her owner continued with us, the better to animate him to play the honest man (though we trusted him no further then we saw him, for we presently discovered him to be a cunning fellow), and for that his other partner had lost the greatest part of gold, and seemed to be an honest man, as after he prooved by his thankfulnesse in Lyma, we gave them the ship and the greatest part of her loading freely.

Here we supplied our want of anchors, though not ac- Light cording to that which was requisite in regard of the burden anchors brought of our shippe; for in the South sea, the greatest anchor from the North sea. for a shippe of sixe or eight hundreth tunnes, is not a thousand waight; partly, because it is little subject to stormes, and partly, because those they had till our com-ming, were all brought out of the North sea by land; for they make no anchors in those countries. And the first And the first artillerie. artillerie they had was also brought over land, which was small; the carriage and passage from Nombre de Dios, or Porto Velo to Panama, being most difficult and steepe, up hill and downe hill, they are all carried upon negroes backes.

But some years before my imprisonment, they fell to making of artillery, and, since, they forge anchors also. Wee furnished our shippe also with a shift of sayles of Sayles of cotton cloth. cotton cloth, which are farre better in that sea then any of our double sayles; for that in all the navigation of that sea they have little rayne and few stormes; but where rayne and stormes are ordinary, they are not good; for with the wett they grow so stiffe they cannot be handled.

SECTION XLIII.

I CONCLUDED the ransome of the shippes with an auncient captaine, and of noble blood, who had his daughter there, ready to be imbarked to go to Lyma, to serve Donia Teruza de Castro, the viceroyes wife, and sister to Don Beltran de Castro. Her apparell and his, with divers other things which they had imbarked in the greatest shippe, we restored, for the good office he did us, and the confidence he had of us, comming and going onely upon my word; for which he was after ever thankefull, and deserved much more.

Another that treated with me was Captaine Iuan Contreres, owner of one of the shippes, and of the iland Santa Maria, in thirtie-seaven degrees and fortie minutes. In treating of the ransomes, and transporting and lading the provisions we made choyce of, wee spent some sixe or eight dayes; at the end whereof, with reputation amongst our enemies, and a good portion towards our charges, and our shippe as well stored and victualled as the day we departed from England, we set sayle.

The time wee were in this port, I tooke small rest, and so did the master of our shippe, Hugh Cornish, a most carefull, orderly, and sufficient man, because we knew our owne weaknesse; for entring into the harbour, we had but seaventie five men and boyes, five shippes to guard, and every one moored by himselfe; which, no doubt, if our enemies had knowne, they would have wrought some stratagem upon us; for the governour of Chily was there on shore in view of us, an auncient Flanders soldier, and of experience, wisedome, and valour, called Don Alonso de Soto Mayor, of the habit of Saint Iago, who was after captaine generall in Terra Firme, and wrought all the inventions upon the river of Chagree, and on the shore, when

Sir Francis Drake purposed to goe to Panama, in the voy- Sect. xliv.
age wherein he died ; as also, at my comming into Spaine,
he was president in Panama, and there, and in Lyma, used
me with great courtesie, like a noble souldier and liberall The noble-
ness of
gentleman. He confessed to me after, that he lay in am- Alonso de
Soto.
bush with three hundreth horse and foote, to see if at any
time wee had landed or neglected our watch, with balsas,
(which is a certaine raffe made of mastes or trees fastened
together), to have attempted something against us. But
the enemy I feared not so much as the wine ; which, not- The enemy
less danger-
withstanding all the diligence and prevention I could use ous then the
wine.
day and night, overthrew many of my people. A foule
fault, because too common amongst sea-men, and deserveth
some rigorous punishment, with severitie to be executed;
for it hath beene, and is daily, the destruction of many
good enterprises, amidst their best hopes. And besides
the ordinary fruites it bringeth forth, of beggery, shame,
and sicknesse, it is a most deadly sinne. A drunkard is
unfit for any government, and if I might be hired with
many thousands, I would not carry with me a man known
to put his felicitie in that vice, instiling it with the name
of good fellowship ; which in most well governed common-
wealths, hath beene a sufficient blemish to deprive a man
of office, of honour, and estimation. It wasteth our kingdome more then is well understood, as well by the infirmities it causeth, as by the consumption of wealth, to the
impoverishing of us, and the enriching of other kingdomes.

And though I am not old, in comparison of other Spanish
wines and
auncient men, I can remember Spanish wine rarely to burning
be found in this kingdome. Then hot burning feavers feavers un-
knowne in
England.
were not knowne in England, and men lived many moe
yeares. But since the Spanish sacks have beene common
in our tavernes, which, for conservation, is mingled with
lyme[1] in its making, our nation complaineth of calenturas,

[1] Lime was added to sack, not to preserve it, apparently, but for the

of the stone, the dropsie, and infinite other diseases, not heard of before this wine came in frequent use, or but very seldome.   To confirme which my beliefe, I have heard one of our learnedst physitians affirme, that he thought there died more persons in England of drinking wine and using hot spices in their meats and drinkes, then of all other diseases.   Besides there is no yeare in which it wasteth not two millions of crownes of our substance, by convayance into forraine countries ; which in so well a governed common-wealth as ours is acknowledged to be through the whole world, in all other constitutions, in this onely remaineth to be looked into and remedied.   Doubtlesse, whosoever should be the author of this reformation, would gaine with God an everlasting reward, and of his country a statua of gold, for a perpetuall memory of so meritorious a worke.

And consumeth treasure.

SECTION XLIV.

Description of the bay. A LEAGUE or better before a man discover this baye to the south-wards, lyeth a great rocke, or small iland, neere the shore ; under which, for a need, a man may ride with his shippe.   It is a good marke, and sure signe of the port, and discovering the bay a man must give a good birth to the poynt of the harbour; for it hath perilous rockes lying a good distance off.   It neither ebbeth nor floweth in this port, nor from this till a man come to Guayaquill, which is three degrees from the equinoctiall lyne to the south-wards.   Let this be considered.   It is a good harbour for all windes that partake not of the north; for it runneth up

same purpose that drugs are mixed in beer and spirits by brewers, publicans, and rectifiers, at the present day.

Falstaff.   Villain, there's lime in this sack.—*Hen. IV.*

Host.   I have spoke ; let him follow ; let me see thee
Froth and lime.—   *Merry Wives of Windsor.*

south and by west, and south south-west, but it hath much
fowle ground.

In one of these shippes we found a new devise for the
stopping of a sodaine leake in a shippe under water, without
board, when a man cannot come to it within board; which
eased us of one that we had from the day we departed from
Detford, caused by the touching a-ground of our shippe at
low water, being loaden and in the neap streames, comming
a-ground in the sterne, the force of the tyde caused to cast
thwart, wrested her slegg, and that in such sort, as it made
a continuall leake, though not much. And for that others
may profit themselves of the like, I thinke it good to set
downe the manner of it : which was, taking a round wicker
basket, and to fill it with peeces of a junke or rope, chopped
very small, and of an inch long, and after tozed all as
oacombe ;[2] then the basket is to be covered with a nett,
the meshes of it being at the least two inches square, and
after to be tied to a long pike or pole, which is to goe
a crosse the baskets mouth; and putting it under water,
care is to be had to keepe the baskets mouth towardes the
shippes side. If the leake be any thing great, the oacombe
may be somewhat longer, and it carrieth likelihood to doe
good, and seemeth to be better then the stitching of a
bonnet, or any other diligence which as yet I have seene.

Another thing I noted of these shippes, which would be
also used by us ; that every shippe carrieth with her a spare
rudder, and they have them to hange and unhange with
great facilitie : and besides, in some parts of the shippe
they have the length, breadth, and proportion of the rudder marked out, for any mischance that may befall them ;
which is a very good prevention.[3]

Tenne leagues to the north-wards of this harbour, is the

[2] *Teased*, pulled, or unravelled. Oakum is made from rope yarns
teased or untwisted.

[3] We owe many good hints to Spanish seamen : this among others is
used to this day.

Bay of
Quintera.

*Nota verum
hispanum.*

Coquiubo.

bay of Quintera, where is good anchoring, but an open bay; where master Thomas Candish (for the good he had done to a Spaniard, in bringing him out of the Straits of Magellan, where, otherwise, he had perished with his company),[4] was by him betrayed, and a dozen of his men taken and slaine. But the judgement of God left not his ingratitude unpunished; for in the fight with us, in the vice-admirall, he was wounded and maymed in that manner, as, three yeares after, I saw him begge with crutches, and in that miserable estate, as he had beene better dead then alive.

From Balparizo wee sailed directly to Coquinbo,[5] which is in thirtie degrees; and comming thwart the place, wee were becalmed, and had sight of a shippe: but for that shee was farre off, and night at hand, shee got from us, and wee having winde, entered the port, thinking to have had some shipping in it; but we lost our labour: and for that the towne was halfe a league upp in the countrey, and wee not manned for any matter of attempt, worthy prosecution, we made no abode on the shore, but presently set sayle for the Peru. This is the best harbour that I have seene in the South sea, it is land-locked for all winds, and capeable of many shippes; but the ordinary place where the shippes lade and unlade, and accommodate themselves, is betwixt a rocke and the mayne on the wester side, some halfe a league up within the entrance of the port, which lyeth south and south, and by east and north, and by west.

In the in-country, directly over the port, is a round piked hill, like a sugar loafe, and before the entrance on the southern poynt of the port, comming in out of the sea, is a great rocke, a good birth from the shore; and these are the markes of the port as I remember.

---

[4] This was one of Sarmiento's unfortunate colonists.
[5] Coquimbo, or la Serena.

Being cleere of this port, wee shaped our course for Arica, Sect. XLIV.
and leaft the kingdomes of Chily, one of the best countries Arica in Chily much commended.
that the sunne shineth on ; for it is of a temperate clymate,
and abounding in all things necessary for the use of man,
with infinite rich mines of gold, copper, and sundry other
mettals.[6]

The poorest houses in it, by report of their inhabitants,
have of their owne store, bread, wine, flesh, and fruite ;
which is so plentifull, that of their superfluitie they supply
other partes. Sundry kindes of cattell, as horses, goates,
and oxen, brought thither by the Spaniards, are found in
heardes of thousands, wilde and without owner ; besides For all sorts of fruits.
those of the countrey, which are common to most partes
of America : in some of which are found the bezar stones,
and those very good and great.

Amongst others, they have little beastes like unto a
squirrell, but that hee is gray; his skinne is the most delicate, soft, and curious furre that I have seene, and of much
estimation (as is of reason) in the Peru ; few of them come
into Spaine, because difficult to be come by; for that the
princes and nobles laie waite for them. They call this beast
chinchilla, and of them they have great abundance.

All fruites of Spaine they have in great plentie, saving
stone fruite and almonds; for in no part of the Indies have
I knowne that plumbes, cherries, or almondes have borne
fruit : but they have certaine little round cocos, as those of
Brasill, of the bignesse of a wall-nut, which is as good as
an almond ; besides it hath most of the fruites naturall to
America, of which in another place I shall, God willing,
speake particularly.

The gold they gather is in two manners : the one is And plenty of gold.
washing the earth in great trayes of wood in many waters ;
as the earth washeth away, the gold in the bottome re-

---

[6] Thirty years back, two or three ships sufficed for the trade of this
coast with Great Britain. At present above three hundred are employed,
carrying copper ore, wool, guano, nitrate of soda, etc.

maineth.   The other is, by force of art to draw it out of the mynes, in which they finde it.   In most partes of the countrie, the earth is mingled with gold; for the butizias, in which the wine was, which wee found in Balparizo, had many sparkes of gold shining in them.   Of it the gold-smiths I carryed with me, for like purposes, made experience.

When Baldivia and Arawca were peaceable, they yeelded greatest plentie, and the best : but now, their greatest mynes are in Coquinbo, as also the mines of copper, which they carry to the Peru, and sell it better cheape then it is ordinarily sold in Spaine.

The Indians forbid the search of gold.

The Indians knowing the end of the Spaniards molestation to be principally the desire of their riches, have enacted, that no man, upon paine of death, doe gather any gold.

Every showre a showre of gold.

In Coquinbo it rayneth seldome, but every shower of rayne is a shower of gold unto them ; for with the violence of the water falling from the mountaines, it bringeth from them the gold; and besides, gives them water to wash it out, as also for their ingenious to worke; so that ordinarily every weeke they have processions for rayne.

Linnen and woollen cloth made in Coquinbo.

In this kingdome they make much linnen and woollen cloth, and great store of Indian mantles, with which they furnish other partes ; but all is course stuffe.   It hath no silke, nor iron, except in mynes, and those as yet not discovered.   Pewter is well esteemed, and so are fine linnen, woollen cloth, haberdashers wares, edge tooles, and armes, or munition.

It hath his governour, and *audiencia,* with two bishoppes: the one of Saint Iago, the other of the Imperiall; all under the vice-roy, *audiencia,* and primate of Lyma.   Saint Iago is the metropolitan and head of the kingdome, and the seate of justice, which hath its appellation to Lyma.

The valour of the Arawcans.

The people are industrious and ingenious, of great strength, and invincible courage ; as in the warres, which they have susteyned above fortie yeares continually against the Spaniards, hath beene experienced. For confirmation whereof, I will alledge onely two proofes of many; the one was of an Indian captaine taken prisoner by the Spaniards; and for that he was of name, and knowne to have done his devoire against them, they cut off his hands, thereby intending to disenable him to fight any more against them : but he returning home, desirous to revenge this injury, to maintaine his libertie, with the reputation of his nation, and to helpe to banish the Spaniard, with his tongue intreated and incited them to persevere in their accustomed valour and reputation; abasing the enemy, and advancing his nation; condemning their contraries of cowardlinesse, and confirming it by the crueltie used with him, and others his companions in their mishaps; shewing them his armes without hands, and naming his brethren whose halfe feete they had cut off, because they might be unable to sit on horsebacke: with force arguing, that if they feared them not, they would not have used so great inhumanitie; for feare produceth crueltie, the companion of cowardize. Thus incouraged he them to fight for their lives, limbes, and libertie, choosing rather to die an honourable death fighting, then to live in servitude, as fruitlesse members in their common-wealth. Thus, using the office of a sergeant major, and having loaden his two stumpes with bundles of arrowes, succoured those who in the succeeding battaile had their store wasted, and changing himselfe from place to place, animated and encouraged his countri-men with such comfortable perswasions, as it is reported, and credibly beleeved, that he did much more good with his words and presence, without striking a stroake, then a great part of the armie did with fighting to the utmost.[7]

[7] This reminds us of the familiar lines :

> " For Widdrington needs must I wail,
>   As one in doleful dumps ;
> For when his legs were smitten off,
>   He fought upon his stumps."—*Chevy Chace.*

The other proofe is, that such of them as fight on horse-backe, are but slightly armed, for that their armour is a beasts hide, fitted to their bodie greene, and after worne till it be dry and hard.   He that is best armed, hath him double; yet any one of them with these armes, and with his launce, will fight hand to hand with any Spaniard armed from head to foote.   And it is credibly reported, that an Indian being wounded through the body by a Spaniards launce, with his owne hands hath crept on upon the launce, and come to grapple with his adversary, and both fallen to the ground together.   By which is seene their resolution and invincible courage, and the desire they have to maintaine their reputation and libertie.

SECTION XLV.

LEAVING the coast of Chily, and running towards that of Peru, my company required the third of the gold we had gotten, which of right belonged unto them; wherein I desired to give them satisfaction of my just intention, but not to devide it till we came home, and so perswaded them with the best reasons I could; alledging the difficultie to devide the barres, and being parted, how easie it was to be robbed of them, and that many would play away their portions, and come home as beggerly as they came out; and that the shares could not be well made before our returne to England, because every mans merites could not be discerned nor rewarded till the end of the voyage.   In conclusion, it was resolved, and agreed, that the things of price, as gold and silver, should be put into chests with three keyes, whereof I should have the one, the master another, and the third, some other person whom they should name. This they yeelded unto with great difficultie, and not with-

out reason; for the bad correspondence used by many captaines and owners with their companies upon their returne,
defrauding them, or diminishing their rights, hath hatched
many jealousies, and produced many disorders, with the
overthrow of all good discipline and government, as experience teacheth; for where the souldier and mariner is
unpaide, or defrauded, what service or obedience can be
required at his hands?

The covetous captaine or commander looseth the love of
those under his charge: yea, though he have all the parts
besides required in a perfect commander, yet if he preferre
his private profite before justice, hardly will any man follow such a leader, especially in our kingdome, where more
absolute authoritie and trust is committed to those who
have charge, then in many other countries.

And therefore in election of chieftaines, care would be
had in examination of this poynt. The shamefull fruites
whereof (found by experience of many yeares, wherein I
have wandred the world), I leave to touch in particular;
because I will not diminish the reputation of any. But
this let me manifest, that there have bin, and are, certaine
persons, who, before they goe to sea, either robbe part of
the provisions, or in the buying, make penurious, unhol-
some, and avaritious penny-worths; and the last I hold to
be the least: for they robbe onely the victuallers and
owners; but the others steale from owners, victuallers,
and companie, and are many times the onely overthrowers
of the voyage; for the company thinking themselves to be
stored with foure or sixe moneths victualls, upon survay,
they finde their bread, beefe, or drinke short, yea, perhaps
all, and so are forced to seeke home in time of best hopes
and imployment. This mischiefe is most ordinary in great
actions.

Lastly, some are so cunning, that they not onely make
their voyage by robbing before they goe to sea, but of that

L

also which commeth home.   Such gamsters, a wise man of
our nation resembled to the mill on the river of Thames,
for grinding both with flood and ebbe: so these at their
going out, and comming home, will be sure to robbe all
others of their shares.   Although this be a great abuse
amongst us, and but of late dayes practised, and by me
spoken unto by way of animadversion, either in hope of
redresse, or for infliction of punishment ; yet I would have
the world know, that in other countries the fault is farre
more insufferable.   And the principall cause which I can
finde for it, is that our country imployeth her nobles, or
men of credite in all actions of moment, who rather chuse
to spend wealth and gaine honor, then to gaine riches without reputation : whereas in Spaine, and other partes, the
advancement of poore men and meane persons by favour
and interest, produceth no other end, but private and particular respects to enrich themselves ; yet the nobilitie
themselves, for the most part, in all occasions pretend re-
wards for any small service whatsoever, which with us as
yet is not in use.

Of detayning
and defraud-
ing of wages.   But the greatest and most principall robbery of all, in
my opinion, is the defrauding or detaining of the companies
thirdes[1] or wages, accursed by the just God, who forbiddeth
the hyre of the labourer to sleepe with us.   To such I
speake as either abuse themselves in detayning it ; or else
to such as force the poore man to sell it at vile and low
prices ; and lastly, to such as upon fained cavils and sutes,
doe deterre the simple and ignorant sort from their due
prosecutions ; which being too much in use amongst us,
hath bred in those that follow the sea a jealousie in all imployments, and many times causeth mutenies and infinite
inconveniences.   A poynt deserving consideration and reformation, and which with great facilitie may be remedied,

---

[1] " Going by thirds" means that the crew have a certain per cent-
age on the profits of the voyage, in lieu of wages ; thus their remu-
neration partly depends on their own exertions.

if upright justice would put it selfe as stickler betwixt the
owners and company.

No lesse worthie of reformation are the generall abuses
of mariners and souldiers, who robbe all they can, under
the colour of pillage, and after make ordinance, cables,
sayles, anchors, and all above deckes, to belong unto them
of right, whether they goe by thirdes or wages : this proceedeth from those pilfering warres, wherein every gallant
that can arme out a shippe, taketh upon him the name and
office of a captaine, not knowing what to command, nor
what to execute. Such commanders, for the most part,
consort and joyne unto themselves disorderly persons,
pyrates, and ruffians, under the title of men of valour and
experience : they meeting with any prise, make all upon
the deckes theirs of dutie ; viz.—the best peece of ordinance for the captaine ; the second, for the gunner ; the
third, for his mate ; the best cable and anchor for the
master ; the maine topsayle for the botesman :[2] the bon-
netts for the quarter masters ; and the rest of the sayles
for the company. The cardes and instruments of the
master, for the master ; the surgeans instruments and
chest for the surgean ; the carpenters tooles and chest for
the carpenter ; and so consequently of each officer, that
answereth the other in the two shippes.

If one happen upon a bag of gold, silver, pearle, or
precious stones, it is held well gotten, provided it be cleanly
stolne, though the shippe and all her loading besides be not
worth so much ; little considering the common injury in defrauding the owners, victuallers, and whole companie : and
forgetting, that if himselfe were a jury-man upon another
in like case, he would adjudge him to the gallows. But I
would advise such novices to know, that our true and
auncient discipline of warre is farre different, and being
understood, is much more better for the generall. Besides it

[2] Boatswain ?

is grounded on Gods law (from whence all lawes should be derived), and true justice, which distributeth to every one that which to him belongeth of right, and that in due season.

In the time of warre in our country, as also in others by the lawes of Oleron, which to our auncient sea-men were fundamental, nothing is allowed for pillage but apparell, armes, instruments, and other necessaries belonging to the persons in that shippe which is taken; and these too when the shippe is gained by dint of sword; with a proviso, that if any particular pillage exceed the valew of sixe crownes, it may be redeemed for that valew by the generall stocke, and sould for the common benefit.

If the prise render it selfe without forcible entry, all in generall ought to be preserved and sould in masse, and so equally devided; yea though the shippe be wonne by force and entry, yet whatsoever belongeth to her of tackling, sayles, or ordinance, is to bee preserved for the generalitie: saving a peece of artillery for the captaine, another for the gunner, and a cable and anchor for the master; which are the rights due unto them: and these to be delivered when the shippe is in safety, and in harbour, eyther unloaden or sould. Which law or custome, well considered, will rise to be more beneficiall for the owners, victuallers, and company, then the disorders newly crept in and before remembred.

For the sayles, cables, anchors, and hull, being sould every one a part, yeeld not the one halfe which they would doe if they were sould altogether; besides the excusing of charges and robberies in the unloading and parting.

In the warres of Fraunce, in the time of queen Mary, and in other warres, as I have heard of many auncient captaines, the companie had but the fourth part, and every man bound to bring with him the armes with which hee would fight; which in our time I have knowne also used in Fraunce: and if the company victualed themselves, they

had then the one halfe, and the owners the other halfe for
the shippe, powder, shott, and munition. If any prise were
taken, it was sould by the tunne, shippe and goods, so as
the loading permitted it ; that the marchant having bought
the goods, hee might presently transport them whethersoever he would. By this manner of proceeding, all rested
contented, all being truely paid; for this was just dealing:
if any deserved reward, he was recompensed out of the
generall stocke; if any one had filched or stolne, or committed offence, hee had likewise his desert. And who once
was knowne to be a disordered person, or a theefe, no man
would receive him into his shippe; whereas, now a dayes
many vaunt themselves of their theftes and disorders : yea
I have seene the common sort of mariners, under the
name of pillage, maintaine and justify their robberies
most insolently, before the queens majesties commissioners,
with arrogant and unseemly termes, for that they would
not condiscend to their unreasonable challenges. The demaunds being better worth then five hundreth poundes,
which some one pretended to be his; and that of the
choysest marchandize, and most of it robbed out of that
part of the shippe, which they themselves, and all the
world, cannot but confesse to be marchandize.

My opinion is, that such malaperts deserve most justly
to have their spoyle taken from them, or some worse
consideration, and afterwards to be severely punished, in
prevention of greater prejudices, then can by paper be
well declared.

But I must tell you withall, such hath beene the partiallitie of some commissioners in former times, that upon
information, in lieu of punishment, opinion hath held them
for tall fellowes, when, in truth, they never prove the best
men in difficult occasions. For their mindes are all set
on spoyle, and can bee well contented to suffer their associates to beare the brunt, whillest they are prolling after

pillage, the better to gaine and mainetaine the aforesaid attributes in tavernes and disorderly places.

For the orderly and quiet men I have ever found in all occasions to bee of best use, most valiant, and of greatest sufficiency. Yet I condemne none, but those who will be reputed valiant, and are not: examine the accusation.

What ought to be reputed pillage.

All what soever is found upon the decke going for marchandize, is exempted out of the censure of pillage: silks, linnen, or woollen cloth in whole peeces, apparell, that goeth to be sold, or other goods whatsoever, though they be in remnants, manifestly knowne to be carryed for that end; or being comprehended in the register, or bils of lading, are not to bee contayned under the name of pillage.

Against the disloyalties of captaines.

But as I have sayd of the consort, so can I not but complaine of many captaines and governours, who, overcome with like greedie desire of gaine, condiscend to the smoothering and suppressing of this auncient discipline, the clenlier to smother their owne disloyalties, in suffering these breake-bulks to escape and absent themselves, till the heate be past and partition made.

Concealment of much more value then the trading.

Some of these cause the bils of lading to be cast into the sea, or so to bee hidden that they never appeare. Others send away their prisoners, who sometimes are more worth then the shippe and her lading, because they should not discover their secret stolne treasure; for many times that which is leaft out of the register or bils of lading, with purpose to defraud the prince of his customes (in their conceits held to be excessive), is of much more value then that which the shippe and lading is worth. Yea I have knowne shippes worth two hundreth thousand pounds, and better, cleane swept of their principall riches, nothing but the bare bulke being leaft unsacked. The like may be spoken of that which the disorderly mariner and the souldier termeth pillage; yet all winked at and unpunished, although such prizes have beene rendred without stroake stricken.

This, doubtlesse, cannot but be a hearts greife and discouragement to all those who vertuously and truely desire to observe the auncient discipline of our nation, their owne honours, and the service of their soveraigne.

But to prevent these unknowne mischiefes, and for his The prevention of undue pillagings. better discharge, I remember that my father, Sir John Hawkins, in his instructions, in actions under his charge, had this particular article : that whosoever rendred or tooke any shippe, should be bound to exhibite the bils of lading; to keepe the captaine, master, marchants, and persons of account, and to bring them to him to be examined, or into England. If they should bee by any accident seperated from him, whatsoever was found wanting (the prisoners being examined), was to bee made good by the captaine and company which tooke the shippe, and this upon great punishments. I am witness, and avow that this course did redownd much to the benefitte of the generall stocke ; to the satisfaction of her majestie and counsell, the justification of his government, and the content of his followers.

Thus much have I set downe concerning these abuses and the reformation thereof, for that I have neither seene them divulged by any with whom I have gone to sea, neither yet recorded in writing by any mans pen. Let consideration present them to the eares of the powerfull. But now to our voyage.

SECTION XLVI.

RUNNING alongst the coast till wee came within few leagues of Arica, nothing happened unto us of extraordinary noveltie or moment, for we had the brese favourable, which seldome happeneth in this climate; finding ourselves in nineteene degrees, wee haled the shore close abourd, purposing to see if there were any shipping in the road of

Arica. Arica. It standeth in a great large bay, in eighteene degrees: and before you come to it, a league to the southwards of the roade and towne, is a great round hill, higher then the rest of the land of the bay, neere about the towne; which wee having discovered, had sight presently of a small barke, close abourd the shore, becalmed. Manning our boate, wee tooke her, being loaden with fish, from Moromereno[1]; which is a goodly head-land, very high, and lyeth betwixt twenty-foure and twenty-five degrees, and whether ordinarily some barkes use to goe a fishing every yeare.

In her was a Spaniard and sixe Indians. The Spaniard, for that hee was neere the shore, swam unto the rockes; and though wee offered to returne him his barke and fish (as was our meaning), yet hee refused to accept it, and made us answere, that hee durst not, for feare least the

The severity justice should punish him. In so great subjection are the of Spaine. poore unto those who have the administration of justice in those partes, and in most partes of the kingdomes and countries subject to Spaine. Insomuch, that to heare the justice to enter in at their doores, is to them destruction and desolation : for this cause wee carried her alongst with us.

In this meane while wee had sight of another tall shippe, comming out of the sea, which wee gave chase unto, but could not fetch upp, beeing too good of sayle for us. Our small prize and boate standing off unto us, descryed another shippe, which they chased and tooke also, loaden with fish, comming from the ilands of Iuan Fernandes.

After wee opened the bay and port of Arica; but seeing it cleane without shipping, wee haled the coast alongst, and going aboord to visit the bigger prize, my company saluted me with a volley of small shot. Amongst them,

[1] Monte Morena.

one musket brake, and carryed away the hand of him that Sect. xlvi. shot it, through his owne default, which for that I have seene to happen many times, I thinke it necessary to note in this place, that others may take warning by his harme.

The cause of the muskets breaking, was the charging Over-charging of artilleries. with two bullets, the powder being ordayned to carry but the waight of one, and the musket not to suffer two charges of powder or shott. By this oversight, the fire is restrayned with the overplus of the waight of shott, and not being able to force both of them out, breaketh all to peeces, so to find a way to its owne center.

And I am of opinion, that it is a great errour to prove great ordinance, or small shot, with double charges of powder or shot; my reason is, for that ordinarily the mettall is proportioned to the waight of the shot which the peece is to beare, and the powder correspondent to the waight of the bullet; and this being graunted, I see no reason why any man should require to prove his peece with more then is belonging to it of right : for I have seene many goodly peeces broken with such tryals, being cleane without hony combes, cracke, flawe, or other perceavable blemish, which no doubt, with their ordinary allowance, would have servea many yeares. Yea, I have beene certified by men of credit, that some gunners have taken a glory for breaking many peeces in the tryall ; which is easie to be done by sundry slights and meanes not fitt to bee published, much lesse to bee exercised, being prejudiciall to the seller, and charge-able to the conscience of the practiser; therefore it were good, this excessive tryall by double charges were cleane abolished.[2] If I should make choyce for my selfe, I would not willingly, that any peece should come into fort or shippe, under my charge, which had borne at any time

[2] It is still the custom to prove ordnance with a heavier charge than they are expected to carry on service. It seems quite possible that a piece may bear the proof, and yet the particles be so disarranged, that it fail afterwards.

more then his ordinary allowance, misdoubting, least, through the violence of the double charge, the peece may be crased within, or so forced, as at another occasion with his ordinary allowance, he might breake in peeces : how many men so many mindes : for to others this may seem harsh, for that the contrary custome hath so long time beene received, and therefore I submit to better experience, and contradict not but that in a demy culvering, a man may put two saker or minion shots, or many of smaller waight : and so in a muskett, two calever shott, or many smaller, so they exceed not the ordinary waight prescribed by proportion, arte, and experience.[3] These experiments I hold convenient upon many occasions, yea, and most necessary ; but the vaine custome of double charges, to cause their peeces thereby to give a better report, I affirme can produce no other effect but danger, losse, and harme.

SECTION XLVII.

HAVING visited our prises, and finding nothing in them but fish, we tooke a small portion for our victualing, and gave the bigger shippe to the Spaniards againe, and the lesser wee kept, with purpose to make her our pinnas. The Indians which wee tooke in her, would by no meanes depart from us, but desired to goe with us to England, The amity of saying that the Indian and English were brothers; and in the Indians. all places where wee came, they shewed themselves much affectionated unto us : these were natives of Moremoreno, and the most brutish of all that ever I had seene ; and except it were in forme of men and speech, they seemed altogether voyde of that which appertained to reasonable

[3] The demy-culverin was about equivalent to the nine-pounder ; a saker to the six-pounder ; and the minion to the four-pounder.

men.   They were expert swimmers; but after the manner of spaniels, they dive and abide under water a long time, and swallow the water of the sea as if it were of a fresh river.   Except a man see them, he would hardly beleeve how they continue in the sea, as if they were mer-maides, and the water their naturall element.

Their countrey is most barren, and poore of foode.   If they take a fish alive out of the sea, or meete with a peece of salted fish, they will devoure it without any dressing, as savourely as if had beene most curiously sodden or dressed, all which makes me beleeve that they sustaine themselves of that which they catch in the sea.

The Spaniards profit themselves of their labour and travell, and recompense them badly : they are in worse condition then their slaves, for to those they give sustenance, house-roome, and clothing, and teach them the knowledge of God : but the other they use as beastes, to doe their labour without wages, or care of their bodies or soules.

SECTION XLVIII.

Thwart of Ariquipa,[1] the shippe we brought with us from Balparizo being very leake, and my companie satisfied that their hope to find any thing of worth in her was vaine, having searched her from post to stemme, condiscended to fire her; and the rather to keepe our company together, which could not well suffer any devision more then of meere necessity : so by generall accord we eased ourselves of her, and continued our course alongst the coast, till we came thwart of the bay of Pisco, which lyeth within fifteene degrees and fifteene minutes.

Presently after wee were cleare of Cape Saugalean,[2] and

---

[1] Arequipa.   [2] Sangallan.

his ilands, wee ranged this bay with our boate and pinnace. It hath two small ilands in it, but without fruite; and being becalmed, we anchored two dayes thwart of Chilca.

Advise given by sea and land. By sea and by land, those of Chyly had given advise to Don Garcia Hurtado de Mendoça, marquis of Cavete, vice-roy of Peru, resident in Lima, of our being on the coast. Hee presently with all possible diligence, put out sixe shippes in warlike order, with well neere two thousand men, and dispatched them to seeke us, and to fight with us, under the conduct of Don Beltrian de Castro Ydelaluca, his wives brother; who departing out of the port of Callao, turned to wind-ward in sight over the shore, from whence they had dayly intelligence where wee had beene discovered. And the next day after our departure out of Chilca, about the middle of May, at breake of day, wee had sight each of other, thwart of Cavete, wee being to windwards of the Spanish armado some two leagues, and all with little or no winde. Our pinnace or prise being furnished with oares came unto us, out of which we thought to have taken our men, and so to leave her; but being able to come unto us at all times, it was held for better to keepe her till necessity forced us to leave her: and so it was determined that if we came to likelihood of boording, shee should lay our boate aboord, and enter all her men, and from thence to enter our shippe, and so to forsake her. Although, by the event in that occasion this proved good, notwithstanding I hold it to bee reproved where the enemie is farre superiour in multitude and force, and able to come and bourd if hee list; and that the surest course is to fortifie the principall the best that may bee, and to cut of all impediments, where a man is forced to defence: for that no man is assured to have time answerable to his purpose and will; and upon doubt whether the others, in hope to save themselves, will not leave him in greatest extremitie.

SECTION XLIX.

Wee presently put ourselves in the best order wee could to fight and to defend ourselves : our prayers we made unto the Lord God of battails, for his helpe and our deliverance, putting our selves wholy into his hands. About nine of the clocke, the brese began to blow, and wee to stand off into the sea, the Spaniards cheeke by jole with us, ever getting to the wind-wards upon us ; for that the shipping of the South sea is ever moulded sharpe under water, and long ; all their voyages depending upon turning to wind-wardes, and the brese blowing ever southerly.

As the sunne began to mount aloft, the wind began to fresh; which together with the rowling sea that ever beateth upon this coast, comming out of the westerne-bourd, caused a chapping sea, wherewith the admirall of the Spaniards snapt his maine mast asunder, and so began to lagge a sterne, and with him other two shippes. The vice-admirall split her maine-sayle, being come within shott of us upon our broad side, but to lee-wards : the reare-admirall cracked her maine-yard asunder in the middest, being a head of us. One of the armado, which had gotten upon the broad side of us, to wind-wards, durst not assault us.

With these disgraces[1] upon them, and the hand of God helping and delivering us, night comming, we began to consult what course was best to be taken to free our selves; wherein were divers opinions : some sayd it was best to stand off to the sea close by all the night; others to lye it a hull ; others to cast about to the shoare-wards two glasses, and after all the night to stand off to sea close by. The admirall of the Spaniards, with the other two, were a sterne of us some foure leagues ; the vice-admirall a mile right to le-wards of us; the reare-admirall in a manner

1 Used in the sense of misfortunes.

right a head, some culvering shott; and one upon our loofe, within shott also. The moone was to rise within two houres. After much debating, it was concluded that wee should beare up before the winde, and seeke to escape betwixt the admirall and the vice-admirall, which wee put in execution, not knowing of any other disgrace befallen them, but that of the reare-admirall, till after our surrender, when they recounted unto us all that had past. In the morning at breake of day, wee were cleare of all our enemies, and so shaped our course alongst the coast, for the bay of Atacames, where we purposed to trim our pinnace, and to renue our wood and water, and so to depart upon our voyage with all possible speede.

The Spanish armado returned presently to Callao, which is the port of Lyma, or of the Citty of the Kings. It was first named Lyma, and retayneth also that name of the river, which passeth by the citty called Lyma. The Spanish armado being entred the port, the people began to goe ashore, where they were so mocked and scorned by the women, as scarce any one by day would shew his face: they reviled them with the name of cowards and golnias, and craved licence of the vice-roy to bee admitted in their roomes, and to undertake the surrendry of the English shippe. I have beene certified for truth, that some of them affronted their souldiers with daggers and pistols by their sides.

This wrought such effects in the hearts of the disgraced, as they vowed eyther to recover their reputation lost, or to follow us into England; and so with expedition, the viceroy commaunded two shippes and a pinnace to be put in order, and in them placed the chiefe souldiers and marriners of the rest, and furnished them with victuals and munition.

The foresayd generall is once againe dispatched to seeke us; who ranged the coastes and ports, enforming himselfe what hee could. Some fiftie leagues to the north-wards of Lyma, in sight of Mongon, wee tooke a shippe halfe loaden with wheate, sugar, miell de canas, and cordovan skins: which for that shee was leake, and sayled badly, and tackled in such maner as the marriners would not willingly put themselves into her, wee tooke what was necessary for our provision and fired her.

Thwart of Truxillo, wee set the companie of her a shore, with the pilot which we had taken in Balparizo, reserving the pilot of the burnt shippe, and a Greeke, who chose rather to continue with us, then to hazard their lives in going a shore; for that they had departed out of the port of Santa, which is in eight degrees, being required by the justice not to weigh anchor before the coast was knowne to be cleere.

It is a thing worthy to be noted, and almost incredible, with how few men they use to sayle a shippe in the South sea; for in this prise, which was above an hundred tuns, were but eight persons: and in a shippe of three hundreth tuns, they use not to put above foureteene or fifteene persons; yea, I have beene credibly enformed, that with foureteene persons, a shippe of five hundreth tuns hath beene carried from Guayaquil to Lyma, deepe loaden, (which is above two hundreth leagues): and are forced ever to gaine their voyage by turning to wind-wards, which is the greatest toyle and labour that the marriners have; and slow sometimes in this voyage foure or five moneths, which is generall in all the navigations of this coast.[2] But the security from stormes, and certainty of the breze, with the desire to make their gaine the greater, is the cause that every man forceth himselfe to the uttermost, to doe the labour of two men.

[2] The plan pursued at that day was to beat to wind-ward in shore: now, by standing out boldly to the westward, the voyage to the south-ward, against the prevailing wind, is much shortened.

SECTION L.

IN the height of this port of Santa, some seven hundreth and fiftie leagues to the west-wards, lie the ilands of Salomon, of late yeares discovered. At my being in Lyma, a fleete of foure sayle was sent from thence to people them; which through the emulation and discord that arose amongst them, being landed and setled in the countrey, was utterly overthrowne; onely one shippe, with some few of the people, after much misery, got to the Philippines. This I came to the knowledge of·by a large relation written from a person of credit, and sent from the Philippines to Panama. I saw it at my being there, in my voyage towards Spaine.

Having edged neere the coast to put the Spaniards on shore, a thicke fogge tooke us, so that wee could not see the land; but recovering our pinnace and boate, we sayled on our course, till we came thwart of the port called Malabrigo: it lyeth in seaven degrees.

In all this coast the currant runneth with great force, but never keepeth any certaine course, saving that it runneth alongst the coast, sometimes to the south-wards, sometimes to the north-wards; which now running to the north-wards, forced us so farre into the bay, which a point of the land causeth, that they call Punta de Augussa,[1] as thinking to cleere ourselves by roving north-west, wee could not double this point, making our way north northwest. Therefore speciall care is ever to bee had of the current: and doubtlesse, if the providence of Almighty God had not freede us, wee had runne ashore upon the land, without seeing or suspecting any such danger. His name bee ever exalted and magnified for delivering us from the unknowne daunger, by calming the winde all night: the sunnes rising manifested unto us our errour and perill,

[1] Punta de Ahuja?

by discovering unto us the land within two leagues, right
a head. The current had carried us without any wind, at
the least foure leagues; which seene, and the winde beginning to blow, wee brought our tackes abourd, and in
short time cleared our selves.

Thwart of this point of Augussa, lie two desert ilandes;
they call them Illas de Lobos, for the multitude of seales
which accustome to haunt the shore. In the bigger is
very good harbour, and secure: they lie in sixe degrees and
thirtie minutes.

The next day after, wee lost sight of these ilands, being
thwart of Payta, which lyeth in five degrees; and having
manned our pinnace and boate to search the port, wee had
sight of a tall shippe, which having knowledge of our
being on the coast, and thinking her selfe to be more safe
at sea then in the harbour, put her selfe then under sayle:
to her wee gave chase all that night and the next day, but
in fine she being better of sayle then wee, shee freed her
selfe. Thus being too lee-ward of the harbour and discovered, we continued our course alongst the shore. That
evening wee were thwart of the river of Guayaquill, which
hath in the mouth of it two ilands: the souther-most and
biggest, called Puma,[1] in three degrees; and the other, to
the north-wards, Santa Clara.

Puma is inhabited, and is the place where they build
their principall shipping; from this river, Lyma and all
the valleys are furnished with timber, for they have none
but that which is brought from hence, or from the kingdome of Chile. By this river passeth the principall trade
of the kingdome of Quito; it is navigable some leagues
into the land, and hath great abundance of timber.

Those of the Peru, use to ground and trim their shippes
in Puma, or in Panama, and in all other partes they are
forced to carene their shippes. In Puma, it higheth and

Puma.

---

[1] Puna.

falleth fifteene or sixteene foote water, and from this iland
till a man come to Panama, in all the coast it ebbeth and
floweth more or lesse, keeping the ordinary course which
the tides doe in all seas. The water of this river, by experience, is medicinable, for all aches of the bones, for the
stone, and strangurie : the reason which is given is, because all the bankes and low lands adjoining to this river,
are replenished with salsaperillia ;[2] which lying for the most
part soaking in the water, it participateth of this vertue,
and giveth it this force.

In this river, and all the rivers of this coast, are great
abundance of *alagartoes* ;[3] and it is sayd that this exceedeth
the rest ; for persons of credit have certified mee, that as
small fishes in other rivers abound in scoales, so the alagartoes in this. They doe much hurt to the Indians and
Spaniards, and are dreadfull to all whom they catch within
their clutches.

<hr>

SECTION LI.

SOME five or six leagues to the north-wards of Puma, is
la Punta de Santa Elena; under which is good anchoring,
cleane ground, and reasonable succour. Being thwart of
this point, wee had sight of a shippe, which wee chased;
but being of better saile then we, and the night comming
on, we lost sight of her, and so anchored under the Isla de
Plata, to recover our pinnace and boate, which had gone
about the other point of the iland, which lyeth in two degrees and fortie minutes.

Puerto Viejo The next day we past in sight of Puerto Viejo, in two
degrees and ten minutes; which lying without shipping,
wee directed our course for Cape Passaos.[1] It lyeth directly

under the equinoctiall lyne; some fourescore leagues to the west-wards of this cape, lyeth a heape of ilands, the Spaniards call Illas de Los Galapagos : they are desert and bear no fruite. From Cape Passaos, wee directed our course to Cape Saint Francisco, which lyeth in one degree to the north-wardes of the lyne; and being thwart of it, wee descried a small shippe, which wee chased all that day and night; and the next morning our pinnace came to bourd her; but being a shippe of advise, and full of passengers, and our ship not able to fetch her up, they entreated our people badly, and freed themselves; though the feare they conceived, caused them to cast all the dispatches of the king, as also of particulars, into the sea, with a great part of their loading, to bee lighter and better of sayle; for the shippes of the South sea loade themselves like lighters, or sand barges, presuming upon the securitie from stormes.

SECTION LII.

BEING out of hope to fetch up this shippe, wee stood in with the cape, where the land beginneth to trend about to the east-wards. The cape is high land, and all covered over with trees, and so is the land over the cape; and all the coast, from this cape to Panama, is full of wood, from the Straites of Magelan to this Cape of San Francisco. In all the coast from head-land to head-land, the courses lye betwixt the north, and north and by west, and sometimes more westerly, and that but seldome. It is a bold coast, and subject to little foule weather or alteration of windes, for the brese, which is the sowtherly wind, bloweth continually from Balparizo to Cape San Francisco, except it be a great chance.

Trending about the cape, wee haled in east north-east,

to fetch the bay of Atacames, which lyeth some seaven leagues from the cape. In the mid-way, some three leagues from the shore, lyeth a banke of sand, whereof a man must have a care; for in some parts of it, there is but little water.

The tenth of June, wee came to an anchor in the bay of Atacames, which on the wester part hath a round hammock. It seemeth an iland, and in high springes I judge that the sea goeth round about it. To the east-wards it hath a high sandie cliffe, and in the middest of the bay, a faire birth from the shore, lyeth a bigge black rocke above water : from this rocke to the sandie cliffe, is a drowned marsh ground, caused by his lownesse ; and a great river, which is broad, but of no depth.

Manning our boate, and running to the shore, we found presently, in the westerne bight of the bay, a deepe river, whose indraught was so great that we could not benefit our selves of it, being brackish, except at low water, which hindred our dispatch ; yet in five dayes, wee filled all our emptie caske, supplied our want of wood, and grounded and put in order our pinnace.

They dismisse their Indians. Here, for that our Indians served us to no other use but to consume our victuals, we eased our selves of them ; gave them hookes and lines which they craved, and some bread for a few dayes, and replanted them in a farre better countrey then their owne, which fell out luckely for the Spaniards of the shippe which wee chased thwart of Cape San Francisco ; for victuals growing short with her, having many mouthes, shee was forced to put a shore fiftie of her passengers neere the cape ; whereof more than the one halfe dyed with famine and continual wading through rivers and waters : the rest, by chance, meeting with the Indians which wee had put a shore, with their fishing, guide, and industry, were refreshed, susteyned, and brought to habitation.

SECTION LIII.

OUR necessary busines being ended, wee purposed the fifteenth day of May, in the morning, to set sayle; but the foureteenth in the evening, we had sight of a shippe, some three leagues to sea-wards; and through the importunitie of my captaine and companie, I condiscended that our pinnas should give her chase: which I should not have done, for it was our destruction. I gave them precise order, that if they stood not in againe at night, they should seeke mee at Cape San Francisco, for the next morning I purposed to set sayle without delay. And so seeing that our pinnas slowed her comming, at nine of the clocke in the morning wee weyed our anchors, and stood for the cape, where wee beate off and on two dayes; and our pinnas not appearing, wee stood againe into the bay, where wee descried her turning in without a maine mast, which standing off to the sea close by, with much winde, and a chapping sea, bearing a taunt-sayle, where a little was too much (being to small purpose), sodainely they bare it by the bourd; and standing in with the shore, the winde, or rather God blinding them for our punishment, they knewe not the land; and making themselves to bee to wind-wards of the bay, bare up, and were put into the bay of San Mathew. It is a goodly harbour, and hath a great fresh river, which higheth fifteene or sixteene foote water, and is a good countrey, and well peopled with Indians: they have store of gold and emeralds. Heere the Spaniards from Guayaquill made an habitation, whilst I was prisoner in Lyma, by the Indians consent; but after, not able to suffer the insolencies of their guests, and being a people of stomacke and presumption, they suffered themselves to bee perswaded and led by a Molato. This leader many yeares before had fled unto them from the Spaniards: him they had long time held in reputation of their captaine generall, and was admitted also unto a chiefe office by the Spaniardes, to gaine him unto them.

But now the Indians uniting themselves together, presuming that by the helpe of this Molato, they should force the Spaniards out of the countrey, put their resolution into execution, drove their enemies into the woods, and slue as many as they could lay hands on ; some they killed, few escaped with life ; and those who had that good happe, suffered extreame misery before they came to Quito, the place of neerest habitation of Spaniards.

To this bay, assoone as our people in the pinnas saw their errour, they brought their tackes abourd, and turned and tyded it up, as they could. Assoone as we came to anchor, I procured to remedie that was amisse; in two daies wee dispatched all we had to doe, and the next morning wee resolved to set sayle, and to leave the coast of Peru and Quito.

The day appearing, we began to weigh our anchors, and being a pike, ready to cut sayle, one out of the toppe de-
Spanish
Armado. scryed the Spanish armado, comming about the cape; which by the course it kept, presently gave us to understand who they were : though my company, as is the custome of seamen, made them to be the fleete bound for Panama, loaden with treasure, and importuned that in all hast we should cut sayle and stand with them; which I contradicted, for that I was assured, that no shipping would stirre upon the coast till they had securitie of our departure (except some armado that might be sent to seeke us), and that it was not the time of the yeare to carry the treasure to Panama. And besides, in riding still at an anchor, they ever came neerer unto us; for they stood directly with us, and wee kept the weather gage ; where if we had put our selves under sayle, the ebbe in hand, wee should have given them the advantage, which we had in our power, by reason of the point of the bay. And being the armado, as it was, we gained time to fit ourselves, the better to fight. And truly (as before, to a stiffe-necked horse), so now againe

I cannot but resemble the condition of the mariner to any
thing better, then to the current of a furious river, re-
pressed by force or art, which neverthelesse ceaseth not to
seeke a way to overthrow both fence and banke : even so
the common sort of sea-men, apprehending a conceite in
their imaginations, neither experiment, knowledge, examples, reasons, nor authority, can alter and remoove them
from their conceited opinions. In this extremitie, with
reason I laboured to convince them, and to contradict
their pretences : but they altogether without reason, or
against reason, breake out, some into vaunting and brag-
ging, some into reproaches of want of courage, others into
wishings that they had never come out of their countrey,
if we should refuse to fight with two shippes whatsoever.
And to mend the matter, the gunner, for his part, assured
me that with the first tire[1] of shott, he would lay the one of
them in the sods : and our pinnace, that she would take
the other to taske. One promised that he would cut
downe the mayne yard ; another that he would take their
flagge ; and all in generall shewed a great desire to come
to tryall with the enemy. To some I turned the deafe eare,
with others I dissembled, and armed myselfe with patience
(having no other defence nor remedie for that occasion),
soothing and animating them to the execution of what they
promised, and perswaded them to have a little sufferance,
seeing they gained time and advantage by it.

And to give them better satisfaction, I condiscended that
our captaine, with a competent number of men, should with
our pinnace goe to discover them ; with order that they
should not engage themselves in that manner as they might
not be able to come unto us, or we to succour them. In all
these divisions and opinions, our master, Hugh Dormish,[2]
who was a most sufficient man for government and valour,
and well saw the errors of the multitude, used his office as
became him ; and so did all those of best understanding.

---

[1] The first broadside—*tirer* (French).   [2] Cornish ? See page 24.

Sect. LIII.   In short space our pinnace discovered what they were, and casting about to returne unto us, the vice-admirall, being next her, began with her chace to salute her with three or foure peeces of artillery, and so continued chasing her and gunning at her.   My company seeing this, now began to change humour; and I then to encourage and perswade them to performe the execution of their promises and vaunts of valour, which they had but even now protested, and given assurance of by their proferres and forwardnesse.

And that we might have sea-roome to fight, we presently weighed anchor, and stood off to sea with all our sayles, in hope to get the weather gage of our contraries.   But the winde scanting with us, and larging with them, we were *The beginning of the fight.* forced to lee-ward.   And the admirall weathering us, came rome[3] upon us : which being within musket shott, we hayled first with our noise of trumpets, then with our waytes, and after with our artilery : which they answered with artilery, two for one.   For they had double the ordinance we had, and almost tenne men for one.   Immediately they came shoring[4] abourd of us, upon our lee quarter, contrary to our expectation, and the custome of men of warre. *The inexperience of the Spaniards.* And doubtlesse, had our gunner beene the man he was reputed to be, and as the world sould him to me, shee had received great hurt by that manner of bourding.   But *And carelesnesse of the English.* contrary to all expectation, our stearne peeces were unprimed, and so were all those which we had to lee-ward, save halfe one in the quarter, which discharged, wrought that effect in our contraries as that they had five or sixe foote water in hold, before they suspected it.

How farre a commander is to trust his officers. Hereby all men are to take warning by me, not to trust any man in such extremities, when he himselfe may see it done : and comming to fight, let the chieftaine himselfe be

---

[3] Down ?

[4] To sheer, or shore, means to *separate*—we use the term "sheer to", but "sheer off" appears to be the only sense in which it should be applied.

sure to have all his artilery in a readinesse upon all occasions. This was my oversight, this my overthrow. For
I and all my company had that satisfaction of the sufficiencie and the care of our gunner, as not any one of us ever
imagined there would be any defect found in him. For
my part, I with the rest of our officers, occupied our selves
in cleering our deckes, laceing our nettings, making of
bulwarkes, arming our toppes, fitting our wast-cloathes,
tallowing our pikes, slinging our yards, doubling our
sheetes, and tackes, placing and ordering our people, and
procuring that they should be well fitted and provided of
all things; leaving the artilery, and other instruments of
fire, to the gunners dispose and order, with the rest
of his mates and adherents; which, as I said, was part
of our perdition. For bearing me ever in hand, that he
had five hundred cartreges in a readinesse, within one
houres fight we were forced to occupie three persons onely
in making and filling cartreges; and of five hundred elles
of canvas and other cloth given him for that purpose, at
sundry times, not one yard was to be found. For this we
have no excuse, and therefore could not avoyd the danger,
to charge and discharge with the ladell, especially in so
hotte a fight.[5] And comming now to put in execution the
sinking of the shippe, as he promised, he seemed a man
without life or soule. So the admirall comming close unto
us, I myselfe, and the master of our shippe, were forced to
play the gunners.

Those instruments of fire wherein he made me to spend
excessively, before our going to sea, now appeared not;
neither the brasse balles of artificiall fire, to be shott with
slurbowes (whereof I had six bowes, and two hundreth bals,
and which are of great account and service, either by sea
or land); he had stowed them in such manner, though in

[5] The greater part of the powder on board men-of-war, is made up
into cartridges, to avoid delay in filling during action, and danger from
using loose powder in a ladle.

Sect. LIII. double barrels, as the salt water had spoyled them all; so that comming to use them, not one was serviceable. Some of our company had in him suspition to be more friend to the Spaniards then to us; for that he had served some yeares in the *Tercera*, as gunner, and that he did all this of purpose. Few of our peeces were cleere, when we came to use them, and some had the shott first put in, and after the powder. Besides, after our surrendry, it was laid to his charge, that he should say, he had a brother that served the king in the *Peru*, and that he thought he was in the armado; and how he would not for all the world he should be slaine. Whether this were true or no, I know not; but I am sure all in generall gave him an ill report, and that he in whose hands the chiefe execution of the whole fight consisted, executed nothing as was promised and expected.

Admonitions for commanders. The griefe and remembrance of which oversights once againe inforceth me to admonish all captaines and commanders hereby to take advice, now and then to survey their officers and store-roomes, the oftener the better; that so their defects and wants may be supplied in time: never relying too much upon the vulgar report, nor giving too much credite to smooth tongues and boasting companions. But to performe this taske, it is requisite that all captaines and commanders were such, and so experimented in all offices, that they might be able as well to controule as to examine all manner of errors in officers. For the government at sea hardly suffereth a head without exquisite experience. The deficiency whereof hath occasioned Who to be accounted a true mariner some ancient sea-men to straighten the attribute of mariner in such sort, as that it ought not to be given but to the man who is able to build his shippe, to fit and provide her of all things necessary, and after to carry her about the world: the residue to be but saylers. Hereby giving us to understand, that though it is not expedient that he His knowledge for materialls. should be an axe-carpenter, to hewe, cut, frame, and mould each timber piece, yet that he should know the parts and peeces of the shippe, the value of the timber, ^{Sect. LIV.} planke, and yron-worke, so to be able as well to build in proportion, as to procure all materialls at a just price. And againe, though it be not expected that he should sowe the sayles, arme the shrowds, and put the tackling over head, yet is it requisite that he should knowe how to cut his sayles, what length is competent to every roape, and to be of sufficiency to reprehend and reforme those who erre and doe amisse. In providing his shippe with victualls, ^{For provisions.} munition, and necessaries, of force it must be expected that he be able to make his estimate, and (that once provided and perfected), in season, and with expedition to see it loden and stowed commodiously, with care and proportion. After that, he is to order the spending thereof, that in nothing he be defrauded at home; and at sea, ever to know how much is spent, and what remaineth unspent.

In the art of navigation, he is bound also to know so ^{For navigation.} much as to be able to give directions to the pilote and master, and consequently to all the rest of inferiour officers.

SECTION LIV.

MY meaning is not that the captaine or governour should be tyed to the actuall toyle, or to intermeddle with all offices, for that were to binde him to impossibilities, to diminish and abase his authoritie, and to deprive the other officers of their esteemes, and of that that belongeth unto them, which were a great absurditie : but my opinion is, that he should be more then superficially instructed and practised in the imployments. Yea, I am verily perswaded, that the more absolute authoritie any commander giveth to his under officers, being worthy of it, the sweeter is the command, and the more respected and beloved the commander.

Sect. LIV.

Office of
the master.
For in matter of guide and disposing of the saylers, with the tackling of the shippe, and the workes which belong thereunto, within bourd and without, all is to be committed to the masters charge.

Office of
the pilot.
The pilote is to looke carefully to the sterridge of the shippe; to be watchfull in taking the heights of sunne and starre; to note the way of his shippe, with the augmenting and lessening of the winde, etc.

The bote
swaine.
The boateswayne is to see his shippe kept cleane; his mastes, yards and tacklings well coated, matted and armed; his shroudes and stayes well set; his sayles repayred, and sufficiently prevented with martnets, blayles, and caskettes; his boate fitted with sayle, oares, thougts, tholes danyd, windles and rother; his anchors well boyed, safely stopped and secured, with the rest to him appertaining.

The steward.
The steward is to see the preservation of vittayles and necessaries committed unto his charge; and by measure and weight to deliver the portions appointed, and with discretion and good tearmes to give satisfaction to all.

The carpenter.
The carpenter is to view the mastes and yards, the sides of the shippe, her deckes, and cabines, her pumpes, and boate; and moreover to occupie him selfe in the most forceible workes, except he be otherwise commanded.

The gunner.
The gunner is to care for the britching and tackling of his artilery; the fitting of his shott, tampkins, coynes, crones,[1] and lin-stockes, etc. To be provident in working his fire workes; in making and filling his cartreges; in accommodating his ladles, sponges, and other necessaries; in sifting and drying his powder; in cleaning the armes, munition, and such like workes, intrusted unto him.

In this manner every officer, in his office, ought to be an absolute commander, yet readie in obedience and love, to sacrifice his will to his superiors command. This cannot but cause unitie; and unitie cannot but purchase a happie issue to dutifull travelles.

[1] Crows or crow-bars?

Lastly, except it be in urgent and precise cases, the head should never direct his command to any but the officers, and these secretly, except the occasion require publication, or that it touch all in generall.

Such orders would be, for the most part, in writing, that all might know what in generall is commanded and required.

SECTION LV.

And as the wise husband-man, in walking from ground to ground, beholdeth one plowing, another harrowing, another sowing, and lopping; another pruning, one hedging, another threshing, and divers occupied in severall labours: some he commendeth, others he reproacheth; others he adviseth, and to another he saith nothing, for that he seeth him in the right way: and all this, for that he knoweth and understandeth what they all doe, better then they themselves, though busied in their ordinary workes: even so a worthy commander at sea, ought to have the eyes, not only of his body, but also of his understanding, continually set (with watchfull care) upon all men, and all their workes under his charge; imitating the wise husband-man; first to know, and then to command: and lastly, to will their obedience voluntary, and without contradiction. For who knoweth not that ignorance many times commandeth that which it understandeth not; which the artist perceiving, first disdaineth, afterwards disteemeth, and finally in these great actions, which admit no temporizing, either he wayveth the respect of dutie, or faintly performeth the behest of his superiour upon every slight occasion, either in publike opposing, or in private murmuring: the smallest of which is most pernicious. Thus much (not amisse) for instruction.

Parts requisite iu a good husband-man.

The like in a good chieftaine.

SECTION LVI.

Sect. LVI.

Why the
Spanish
admirall
came to
lee-wards.

THE reason why the admirall came to lee-wardes, as after I
understood, was for that her artillery being very long, and
the wind fresh, bearing a taunt sayle to fetch us up, and
to keepe us company, they could not use their ordinance to
the weather of us, but lay shaking in the wind : and doubtlesse it is most proper for shippes to have short ordinance,
except in the sterne or chase.　The reasons are many :
viz.—easier charging, ease of the shippes side, better tra-
versing, and mounting ; yea, greater security of the artillery, and consequently of the ship.　For the longer the
peece is, the greater is the retention of the fire, and so the
torment and danger of the peece the greater.

But here will be contradiction by many, that dare avouch
that longer peeces are to be preferred ; for that they burne
their powder better, and carrie the shott further, and so
necessarily of better execution; whereas the short artillery
many times spend much of their powder without burning,
and workes thereby the slenderer effect.

To which I answere, that for land service, fortes, or
castles, the long peeces are to bee preferred : but for shipping, the shorter are much more serviceable.　And the
powder in them, being such as it ought, will be all fiered
long before the shott can come forth ; and to reach farre
in fights at sea, is to little effect.　For he that purposeth
to annoy his enemie, must not shoot at randome, nor at
point blanke, if hee purpose to accomplish with his devoire,
nether must hee spend his shott nor powder, but where a
pot-gun may reach his contrary ; how much the neerer, so
much the better : and this duely executed, the short artillery will worke its effect as well as the long ; otherwise,
neither short nor long are of much importance : but here
my meaning is not to approve the overshort peeces, devised
by some persons, which at every shott they make, daunce

out of their carriages, but those of indifferent length, and
which keepe the meane, betwixt seaven and eight foote.[1]

SECTION LVII.

THE entertainement wee gave unto our contraries, being Intertaine-
ment of
Spaniards. otherwise then was expected, they fell off, and ranged a
head, having broken in peeces all our gallerie; and pre-
sently they cast about upon us, and being able to keepe us
company, with their fighting sayles, lay a weather of us,
ordinarily within musket shott; playing continually with
them and their great artillery; which we endured, and
answered as we could.

Our pinnace engaged herselfe so farre, as that before shee
could come unto us, the vice-admirall had like to cut her
off, and comming to lay us aboord, and to enter her men,
the vice-admirall boorded with her : so that some of our
company entred our ship over her bow-sprit, as they themselves reported.

We were not a little comforted with the sight of our
people in safetie within our shippe ; for in all we were but
threescore and fifteene, men and boyes, when we began to The English
seventy-five.
fight, and our enemies thirteene hundred men and boyes, The Spani-
ards thirteen
hundred.
little more or lesse, and those of the choise of Peru.

SECTION LVIII.

HEERE it shall not be out of the way to discourse a little The Spanish
discipline.
of the Spanish discipline, and manner of their government

---

[1] The additional velocity of the projectile gained by using long guns,
is thought to overbalance the advantage which the short guns possess
by being more easily handled. The usual length of heavy guns at
present, is about nine feet and a half.

in generall; which is in many things different to ours. In this expedition came two generalls : the one Don Beltran de Castro, who had the absolute authoritie and commaund; the other Michael Angell Filipon, a man well in yeares, and came to this preferment by his long and painful service ; who though he had the title of generall by sea, I thinke it was rather of courtesie then by pattent ; and for that hee had beene many yeares generall of the South sea, for the carriage and waftage of the silver from Lyma to Panama. He seemed to bee an assistant, to supply that with his counsell, advice, and experience, whereof Don Beltran had never made tryall (for hee commanded not absolutely, but with the confirmation of Don Beltran), for the Spaniards never give absolute authoritie to more then one. A custome that hath beene, and is approved in all empires, kingdomes, common-wealths, and armies, rightly disciplined : the mixture hath been seldome seene to prosper, as will manifestly appeare, if we consider the issue of all actions and journeys committed to the government of two, or more generally.

Two chieftains joyned in commission, dangerous. The famous victory of Hannibal against the Romane consuls Paulus Emillius and Terrentius Varro, was attributed to their equality of government. The unhappie overthrowe given by the Turke Amurate, to the Christian princes, in the journey of Nicapolis, is held to have proceeded from the difference betwixt the heads, every one leaning to his owne opinion. The overthrow in recoverie of the Holy land, undertaken by king Richard of England, and king Philip of France, sprang from the like differences and dissentions. The victory of the emperour Charles the Fifth, against the Protestant princes of Germanie, is imputed to their distractures arising from parity in command. If we looke into our owne actions, committed to the charge of two generals, the effects and fruits which they have brought forth, for the most part, will be found to be little better : yea, most of them, through emūlation, envie, and pride, overthrowne, and brought to nought ; though to cover their confusions, there have never beene wanting cloakes and colours. The most approoved writers reproove, and call it a monster with two heads, and not without reason. For if the monarchy be generally approoved, for strongest, soundest, and most perfect, and most sufficient to sustaine it selfe ; and the democracie and aristocracie utterly reprooved, as weake, feeble, and subject to innovations and infirmities ; it cannot be but errour, confusion, and imperfection, to differ or dissent from it. For where the supreame government is divided betwixt two or more, the authoritie is diminished, and so looseth his true force ; as a fagget of stickes, whose bond being broken, the entire strength is easily dissolved : but all under correction.

The Spaniards, in their armadoes by sea, imitate the discipline, order, and officers, which are in an army by land, and divide themselves into three bodies ; to wit, souldiers, marriners, and gunners.

Their souldiers ward and watch, and their officers in every shippe round, as if they were on the shoare ; this is the only taske they undergoe, except cleaning their armes, wherein they are not over curious. The gunners are exempted from all labour and care, except about the artillery. The souldier

The gunner.

And these are either Almaynes, Flemmings, or strangers; for the Spaniards are but indifferently practised in this art. The marriners are but as slaves to the rest, to moyle,[1] and to toyle day and night ; and those but few and bad, and not suffered to sleepe or harbour themselves under the deckes. For in faire or fowle weather, in stormes, sunne, or raine, they must passe voyde of covert or succour. The marriner.

There is ordinarily in every shippe of warre, a captaine, whose charge is as that of our masters with us, and also a captaine of the souldiers, who commandeth the captaine of Officers in a shippe of war. Captaine of the shippe. Captaine of the souldiers

[1] *To moil* has been supposed to be derived from the French *mouiller*.

the shippe, the souldiers, gunners, and marriners in her; yea, though there be divers captaines, with their companies in one shippe (which is usuall amongst them), yet one hath the supreme authoritie, and the residue are at his *Mastros de campo, &c.* ordering and disposing. They have their *mastros de campo,* seargeant, master, generall (or captaine) of the artillery, with their alfere major, and all other officers, as in a campe.

If they come to fight with another armado, they order themselves as in a battell by land; in a vanguard, rereward, maine battell, and wings, etc. In every particular shippe the souldiers are all set upon the deckes; their forecastle they account their head front, or vanguard of their company; that abaft the mast, the rereward; and the wayste the mayne battell; wherein they place their principall force, and on which they principally relye, which they call their *placa de armas,* or place of armes: which taken, their hope is lost.

The gunners fight not but with their great artillery: the marriners attend only to the tackling of the shippe and handling of the sayles, and are unarmed, and subject to all misfortunes; not permitted to shelter themselves, but to be still aloft, whether it be necessary or needlesse. So ordinarily, those which first fayle, are the marriners and saylers, of which they have greatest neede. They use few close fights or fire-workes; and all this proceedeth, as I judge, of errour in placing land captaines for governours and commanders by sea; where they seldome understand what is to be done or commanded.

Prying of the Spaniards into our discipline. Some that have beene our prisoners, have perfitted[2] themselves of that they have seene amongst us; and others disguised under colour of treaties, for ransoming of prisoners, for bringing of presents, and other imbassages, have noted our forme of shipping, our manner of defences,

[2] Profited.

and discipline. Sithence[3] which espiall, in such actions as *Sect. LIX.*
they have beene imployed in, they seeke to imitate our *Their imita-tion of our discipline.*
government and reformed discipline at sea : which, doubt-
lesse, is the best and most proper that is at this day knowne
or practised in the whole world, if the execution be answerable to that which is knowne and received for true and
good amongst us.

In the captaine (for so the Spaniards call their admirall)
was an English gunner, who to gaine grace with those
under whom hee served, preferred himselfe, and offered to
sinke our shippe with the first shott he made : who, by the
Spaniards relation, being travesing of a peece in the bowe,
to make his shott, had his head carryed away with the first
or second shott made out of our shippe. It slew also two
or three of those which stood next him.

Which may be a good and gentle warning for all those
who mooved either with covetousnesse, or with desire of
revenge, or in hope of worldly promotion, or other respect
whatsoever, doe willingly and voluntarily serve the enemie
against their owne nation : *nulla causa insta videri potest,
adversus patriam arma capiendi.*

And if we consider the end of those who have thus erred, *The ends of fugitives.*
wee shall finde them, for the most part, lamentable and
most miserable. At the least, those whom I have knowne,
have lived to be pointed at with detestation, and ended
their lives in beggery, voyde of reputation.

SECTION LIX.

THE fight continued so hott on both sides, that the artillery
and muskets never ceased playing. Our contraries, towards the evening, determined the third time to lay us

3 Since.

abourd, with resolution to take us or to hazard all. The order they set downe for the execution hereof, was, that the captaine (or admirall) should bring himselfe uppon our weather bowe, and so fall abourd of us, upon our broad side : and that the vice-admirall should lay his admirall abourd uppon his weather quarter, and so enter his men into her ; that from her they might enter us, or doe as occasion should minister.

The captaine of the vice-admirall being more hardy then considerate, and presuming with his shippe and company to get the price and chiefe honour, wayted not the time to put in execution the direction given, but presently came abourd to wind-wards uppon our broad side. Which, doubtlesse, was the great and especiall providence of Almightie God, for the discouraging of our enemies, and animating of us. For although shee was as long, or rather longer then our shippe, being rarely[1] built, and utterly without fights or defences ; what with our muskets, and what with our fire-works, wee cleered her decks in a moment, so that scarce any person appeared. And doubtlesse if we had entred but a dozen men, we might have enforced them to have rendred unto us, or taken her ; but our company being few, and the principall of them slaine or hurt, we durst not, neither was it wisedome, to adventure the separation of those which remained : and so held that for the best and soundest resolution, to keepe our forces together in defence of our owne.

The Spaniards pay deerely for their rashnesse.

The vice-admirall seeing himselfe in great distresse, called to his admirall for succour ; who presently laid him abourd, and entred a hundreth of his men, and so cleered themselves of us.

In this bourding, the vice-admirall had at the least thirtie and six men hurt and slaine ; and amongst them his pilote shot through the body, so as he died presently.

---

[1] Slightly—or perhaps what we now call " deep-waisted".

And the admirall also received some losse, which wrought
in them a new resolution, onely with their artillery to
batter us; and so with time to force us to surrender, or to
sinke us; which they put in execution: and placing themselves within a musket shott of our weather quarter, and
sometimes on our broad side, lay continually beating upon
us without intermission; which was, doubtlesse, the best
and securest determination they could take; for they
being rare[2] shippes, and without any manner of close fights,
in bourding with us, their men were all open unto us, and
we under covert and shelter. For on all parts our shippe
was musket free, and the great artillery of force must cease
on either side (the shippes being once grapled together),
except we resolved to sacrifice our selves together in fire.
For it is impossible, if the great ordinance play (the shippes
being bourded), but that they must set fire on the shippe
they shoote at; and then no surety can be had to free
himselfe, as experience daily confirmeth. For a peece of
artillery most properly resembleth a thunderclap, which
breaking upwards, or on the side, hurteth not; for that
the fire hath scope to dispence it selfe without finding resistance, till the violence which forceth it taketh end, and
so it mounts to its center: but breaking downe right
or stooping downwards, and finding resistance or impediment, before the violence that forceth it take end, being
so subtill and penetrable a substance, passeth and pierceth
so wonderfully, as it leaveth the effect of his execution in
all points answerable to his levell and nighnesse. For if
the clouds be nigh the earth (as some are higher, some
lower), and breake down-wards, the violence wherewith the
fire breaketh out is such, and of so strange an execution,
that men have beene found dead without any outward signe
in their flesh, and yet all their bones burnt to dust. So
the blade of the sword hath beene found broken all to

[2] See note, page 199.

peeces in the scabard, and the scabard whole without blemish : and a cristall glasse all shivered in peeces, his cover and case remaining sound ; which commeth to passe for that in the flesh, in the scabard, and in the case, the fire being so subtile of nature, findeth easie passage without resistance; but the bones, the blade, the cristall, being of substance more solide, maketh greater resistance, and so the fire with the more fury worketh the more his execution in its objects. As was seene in the Spanish admirall (or captaine), after my imprisonment, crossing from Panama to Cape San Francisco, a rayo (for so the Spaniards call a thunder-clappe), brake over our shippe, killed one in the fore-toppe, astonished either two or three in the shroudes, and split the mast in strange manner : where it entred it could hardly be descerned, but where it came forth, it drave out a great splinter before it ; and the man slaine, was cleane in a manner without signe or token of hurt, although all his bones turned to powder; and those who lived and recovered, had all their bodies blacke, as burnt with fire : which plainly declareth and confirmeth that above said, and may serve to judge in such occasions of persons hurt with thunder ; for if they complaine of their bones, and have little signe of the fire, their hazard of death is the greater, then when the fire hath left greater impressions outward. The fire out of a cloude worketh like effect, only where it leveleth directly, as experience daily teacheth ; killing those who are opposite, hurting those who are neere, and only terrifying those who are further distant.

In like manner the peece of ordinance hurteth not those which stand aside, nor those which stand a slope from his mouth, but those alone which stand directly against the true point of his levell : though sometimes the winde of the shott overthroweth one, and the splinters (being accidents), mayne[3] and hurt others. But principally where the peece doth resemble the thunder clappe, as when the ships are bourded: for then, although the artillery be discharged without shott, the fury of the fire, and his piercing nature is such, as it entreth by the seames, and all parts of the ships sides, and meeting with so fit matter as pitch, tarre, ocombe, and sometimes with powder, presently converteth all into flames.

For avoyding whereof, as also the danger and damage which may come by pikes and other inventions of fire, and if any shippe be oppressed with many shippes at once, and subject by them to be bourded; I hold it a good course to strike his fore and mayne yards close to his decke, and to fight with sprit-saile and myson, and top-sayles loose: so shall he be able to hinder them from oppressing him.

Some have thought it a good pollicy to launce out some ends of mastes or yards by the ports or other parts : but this is to be used in the greater shippes; for in the lesser, though they be never so strong, the waight of the bigger will beate out the opposite sides and doe hurt, and make great spoyle in the lesser. And in bourding, ordinarily the lesser shippe hath all the harme which the one shippe can doe unto the other.

Pollicies to avoid bourdings.

Here is offered to speake of a point much canvassed amongst carpenters and sea captaines, diversly mainetained but yet undetermined: that is, whether the race[4] or loftie built shippe bee best for the merchant, and those which imploy themselves in trading ? I am of opinion that the race shippe is most convenient; yet so as that every perfect shippe ought to have two deckes, for the better strengthening of her; the better succouring of her people ; the better preserving of her merchandize and victuall; and for her greater safetie from sea and stormes.

Disputes concerning ships of trade.

---

[3] Maim.   [4] Probably a misprint for " rare".

Sect. LIX.

Concerning
the prince
his shippes.

But for the princes shippes, and such as are imployed continually in the warres, to be built loftie I hold very necessary for many reasons. First for majestie and terrour of the enemy; secondly, for harbouring of many men; thirdly, for accommodating more men to fight; fourthly, for placing and using more artillery; fiftly, for better strengthening and securing of the shippe; sixtly, for overtopping and subjecting the enemy; seventhly, for greater safeguard and defence of the ship and company. For it is plaine, that the ship with three deckes, or with two and a halfe, shewes more pomp than another of her burthen with a decke and a halfe, or two deckes, and breedeth greater terror to the enemy, discovering herselfe to be a more powerfull ship, as she is, then the other; which being indeed a ship of force, seemeth to be but a barke, and with her low building hideth her burthen. And who doubteth that a decke and a halfe cannot harbour that proportion of men, that two deckes, and two deckes and a halfe can accommodate to fight; nor carry the artillery so plentifully, nor so commodiously. Neither can the ship be so strong with a decke and a halfe as with two deckes; nor with two, as with three; nor carry her masts so taunt; nor spread so great a clue; nor contrive so many fightes, to answer one another for defence and offence. And the advantage the one hath of the other, experience daily teacheth.

All ships of
warre are
not to be
low built.

In the great expedition of eightie eight, did not the *Elizabeth Jonas*, the *Triumph*, and the *Beare*, shew greater majestie then the *Arke Royall* and the *Victorie*, being of equall burthens? did they not cause greater regard in the enemy? did they not harbour and accommodate more men, and much better? did they not beare more artillery? And if they had come to boord with the Spanish high-charged ships, it is not to be doubted but they would have mustred themselves better, then those which could not with their prowesse nor props, have reached to their wastes. The strength of the one cannot be compared with the strength of the other: but in bourding, it goeth not so much in the strength, as in weight and greatnesse. For the greater ship that bourdeth with the lesser, with her mastes, her yardes, her tacklings, her anchors, her ordinance, and with her sides, bruseth and beateth the lesser to peeces, although the lesser be farre stronger according to proportion.

The *Foresight* of his Majesties, and the *Daintie*, were shippes in their proportions farre more stronger then the carake which was taken by them and their consorts, anno 92 : for she had in a manner no strong building nor binding, and the others were strengthened and bound as art was able to affoord; and yet both bourding with her, were so brused, broken, and badly handled, as they had like to have sunke by her side, though bourding with advantage to weather-wards of her. But what would have become of them if she should have had the wind of them, and have come aboord to wind-ward of them? In small time, no doubt, she would have beaten them under water.

Anno 90, in the fleet under the charge of Sir John Hawkins, my father, comming from the south-wards, the *Hope*, of his Majesties, gave chase to a French ship, thinking her to be a Spaniard. She thought to have freed her selfe by her sailing, and so would not availe, but endured the shooting of many peeces, and forced the *Hope* to lay her abourd; of which issued that mischiefe which before I spake off. For in a moment the French ship had all her mastes, yards, and sailes in the sea, and with great difficultie the *Hope* could free herselfe from sinking her.

In the self-same voyage, neere the ilands of Flores and Corvo, the *Rainbow* and the *Foresight* came foule one of another; the *Rainbow,* being the greater shippe, left the *Foresight* much torne; and if God had not beene pleased to seperate them, the lesser, doubtlesse, had sunke in the sea; but in these incounters they received little or no hurt. The boording of the *Rainbow* and *Foresight*, as I was enformed, proceeded of the obstinacie and self will of the captaine or master of the *Foresight*, who would not set sayle in time, to give sea roome to the other, comming driving upon her, for that she was more flotie.[5] This pride I have seene many times to be the cause of great hurt, and is worthy of severe punishment : for being all of one company, and bound every one to helpe and further the good of the other, as members of one body, there ought to be no strayning of courtesie; but all are bound to suppress emulation and particular respect, in seeking the generall good of all, yea, of every particular more ingeniously then that of his owne.

Particular
respects
must give
place to the
generall.

But in equitie and reason, the le-ward shippe ought ever to give way to the weather most, in hulling or trying, without any exception.   First, for that shee advantageth the other in hulling or trying; which is manifest, for that shee to wind-wards drives upon her to le-wards. Secondly, for that the windermost shippe, by opening her sayle, may be upon the other before shee be looked for, either for want of steeridge, not being under way, or by the rowling of the sea, some one sea casting the shippe more to le-wards then ten others.   And thirdly, for that the windermost shippe being neere, and setting sayle, is in possibilitie to take away the winde from her to le-wards comming within danger.   And this by way of argument, for a hull and under-sayle in stormes and fayre weather, in harbour, or at sea.

Humanitie and courtesie are ever commendable and beneficiall to all, whereas arrogancie and ambition are ever accompanied with shame, losse, and repentance.

Arrogancy
of a Spanish
generall.

And though in many examples, touching this point, I have beene an eye witnesse, yet I will record but one,

[5] Did not hold so good a wind, or drove more easily to leeward.

which I saw in the river of Civill,[6] at my comming out of the Indies amongst the galleons loaden with silver. For their wafting, the king sent to the Tercera, eight new galleons, under the charge of Villa Viciosa; who entring the barre of Saint Luar joyntly, the shippes loaden with silver, anchored in the middest of the river in deeper water, and the wafters on either side, neere the shoare. The admirall of the wafters rode close by the galleon in which I was, and had moored her selfe in that manner, as her streame, cable, and anchor, overlayed our land-most. And winding up with the first of the flood, shee her selfe in one of her cables, which together with the great currant of the ebbe, and force of the winde which blewe fresh, caused her to drive, and to dragge home her anchors; and with that which overlay ours, to cause us to doe the like. Whereupon, on both sides was crying out to veere cable: we, for our parts, had lost all our cables in the Terceras, saving those which were a-ground, and those very short, and vered to the better end. The admirall strained courtesie, thinking the other, though loaden with silver, bound to let slippe one, so to give him way; and the generall standing in his gallery, saw the danger which both shippes ranne into, being in a manner bourd and bourd, and driving upon the point of the shoare: yet he commanded to hold fast, and not to vere cable, till he was required and commanded in the kings name, by the captaine of our shippe; protesting, the damage which should ensue thereof to the king and merchants, to runne upon the admirals accompt; and that in his shippe he had no other cable but those which were aground, and that they had vered as much as they could: which the generall knowing, and at last better considering, willed to vere his cable end for

---

[6] Seville was formerly the emporium of the trade of the new world: since the Guadalquiver has become unnavigable for large vessels, its trade has been transferred to Cadiz.

Sect. LIX. end, and so, with some difficultie and dispute, the punto
was remedied; which if he had done at first, he had prevented all other danger, inconvenience, and dispute, by only
weighing of his cable and anchor after the gust was past, and
letting it fall in a place more commodious : whereas, his
vaine glory, stoutnesse, and selfe-will, had put in great
perill two of the kings shippes, and in them above two
millions of treasure.   And it may be, if he had beene one
of the ignorant generalls, such as are sometimes imployed,
whereas he was one of best experience, I doubt not, but
they would have stood so much upon their puntos,[7] as rather
then they would have consented to vere theyr cables (for
that it seemed a diminution of authoritie), they would
rather have suffered all to goe to wracke, without discerning
the danger and damage.

Doubts and
objections
resolved.

But to returne to my former point of advantage, which
the greater shippe hath of the lesser, I would have it to
be understood according to occasion, and to be understood
of ships of warre with ships of warre ; it being no part of
my meaning to maintaine that a small man of warre should

And the duty
of a small
ship against
a greater.

not bourd with a great shippe which goeth in trade.   For I
know, that the war-like shippe that seeketh, is not only
bound to bourd with a greater, but were shee sure to hazard
her selfe, shee ought to bourd where any possibility of surprising may be hoped for.   Witnesse the Biscaine shippes
of five hundreth tunnes, taken by shippes of lesse then a
hundreth.   Such were those which were taken by captaine
George Reymond, and captaine Greenfield Halse ; both
wonne by bourding and force of armes.   And did not
Markes Berry, with a shippe of foure-score tunnes, by
bourding and dent of sword, take a shippe which came
from the Nova Hispania, of neere foure hundreth tunnes ?
To recount all such as have beene in this sort taken by our
countreymen, as also those of great worth they have lost,

[7] Punctilio.

for not hazarding the bourding, were never to make an
end. Yet discretion is ever to be used; for a man that in a
small barke goeth to warre-fare, is not bound to bourd
with a carake, nor with a shippe which he seeth provided
with artillery and other preventions far above his possibilitie.

The Spaniards confesse us to advantage them in our
shipping, and attribute all our victories to that which is
but a masse of dead wood, were it not managed and ordered
by art and experience; affirming, that if we came to handie
strokes and bourding, they should goe farre beyond us,
which to any person of reasonable understanding, cannot
but seeme most vaine-glorious; for we leave not to bourd
with them upon occasion, when otherwise we cannot force
them to surrender : but I conclude it to be great errour,
and want of discretion in any man, to put himselfe, his
shippe, and company in perill, being able otherwise to van-
quish his enemy.[8]

This imagination, so vaine and so voyde of ground, hath
growne from the ignorance of some of our common sort of
marriners and vulgar people, which have beene prisoners
in Spaine : who being examined and asked, why her Majesties shippes in occasions bourd not, have answered and
enformed that it is the expresse order of her Majestie and
counsell, in no case to hazard her shippes by bourding;
yea, I have knowne some captaines of our owne (to colour
their faint proceedings), have averred as much, which is
nothing so. For in the houre that her majestie or counsell
committeth the charge of any of her shippes to any person,
it is left to his discretion to bourd or not to bourd, as the
reason of service requireth. And therefore let no man
hereafter pretend ignorance, nor for this vanitie leave to
doe his duty, or that which is most probable to redound to

[8] This apopthegm is sufficient to stamp Sir Richard Hawkins as a
great commander.

the honour and service of his prince and countrey, and to the damage of his enemy. For in case he excuse himselfe with this allegation, it cannot but redound to his condemnation and disreputation. And I assure all men, that in any reasonable equalitie of shipping, we cannot desire greater advantage, then we have of the Spaniards by bourding. The reasons why, I hold it not convenient to discourse in particular; but experience and tract of time, with that which I have seen amongst them, hath taught me this knowledge; and those who have seene their discipline, and ours, cannot but testifie the same.

SECTION LX.

Courses for artillery after bourding.

AGAINE, all that which hath beene spoken of the danger of the artillery in bourding, it is not to be wrested nor interpreted, to cut of utterly the use of all artillery after bourding, but rather I hold nothing more convenient in shippes of warre, then fowlers and great bases in the cage workes, and murderers in the cobridge heads; for that their execution and speedie charging and discharging, is of great moment.[1]

Disuses of engines of antiquitie.

Many I know have left the use of them, and of sundry other preventions, as of sherehookes, stones in their toppes, and arming them; pikebolts in their wales, and divers other engines of antiquitie. But upon what inducement, I cannot relate, unlesse it be because they never knew their effects and benefit; and may no doubt be used without the inconveniences before mentioned in great ordinance. As also such may be the occasion, that without danger some of the great artillery may be used, and that

----

[1] Fowlers, murderers, etc., were pieces of cannon of the nature of swivels, adapted to close combat. The "cobridge heads" seem to have been bulk heads across the fore and after parts of the vessel.

with great effect, which is in the discretion of the commanders and their gunners, as hath beene formerly seene, and daily is experimented. In the *Revenge* of her Majesties good experience was made, who sunke two of the Spanish armado lying abourd her.

In these bourdings and skirmishes, divers of our men were slaine, and many hurt, and myselfe amongst them received six wounds; one of them in the necke very perillous; another through the arme, perishing the bone, and cutting the sinewes close by the arme-pit; the rest not so dangerous. The master of our shippe had one of his eyes, his nose, and halfe his face shott away. Master Henry Courton was slaine. On these two I principally relyed for the prosecution of our voyage, if God, by sicknesse, or otherwise, should take me away.

The Spaniards with their great ordinance lay continually playing upon us, and now and then parled and invited us to surrender ourselves *a buena querra*.[2] The captaine of our shippe, in whose direction and guide, our lives, our honour, and welfare now remained, seeing many of our people wounded and slaine, and that few were left to sustaine and maintaine the fight, or to resist the entry of the enemy, if he should againe bourd with us, and that our contraries offered us good pertido,[3] came unto me accompanied with some others, and began to relate the state of our shippe, and how that many were hurt and slaine, and scarce any men appeared to traverse the artillery, or to

The Spaniards parley.

[2] *En buena guerra* means by fair or lawful means: it probably implied offering quarter; which means, that if accepted, a certain sum was to be given as ransom.

[3] *Partido* (Spanish), favour or protection.

oppose themselves for defence, if the enemy should bourd
with us againe; and how that the admirall offered us life
and liberty, and to receive us *a buena querra*, and to send
us into our owne country. Saying, that if I thought it so
meete, he and the rest were of opinion that we should put
out a flagge of truce, and make some good composition.
The great losse of blood had weakened me much. The
torment of my wounds newly received, made me faint, and
I laboured for life, within short space expecting I should
give up the ghost.

But this parley pearced through my heart, and wounded
my soule; words failed me wherewith to expresse it, and
none can conceive it but he which findeth himselfe in the
like agonie. Yet griefe and rage ministered force, and
caused me to breake forth into this reprehension and execution following.

"Great is the crosse which Almightie God hath suffered
to come upon me: that assaulted by our professed enemies,
and by them wounded, as you see, in body, lying gasping
for breath, those whom I reputed for my friends to fight
with me; those which I relyed on as my brethren to defend me in all occasions; those whom I have nourished,
cherished, fostered and loved as my children, to succour
me, helpe me, and to sustaine my reputation in all extremities; are they who first draw their swords against
me, are they which wound my heart, in giving me up
into mine enemies hands. Whence proceedeth this ingratitude? whence this faintnesse of heart? whence this
madnesse? Is the cause you fight for unjust? is the
honour and love of your prince and countrey buried in the
dust? your sweete lives, are they become loathsome unto
you? will you exchange your liberty for thraldome? will
you consent to see that which you have sweat for and procured with so great labour and adventure, at the dispose of
your enemies? can you content your selves to suffer my

blood spilt before your eyes, and my life bereft me in your presence, with the blood and lives of your deere brethren to be unrevenged? Is not an honourable death to be preferred before a miserable and slavish life? The one sustaining the honour of our nation, of our predecessors, and of our societie: the other ignominious to our selves, and reproachful to our nation. Can you be perswaded that the enemy will performe his promise with you, that never leaveth to breake it with others, when he thinketh it advantagious? And know you not, that with him, all is convenient that is profitable? Hold they not this for a maxime: that, *nulla fides est servanda cum hereticis?* In which number they accompt us to be. Have you forgotten their faith violated with my father, in Saint John de Ulua, the conditions and capitulations being firmed by the viceroy and twelve hostages, all principall personages given for the more securitie of either party to other? Have you forgotten their promise broken with John Vibao and his company, in Florida, having conditioned to give them shipping and victuals, to carry them into their countrey; immediately after they had delivered their weapons and armes, had they not their throates cut? Have you forgotten how they dealt with John Oxnam and his company, in this sea, yeelded upon composition; and how after a long imprisonment, and many miseries, being carryed from Panama to Lyma, and there hanged with all his company, as pyrates, by the justice?[4] And can you forget how dayly they abuse our noble natures, which being voyde of malice, measure all by sinceritie, but to our losse; for that when we come

---

[4] With respect to the transaction at San Juan de Ulloa, already alluded to at page 10, Sir Richard Hawkins had good reason to be suspicious of the good faith of the Spaniards. From the account given in Hakluyt, from Sir John Hawkins himself, it appears, that " he was attacked after he had been assured on the faith of the Spanish viceroy that no treachery should be used." But in the matter of Oxenham, apparently, they were not to blame. John Oxenham had accompanied

to demand performance, they stoppe our mouthes; either with laying the inquisition upon us, or with delivering us into the hands of the ordinary justice, or of the kings ministers. And then urged with their promises, they shrinke up to the shoulders, and say, that they have now no further power over us; they sorrow in their hearts to see their promise is not accomplished : but now they cannot doe us any good office, but to pray to God for us, and to entreat the ministers in our behalfe.

" Came we into the South sea to put out flags of truce? And left we our pleasant England, with all her contentments, with intention or purpose to avayle our selves of white ragges, and by banners of peace to deliver ourselves for slaves into our enemies hands; or to range the world with the English, to take the law from them, whom by our swords, prowesse, and valour, we have alwaies heretofore bin accustomed to purchase honour, riches, and reputation?   If these motives be not sufficient to perswade you, then I present before your eyes your wives and children, your parents and friends, your noble and sweete countrey, your gracious soveraigne ; of all which accompt yourselves for ever deprived, if this proposition should be put in execution.   But for all these, and for the love and respect you owe me, and for all besides that you esteeme and hold dear in this world, and for Him that made us and all the world, banish out of your imagination such vaine and base thoughts ; and according to your woonted resolution, prosecute the defence of your shippe, your lives, and libertie, with the lives and libertie of your companions ; who by

Drake in his first voyage, in 1574, and after his return, was induced to fit out a small expedition on his own account : he was successful in acquiring booty, but by mismanagement he and all his people fell into the hands of the Spaniards.   At Panama he was examined as to what authority he held from his queen; but not being able to produce any power or commission, he with all his company were sentenced to death, as pirates.

their wounds and hurts are disabled and deprived of all other defence and helpe, save that which lyeth in your discretions and prowesse. And you, captaine,—of whom I made choise amongst many, to be my principall assistant, and the person to accomplish my dutie if extraordinary casualtie should disable me to performe and prosecute our voyage,—tender your obligation; and now in the occasion give testimony, and make proofe of your constancie and valour, according to the opinion and confidence I have ever held of you."

Whereunto he made answere: "My good generall, I hope you have made experience of my resolution, which shall be ever to put in execution what you shall be pleased to command me; and my actions shall give testimonie of the obligation wherein I stand bound unto you. What I have done, hath not proceeded from faintnesse of heart, nor from a will to see imaginations put in execution; for besides the losse of our reputation, liberty, and what good else we can hope for, I know the Spaniard too too well, and the manner of his proceedings in discharge of promises: but only to give satisfaction to the rest of the company, which importuned me to moove this point, I condiscended to that which now I am ashamed of, and grieve at, because I see it disliking to you. And here I vowe to fight it out, till life or lymmes fayle me. Bee you pleased to recommend us to Almightie God, and to take comfort in him, whom I hope will give us victory, and restore you to health and strength, for all our comforts, and the happy accomplishing and finishing of our voyage, to his glory."

I replyed: "This is that which beseemeth you; this sorteth to the opinion I ever held of you; and this will gaine you, with God and man, a just reward. And you the rest, my deere companions and friends, who ever have made a demonstration of desire to accomplish your duties, remember that when we first discryed our enemy, you shewed to have a longing to proove your valours against him : now that the occasion is offered, lay hold of the fore-locke; for if once shee turne her backe, make sure accompt never after to see her face againe : and as true English men, and followers of the steppes of our forefathers, in vertue and valour, sell your bloods and lives deerely, that Spaine may ever record it with sadnesse and griefe. And those which survive, rejoyce in the purchase of so noble a victory, with so small meanes against so powerfull an enemy."

Hereunto they made answere : that as hitherto they had beene conformable to all the undertakings which I had commanded or counselled, so they would continue in the selfe same dutie and obedience to the last breath ; vowing either to remaine conquerours and free-men, or else to sell their lives at that price which their enemies should not willingly consent to buy them at. And with this resolution, both captaine and company tooke their leave of me, every one particularly, and the greater part with teares and imbracings, though we were forthwith to depart the world, and never see one the other againe but in heaven, promising to cast all forepassed imaginations into oblivion, and never more to speake of surrendry.

They resolve to fight it out. In accomplishment of this promise and determination, they persevered in sustaining the fight, all this night, with the day and night following, and the third day after. In which time the enemy never left us, day nor night, beating continually upon us with his great and small shott. Saving that every morning, an hower before the breake of day, he

The enemy breatheth. edged a little from us, to breath, and to remedie such defects as were amisse, as also to consult what they should doe the day and night following.

The English repaire their defects. This time of interdiction, we imployed in repayring our sayles and tacklings, in stopping our leakes, in fishing and wolling our masts and yards, in mending our pumpes, and in fitting and providing our selves for the day to come.

Though this was but little space for so many workes, yet gave it great reliefe and comfort unto us, and made us better able to endure the defence : for otherwise, our ship must of force have suncke before our surrendry, having many shot under water, and our pumpes shot to peeces every day. In all this space, not any man of either part tooke rest or sleepe, and little sustenance, besides bread and wine.

In the second dayes fight, the vice-admirall comming upon our quarter, William Blanch, one of our masters mates, with a luckie hand, made a shot unto her with one of our sterne peeces ; it carried away his maine mast close by the decke : wherewith the admirall beare up to her, to see what harme shee had received, and to give her such succour as shee was able to spare ; which we seeing, were in good hope that they would have now left to molest us any longer, having wherewithall to entertaine themselves in redressing their owne harmes. And so we stood away from them close by as we could ; which we should not have done, but prosecuted the occasion, and brought our selves close upon her weather gage, and with our great and small shot hindered them from repairing their harmes : if we had thus done, they had beene forced to cut all by the bourd ; and it may bee, lying a hull or to le-wards of us, with a few shot wee might have suncke her. At the least, it would have declared to our enemies that wee had them in little estimation, when, able to goe from them, we would not ; and perhaps bin a cause to have made them to leave us.

But this occasion was let slip, as also that other to fight with them, sayling quarter winds, or before the winde ; for having stood off to sea a day and a night, we had scope to fight at our pleasure ; and no man, having sea roome, is bound to fight as his enemie will, with disadvantage, being able otherwise to deal with equalitie ; contrariwise, every man ought to seeke the meanes hee can for his defence, and greatest advantage, to the annoyance of his contrarie.

Now wee might, with our fore saile low set, have borne upp before the winde, and the enemie of force must have done the like, if he would fight with us, or keepe us company : and then should wee have had the advantage of them. For although their artillery were longer, waightier, and many more then ours, and in truth did pierce with greater violence; yet ours being of greater bore, and carrying a waightier and greater shot, was of more importance and of better effect for sinking and spoyling : for the smaller shot passeth through, and maketh but his whole, and harmeth that which lyeth in his way; but the greater shaketh and shivereth all it meeteth, and with the splinters, or that which it encountreth, many times doth more hurt then with his proper circumference : as is plainely seene in the battery by land, when the saker, the demy-colverin, the colverin, and demi-cannon (being peeces that reach much further point blanke then the cannon), are nothing of like importance for making the breach, as is the cannon; for that this shot being ponderous, pierceth with difficultie, yea worketh better effects, tormenting, shaking, and over-throwing all; whereas the others, with their violence, pierce better, and make onely their hole, and so hide themselves in the wooll or rampire.[5]

Besides, our ship being yare[6] and good of steeridge, no doubt but we should have played better with our ordinance, and with more effect then did our enemies; which was a great errour, being able to fight with lesse disadvantage, and yet to fight with the most that could be imagined, which I knew not off, neither was able to direct though I had knowne it, being in a manner senselesse, what with my wounds, and what with the agony of the surrendry pro-

The difference of shot.

Their effects

Errors in fight,

[5] *Wool* probably means the covering or planking. *Rampire* (for rampart?) what is now termed the bulwark. [6] Ready.

pounded, for that I had seldome knowne it spoken of, but that it came afterwards to be put in execution.

The generall not being able to succour his vice-admirall, except he should utterly leave us, gave them order to shift as well as they could for the present, and to beare with the next port, and there to repayre their harmes. Himselfe presently followed the chase, and in short space fetched us up, and beganne a fresh to batter us with his great and small shott. The vice-admirall, having saved what they could, cutt the rest by the bourd, and with fore-sayle and myson came after us also; and before the setting of the sunne, were come upon our broad side, wee bearing all our sayles, and after kept us company, lying upon our weather quarter, and annoying us what shee could.

Here I hold it necessary, to make mention of two things which were most prejudiciall unto us, and the principall causes of our perdition; the errours and faults of late dayes, crept in amongst those who follow the sea, and learned from the Flemings and Easterlings. I wish that by our misfortunes others would take warning, and procure to redresse them, as occasions shall be offered. *learned from the Flemings and Easterlings.*

The one, is to fight unarmed, where they may fight armed. The other is, in comming to fight, to drinke themselves drunke. Yea, some are so madd, that they mingle powder with wine, to give it the greater force, imagining that it giveth spirit, strength, and courage, and taketh away all feare and doubt. The latter is for the most part true, but the former is false and beastly, and altogether against reason. For though the nature of wine, with moderation, is to comfort and revive the heart, and to fortifie and strengthen the spirit; yet the immoderate use thereof worketh quite contrary effects. *1. To fight unarmed. 2. To drinke to excesse.*

In fights, all receipts which add courage and spirit, are of great regard, to be allowed and used; and so is a draught of wine, to be given to every man before he come to action, but more then enough is pernicious; for exceeding the same, it offendeth, and enfeebleth the sences, converting the strength (which should resist the force of the enemy) into weaknesse : it dulleth and blindeth the understanding, and consequently depraveth any man of true valour; for that he is disenabled to judge and apprehend the occasion which may be offered, to assault and retyre in time convenient; the raynes of reason being put into the hands of passion and disorder. For after I was wounded, this *nimium* bred great disorder and inconvenience in our shippe; the pott continually walking, infused desperate and foolish hardinesse in many, who blinded with the fume of the liquor, considered not of any danger, but thus and thus would stand at hazard; some in vaine glory vaunting themselves; some other rayling upon the Spaniards; another inviting his companion to come and stand by him, and not to budge a foote from him; which indiscreetly they put in execution, and cost the lives of many a good man, slaine by our enemies muskettiers, who suffered not a man to shew himselfe, but they presently overthrew him with speed and watchfullnesse. For prevention of the second errour, although I had great preparation of armours, as well of proofe, as of light corseletts, yet not a man would use them; but esteemed a pott of wine a better defence then an armour of proofe. Which truely was great madnesse, and a lamentable fault, worthy to be banished from amongst all reasonable people, and well to be weighed by all commanders.

For if the Spaniard surpasseth us in any thing, it is in his temperance and suffering : and where he hath had the better hand of us, it hath beene, for the most part, through our own folly; for that we will fight unarmed with him being armed. And although I have heard many men maintaine, that in shipping, armour is of little profit : all men of good understanding will condemne such desperate ignorance. For besides, that the sleightest armour secureth

the parts of a mans body, which it covereth, from pike,
sword, and all hand weapons, it likewise giveth boldnesse
and courage: a man armed, giveth a greater and a waightier
blow, then a man unarmed; he standeth faster, and with
greater difficultie is to be overthrowne.

And I never read, but that the glistering of the armour The use and
profit of
arming,
hath beene by authors observed, for that, as I imagine,
his show breedeth terror in his contraries, and despayre to
himselfe if he be unarmed. And therefore in time of
warre, such as devote themselves to follow the profession
of armes, by sea or by land, ought to covet nothing more
then to be well armed; for as much as it is the second
meanes, next Gods protection, for preserving and prolong-
ing many mens lives.[7]

Wherein the Spanish nation deserveth commendation exactly ob-
served by
the Spanish.
above others; every one, from the highest to the lowest,
putting their greatest care in providing faire and good
armes. He which cannot come to the price of a corslet,
will have a coat of mayle, a jackett, at least a buffe-jerkin,
or a privie coate. And hardly will they be found without
it, albeit they live and serve, for the most part, in extreame
hott countries.

Whereas I have knowne many bred in cold countries,
in a moment complaine of the waight of their armes,
that they smoother them, and then cast them off, chusing
rather to be shott through with a bullet, or lanched through
with a pike, or thrust through with a sword, then to endure
a little travaile and suffering. But let me give these lazie
ones this lesson, that he that will goe a warre-fare, must
resolve himselfe to fight; and he that putteth on this resolution, must be contented to endure both heate and waight:
first for the safeguard of his life, and next for subduing of
his enemie; both which are hazarded, and put into great
danger, if he fight unarmed with an enemy armed.

7 " Thrice is he armed who hath his quarrel just."—*Henry V.*

Sect. LXI.

Armes more
necessary by
sea, then at
land
Now for mine owne opinion, I am resolved that armour is more necessary by sea then by land, yea, rather to be excused on the shore then in the shippe. My reason is, for that on the shore, the bullet onely hurteth, but in the shippe I have seene the splinters kill and hurt many at once, and yet the shott to have passed without touching any person. As in the galeon in which I came out of the Indies, in anno 1597, in the rode of Tercera, when the Queenes Majesties shippes, under the charge of the Earle of Essex, chased us into the rode, with the splinters of one shott, were slaine, maymed, and sore hurt, at the least a dozen persons, the most part whereof had beene excused, if they had beene armed.

And doubtlesse, if these errours had beene foreseene, and remedied by us, many of those who were slaine and hurt, had beene on foote, and we inabled to have sustained and maintained the fight much better and longer, and perhaps at last had freed our selves. For if our enemy had come to bourd with us, our close fights were such, as we were secure, and they open unto us. And what with our cubridge heads, one answering the other, our hatches upon bolts, our brackes in our deckes and gunner roome, it was impossible to take us as long as any competent number of men had remained : twentie persons would have sufficed for defence ; and for this, such ships are called impregnable, and are not to be taken, but by surrender, nor to be over-come but with bourding or sinking, as in us by experience was verified. And not in us alone, but in the *Revenge* of the Queenes Majestie, which being compassed round about with all the armado of Spaine, and bourded sundry times by many at once, is said to have sunke three of the armado by her side.

And in this conflict, having lost all her mastes, and being no other then a logge in the sea, could not be taken with all their force and pollicie, till she surrendred her selfe by an honourable composition.

By these presidents,[8] let governours by sea take speciall care, above all, to preserve their people, in imitation of the French; who carrie many souldiers in their shippes of warre, and secure them in their holdes, till they come to entring, and to prove their forces by the dint of sword.

But here the discreete commaunders are to put differ- *A difference for commaunders.* ence, betwixt those which defend, and those which are to offend, and betwixt those which assault, and those which are assaulted. For, as I have sayd, no government whatsoever, better requireth a perfect and experimented commaunder, then that of the sea. And so no greater errour can be committed, then to commend such charges to men unexperimented in this profession.

A third and last cause, of the losse of sundry of our men, *Race-ships of warre disliked.* most worthy of note for all captaines, owners, and carpenters, was the race[9] building of our shippe, the onely fault shee had; and now a-dayes, held for a principall grace in any shippe: but by the experience which I have had, it seemeth for sundry reasons verie prejudiciall for shippes of warre. For in such, those which tackle the sayles, of force must bee upon the deckes, and are open without shelter or any defence: yet here it will be objected, that for this inconvenience, wast clothes are provided, and for want of *Wast clothes not so useful* them, it is usuall to lace a bonnet, or some such shadow for the men: worthily may it bee called a shadow, and one of the most pernitious customes that can be used; for this shadow, or defence, being but of linnen or wollen cloth, emboldeneth many, who without it would retire to better securitie; whereas, now thinking themselves unseene, they become more bould then otherwise they would, and thereby shot through when they least thinke of it. Some captaines observing this errour, have sought to remedie it in some of his Majesties shippes; not by altering the building, but by devising a certaine defence, made of foure or five inch *as other devises.*

---

[8] Precedents. [9] The term "race" is here repeated: if not a misprint (see note, page 199), can "a race ship" mean one built for speed?

planckes, of five foote high, and sixe foote broad, running upon wheeles, and placed in such partes of the shippe as are most open. These they name blenders, and made of elme for the most part; for that it shivers not with a shot, as oake and other timber will doe, which are now in use and service : but best it is, when the whole side hath one blender, and one armour of proofe, for defence of those which of force must labour and be aloft.

This race building, first came in by overmuch homing[10] in of our shippes; and received for good, under colour of making our shippes thereby the better sea-shippes, and of better advantage to hull and trye : but in my judgement, it breedeth many inconveniences, and is farre from working the effect they pretend, by disinabling them for bearing their cage worke correspondent to the proportion and mould of the shippe, making them tender sided, and unable to carry sayle in any fresh gaile of winde, and diminishing the play of their artillery, and the place for accommodating their people to fight, labor, or rest.

And I am none of those who hold opinion that the overmuch homing in, the more the better, is commodious and easier for the shippe ; and this out of the experience that I have learned, which with forcible reasons I could prove to be much rather discomodious and worthy to be reformed. But withall, I hold it not necessary to discourse here of that particularitie, but leave the consequence to men of understanding, and so surcease.

SECTION LXII.

ALL this second day, and the third day and night, our captaine and company susteined the fight, notwithstanding the disadvantage where with they fought; the enemie being

---

[10] Tumbling home (?) ; applied to the inclination inward, given to a ship's topsides.

ever to wind-ward, and wee to lee-ward, their shott much
damnifying us, and ours little annoying them; for when- The disad-
tage of ships
soever a man encountreth with his enemie at sea, in to lee-ward.
gayning the weather gage, hee is in possibilitie to sinke his
contrary, but his enemie cannot sinke him; and therefore
hee which is forced to fight with this disadvantage, is to And the best
procure by all meanes possible to shoote downe his con- remedie.
traries masts or yards, and to teare or spoyle his tackling
and sayles; for which purpose, billets of some heavy wood
fitted to the great ordinance, are of great importance. And
so are arrowes of fire, to bee shott out of slur-bowes, and
cases of small shott, joyned two and two together, with
peeces of wyer, of five or sixe ynches long, which also shot
out of muskets are of good effect, for tearing the sayles or
cutting the tackling.

Some are of opinion that crosse barres and chaine-shot
are of moment for the spoyling of masts and yards; but
experience dayly teacheth them not to be of great importance, though neere at hand, I confesse, they worke great
execution; but the round shott is the onely principall
and powerfull meane to breake mast or yard.

And in this our fight, the admirall of the Spaniards had The Spaniards fore-
his fore-mast shot through with two round shott, some mast thrice
shot through
three yardes beneath the head; had either of them entred
but foure ynches further into the heart of the mast, without all doubt it had freed us, and perhaps put them into
our hands. The third day, in the after-noone, which was
the 22nd of June 1594, according to our computation,
and which I follow in this my discourse, our sayles being
torne, our mastes all perished, our pumpes rent and shot
to peeces, and our shippe with fourteene shott under
water and seven or eight foote of water in hold; many of
our men being slaine, and the most part of them which
remayned sore hurt, and in a manner altogether fruiteles,
and the enemie offering still to receive us *a buena querra*,

and to give us life and libertie, and imbarkation for our countrey;—our captaine, and those which remayned of our company, were all of opinion that our best course was to surrender our selves before our shippe suncke. And so by common consent agreed the second time to send a servant of mine, Thomas Sanders, to signifie unto mee the estate of our shippe and company: and that it was impossible by any other way to expect for hope of deliverance, or life, but by the miraculous hand of God, in using his Almighty power, or by an honourable surrender: which in every mans opinion was thought most convenient. So was I desired by him to give also my consent, that the captaine might capitulate with the Spanish generall, and to compound the best partido he could by surrendring our selves into his hands, upon condition of life and libertie. This hee declared unto me, being in a manner voyd of sence, and out of hope to live or recover; which considered, and the circumstances of his relation, I answered as I could, that hee might judge of my state, readie every moment to give up the ghost, and unable to discern in this cause what was convenient, except I might see the present state of the shippe. And that the honour or dishonour, the welfare or misery was for them, which should be partakers of life. At last, for that I had satisfaction of his valour and true dealing in all the time hee had served me, and in correspondence of it, had given him (as was notorious) charge and credit in many occasions, I bound him, by the love and regard hee ought me, and by the faith and duty to Almighty God, to tell me truely if all were as he had declared. Whereunto hee made answere, that hee had manifested unto mee the plaine and naked truth, and that hee tooke God to witnesse of the same truth; with which receiving satisfaction, I forced my selfe what I could to perswade him to annimate his companions, and in my name to intreate the captaine and the rest to persevere in defence of their libertie, lives, and reputation, remitting all to his discretion : not doubting but he would be tender of his dutie, and zealous of my reputation, in preferring his liberty, and the liberty of the company, above all respects whatsoever. As for the welfare hoped by a surrender, I was altogether unlikely to be partaker thereof, death threatning to deprive me of the benefit which the enemie offered ; but if God would bee pleased to free us, the joy and comfort I should receive, might perhaps give me force and strength to recover health.

Which answere being delivered to the captaine, hee presently caused a flagge of truce to be put in place of our ensigne, and began to parley of our surrendry, with a Spaniard, which Don Beltran appointed for that purpose, from the poope of the admirall, to offer in his name, the conditions before specified ; with his faithful promise and oath, as the king generall, to take us *a buena querra*, and to send us all into our owne countrey. The promise hee accepted, and sayd that under the same hee yeelded, and surrendred himselfe, shippe, and company. Immediately there came unto me another servant of mine, and told me that our captaine had surrendred himselfe, and our shippe; which understood, I called unto one Juan Gomes de Pineda, a Spanish pilote, which was our prisoner, and in all the fight we had kept close in hold, and willed him to goe to the generall Don Beltran de Castro from mee, to tell him that if he would give us his word and oath, as the generall of the king, and some pledge for confirmation, to receive us *a buena querra*, and to give us our lives and libertie, and present passage into our owne countrey, that we would surrender ourselves and shippe into his hands ; otherwise, that he should never enjoy of us nor ours, any thing but a resolution every man to dye fighting.

With this message I dispatched him, and called unto me

all my company, and encouraged them to sacrifice their lives fighting and killing the enemie, if he gave but a fillip to any of our companions. The Spaniards willed us to hoise out our boate, which was shott all to peeces, and so was theirs. Seeing that he called to us to amaine our sayles, which we could not well doe, for that they were slung, and wee had not men inough to hand them. In this parley, the vice-admirall comming upon our quarter, and not knowing of what had past, discharged her two chase peeces at us, and hurt our captaine very sore in the thigh, and maimed one of our masters mates, called Hugh Maires, in one of his armes; but after knowing us to be rendred, hee secured us: and we satisfying them that wee could not hoise out our boate, nor strike our sayles, the admirall layd us abourd; but before any man entred, John Gomes went unto the generall, who received him with great curtesie, and asked him what we required; whereunto he made answere that my demand was, that in the Kings name, he should give us his faith and promise to give us our lives, to keepe the lawes of fayre warres and quarter, and to send us presently into our countrey; and in confirmation hereof, that I required some pledge: whereunto the generall made answere: that in the Kings Majesties name, his master, hee received us *a buena querra*, and swore by God Almightie, and by the habit of Alcantara (whereof he had received knighthood, and in token whereof hee wore in his breast a greene crosse, which is the ensigne of that order), that he would give us our lives with good entreatie, and send us as speedily as he could into our owne countrey. In confirmation whereof, he took of his glove, and sent it to mee as a pledge.

With this message John Gomes returned, and the Spaniards entred and tooke possession of our shippe, every one crying, *Buena querra, buena querra! oy por mi, maniana por ti :*[1] with which our company began to secure themselves.

The generall was a principall gentleman of the ancient nobilitie of Spaine, and brother to the Conde de Lemos, whose intention no doubt was according to his promise; and therefore considering that some bad intreaty, and insolency, might be offered unto me in my shippe, by the common souldiers, who seldome have respect to any person in such occasions, especially in the case I was, whereof hee had enformed himselfe : for prevention, hee sent a principall captaine, brought up long time in Flaunders, called Pedro Alveres de Pulgar, to take care of me, and whilest the shippes were one abourd the other, to bring me into his ship; which he accomplished with great humanitie and courtesie; despising the barres of gold which were shared before his face, which hee might alone have enjoyed if he would. And truely hee was, as after I found by tryall, a true captaine, a man worthy of any charge, and of the noblest condition that I have knowne any Spaniard.

The generall received me with great courtesie and compassion, even with teares in his eyes, and words of great consolation, and commaunded mee to bee accommodated in his owne cabbine, where hee sought to cure and comfort mee the best he could : the like hee used with all our hurt men, six and thirtie at least. And doubtlesse, as true courage, valour, and resolution, is requisit in a generall in the time of battle, so humanitie, mildnes, and courtesie, after victorie.

The mildnes of a generall after victorie

SECTION LXIII.

WHILST the shippes were together, the maine-mast of the *Daintie* fell by the bourd, and the people being occupied in

[1] *Hoy por mi, manana por ti :* which may be freely translated, "my turn to-day, yours to-morrow."

Sect. LXIII. ransacking and seeking for spoile and pillage, neglected the principall; whereof ensued, that within a short space the *Daintie* grew so deepe with water, which increased for want of prevention, that all who were in her desired to forsake her, and weaved and cryed for succour to bee saved, being out of hope of her recoverie.

The *Daintie* in danger of perishing. Whereupon, the generall calling together the best experimented men hee had, and consulted with them what was best to bee done; it was resolved that generall Michaell Angell should goe abourd the *Daintie,* and with him threescore marriners, as many souldiers, and with them the English men who were able to labour, to free her from water, and to put her in order if it were possible; and then to recover Perico the port of Panama; for that, of those to wind-wards, it was impossible to turne up to any of them, and neerer then to le-ward was not any that could supply our necessities and wants; which lay from us east northeast, above two hundreth leagues.

Michaell Arckangell recovereth the ship. Michaell Angell being a man of experience and care, accomplished that he tooke in hand; although in clearing and bayling the water, in placing a pumpe, and in fitting and mending her fore-saile, he spent above six and thirtie howers.

During which time the shippes lay all a hull; but this worke ended, they set sayle, and directed their course for the iles of Pearles. And for that the *Daintie* sayled badly, what for want of her maine-sayle, and with the advantage which all the South-sea shippes have of all those built in our North-sea, the admirall gave her a tawe;[1] which notwithstanding, the wind calming with us as we approached neerer to the land, twelve dayes were spent before we could fetch sight of the ilands; which lye alongst the coast, beginning some eight leagues, west south-west from Panama, and run to the south-wards neere thirtie leagues. They

---

[1] Tow or tug.

are many, and the most unhabited ; and those which have people, have some negroes, slaves unto the Spaniards, which occupie themselves in labour of the land, or in fishing for pearles.

In times past, many inriched themselves with that trade, but now it is growne to decay. The manner of fishing for pearles is, with certaine long pinaces or small barkes, in which there goe foure, five, sixe, or eight negroes, expert swimmers, and great deevers,[2] whom the Spaniards call *busos* ; with tract of time, use, and continuall practise, having learned to hold their breath long under water, for the better atchieving their worke. These throwing themselves into the sea, with certaine instruments of their art, goe to the bottome, and seeke the bankes of the oysters in which the pearles are ingendred, and with their force and art remouve them from their foundation ; in which they spend more or lesse time, according to the resistance the firmnes of the ground affordeth. Once loosed, they put them into a bagge under their armes, and after bring them up into their boates. Having loaden it, they goe to the shoare ; there they open them and take out the pearles : they lie under the uttermost part of the circuite of the oyster, in rankes and proportions, under a certaine part, which is of many pleights and folds, called the ruffe, for the similitude it hath unto a ruffe.

The pearles increase in bignes, as they be neerer the end or joynt of the oyster. The meate of those which have these pearles is milkie, and not very wholesome to be eaten.

In anno 1583, in the iland of Margarita,[3] I was at the dregging of pearle oysters, after the manner we dregge oysters in England ; and with mine owne hands I opened many, and tooke out the pearles of them, some greater, some lesse, and in good quantitie.

[2] Divers.
[3] This island was probably named after the Latin term "Margaritæ" pearls.

How the pearle is ingendred in the oyster, or mussell, for they are found in both, divers and sundry are the opinions, but some ridiculous : whereof, because many famous and learned men have written largely, I will speake no more then hath beene formerly spoken, but referre their curious desires to Pliny, with other ancient and moderne authors.

The places where pearle are found
They are found in divers parts of the world, as in the West Indies, in the South sea, in the East Indian sea, in the Straites of Magellane, and in the Scottish sea.

Those found neere the pooles[4] are not perfect, but are of a thick colour ; whereas such as are found neere the line, are most orient and transparent : the curious call it their water : and the best is a cleare white shining, with fierie flames. And those of the East India have the best reputation, though as good are found in the West India; the choice ones are of great valew and estimation ; but the greatest that I have read or heard of, was found in these ilands of Pearles ; the which king Phillip the Second of Spaine gave to his daughter Elizabeth, wife to Albertus, arch-duke of Austria, and governour of the states of Flaunders ; in whose possession it remaineth, and is called *la peregrina*,[5] for the rarenes of it ; being as bigge as the pomell of a poniard.

SECTION LXIV.

The generall continueth his honourable usage towards the sicke and wounded.
In this navigation, after our surrender, the generall tooke especial care for the good intreaty of us, and especially of

[4] Poles.

[5] Rare--wonderful : this pearl was found at Santa Margarita ; weighed two hundred and fifty carats, and was valued at thirty thousand pounds. Tavernier purchased one at Katifa, in Arabia, for upwards of one hundred thousand pounds. The Ceylon pearls are most valued in England.

those who were hurt. And God so blessed the hands of our
surgians (besides that they were expert in their art), that
of all our wounded men not one died that was alive the day
after our surrendry: the number whereof was neere fortie;
and many of them with eight, ten, or twelve wounds, and
some with more. The thing that ought to move us to give
God Almighty especiall thankes and prayses, was, that they
were cured in a manner without instruments or salves.
For the chests were all broken to peeces, and many of their
simples and compounds throwne into the sea; those which
remained, were such as were throwne about the shippe in
broken pots and baggs; and such as by the Divine Providence were reserved, at the end of three dayes, by order
from the generall, were commaunded to be sought and
gathered together. These with some instruments of small
moment, bought and procured from those who had reserved
them to a different end, did not onely serve for our cures,
but also for the curing of the Spaniards, being many more
then those of our company.

For the Spanish surgians were altogether ignorant in
their profession, and had little or nothing wherewith to
cure. And I have noted, that the Spaniards, in generall,
are nothing so curious in accommodating themselves with
good and carefull surgeans, nor to fit them with that which
belongeth to their profession, as other nations are, though
they have greater neede then any that I do know.

At the time of our surrender, I had not the Spanish
tongue, and so was forced to use an interpreter, or the
Latine, or French, which holpe me much for the understanding of those which spake to me in Spanish, together
with a little smattering I had of the Portugall.

Through the noble proceeding of Don Beltran with us,
and his particular care towards me, in curing and comforting me, I began to gather heart, and hope of life, and
health; my servants, which were on foote, advised me

ordinarily of that which past.   But some of our enemies, badly inclined, repined at the proceedings of the generall, and sayd he did ill to use us so well; that we were Lutherans; and for that cause, the faith which was given us, was not to be kept nor performed.   Others, that wee had fought as good souldiers, and therefore deserved good quarter : others nicknamed us with the name of *corsarios*, or pirats; not discerning thereby that they included themselves within the same imputation. Some were of opinion, that from Panama, the generall would send us into Spaine: others sayd that he durst not dispose of us but by order from the vice-roy of Peru, who had given him his authority.   This hit the nayle on the head.

To all I gave the hearing, and laid up in the store-house of my memory that which I thought to be of substance ; and in the store-house of my consideration, endevoured to frame a proportionable resolution to all occurants, conformable to Gods most holy will.   Withall I profitted my selfe of the meanes which should be offered, and beare greatest probabilitie to worke our comfort, helpe, and remedie.   And so as time ministered opportunitie, I began, and endevoured to satisfie the generall and the better sort in the points I durst intermeddle.   And especially to perswade, by the best reasons I could, that wee might be sent presently from Panama ; alleaging the promise given us, the cost and charges ensuing, which doubtles would be such as deserved consideration and excuse : besides, that now whilest he was in place, and power and authority in his hands, to performe with us, that hee would looke into his honour, and profit himselfe of the occasion, and not put us into the hands of a third person ; who perhaps being more powerfull then himselfe, he might be forced to pray and intreate the performance of his promise : whereunto hee gave us the hearing, and bare us in hand that hee would doe what hee could.

The generall, and all in generall, not onely in the Peru,
but in all Spaine, and the kingdomes thereof, before our
surrendry, held all English men of warre to be corsarios,
or pirats ; which I laboured to reforme, both in the Peru,
and also in the counsels of Spaine, and amongst the chieftaines, souldiers, and better sort, with whom I came to
have conversation : alleadging that a pirate or corsario, is
hee, which in time of peace or truce, spoyleth or robbeth ^{What a pirate is}
those which have peace or truce with them : but the
English have neyther peace nor truce with Spaine, but
warre ; and therefore not to be accounted pirats. Besides,
Spaine broke the peace with England, and not England
with Spaine; and that by ymbargo,[1] which of all kindes of
defiances is most reproved, and of least reputation; the ^{Three sorts of defiances}
ransoming of prysoners, and that by the cannon being
more honorable; but above all, the most honorable is with
trumpet and herald to proclaime and denounce the warre
by publicke defiance. And so if they should condemne
the English for pirats, of force they must first condemne
themselves.

Moreover, pirats are those who range the seas without
licence from their prince ; who when they are met with,
are punished more severely by their owne lords, then when
they fall into the hands of strangers : which is notorious
to be more severely prosecuted in England, in time of
peace, then in any of the kingdomes of Christendome.

But the English have all licence, either immediately
from their prince, or from others thereunto authorized, and
so cannot in any sence be comprehended under the name
of pirats, for any hostility undertaken against Spaine or
the dependancies thereof.

And so the state standing as now it doth ; if in Spaine a ^{The custom of Spaine for of warre.}
particular man should arm a shippe, and goe in warre-fare

---

[1] Imbargo—embargo : laying on an embargo, means issuing an order
to prevent the sailing of vessels.

with it against the English, and happened to be taken by them ; I make no question, but the company should bee intreated according to that manner, which they have ever used since the beginning of the warre, without making further inquisition.

Then if hee were rich or poore, to see if hee were able to give a ransome, in this also they are not very curious. But if this Spanish shippe should fall athwart his King's armado or gallies, I make no doubt but they would hang the captaine and his companie for pirates. My reason is, for that by a speciall law, it is enacted, that no man in the kingdomes of Spaine, may arme any shippe, and goe in warre-fare, without the King's speciall licence and commission, upon paine to be reputed a pirate, and to bee chas-
The custome of England. tised with the punishment due to *corsarios*. In England the case is different : for the warre once proclaimed, every man may arme that will, and hath wherewith ; which maketh for our greater exemption from being comprehended within the number of pirates.

With these, and other like arguments to this purpose, (to avoid tediousnes, I omitt): I convinced all those whom I heard to harpe upon this string : which was of no small importance for our good entreatie, and motives for many, to further and favour the accomplishment of the promise lately made unto us.

SECTION LXV.

A disputation concerning *buena querra*. ONE day after dinner, as was the ordinary custome, the generall, his captaines, and the better sort of his followers, being assembled in the cabbin of the poope in conference, an eager contention arose amongst them, touching the capitulation of *buena querra,* and the purport thereof. Some

sayd that onely life and good entreatie of the prisoners was
to be comprehended therein: others enlarged, and restrained
it, according to their humors and experience. In fine, my
opinion was required, and what I had seene and knowne
touching that point: wherein I pawsed a little, and suspecting the worst, feared that it might be a baite layd to
catch me withall, and so excused my selfe, saying : that
where so many experimented souldiers were joyned together,
my young judgement was little to be respected : whereunto
the generall replied, that knowledge was not alwayes
incident to yeares, though reason requireth that the aged
should be the wisest, but an art acquired by action and
management of affaires ; and therefore they would be but
certified what I had seene, and what my judgement was in
this point. Unto which, seeing I could not well excuse
myselfe, I condiscended; and calling my wits together,
holding it better to shoote out my boult by yeelding unto
reason, although I might erre, then to stand obstinate, my
will being at warre with my consent, and fearing my deniall
might be taken for discourtesie, which peradventure might
also purchase me mislike with those who seemed to wish
me comfort and restitution ; I submitted to better judgement, the reformation of the present assembly, saying :
" Syr, under the capitulation of *buena querra,* or fayre
warres, I have ever understood, and so it hath beene observed in these, as also in former times, that preservation
of life and good entreatie of the prisoner have beene comprehended ; and further, by no meanes to be urged to any
thing contrary to his conscience, as touching his religion ;
nor to be seduced or menaced from the allegeance due to
his prince and country ; but rather to ransome him for his
moneths pay. And this is that which I have knowne practised in our times, in generall, amongst all civill and noble
nations. But the English have enlarged it one point more
towards the Spaniards rendred *a buena querra* in these

warres ; have ever delivered them which have beene taken upon such compositions, without ransome : but the covetousnes of our age hath brought in many abuses, and excluded the principall officers from partaking of the benefit of this privilege, in leaving them to the discretion of the victor, being, many times, poorer then the common souldiers, their qualities considered; whereby they are commonly put to more then the ordinary ransome; and not being able of themselves to accomplish it, are forgotten of their princes and sometimes suffer long imprisonment, which they should not."

With this, Don Beltran sayd : " This ambiguitie you have well resolved ;" and, like a worthie gentleman, with great courtesie and liberalitie, added : " let not the last point trouble you, but bee of good comfort; for I here give you my word anew, that your ransome, if any shall be thought due, shall be but a cople of grey-hounds for mee, and other two for my brother, the Conde de Lemos: and this I sweare to you by the habit of Alcantera.   Provided alwayes, that the King, my master, leave you to my dispose, as of right you belong unto me."

For amongst the Spaniards in their armadoes, if there bee an absolute generall, the tenth of all is due to him, and he is to take choise of the best : where in other countries, it is by lot that the generalls tenth is given.   And if they be but two shippes, he doth the like ; and being but one, shee is of right the generalls.   This I hardly believed, until I saw a letter, in which the King willed his vice-roy to give Don Beltran thankes for our shippe and artillerie, which he had given to his Majestie.

I yeelded to the generall most heartie thankes for his great favour, wherewith hee bound mee ever to seeke how to serve him, and deserve it.

SECTION LXVI.

IN this discourse, generall Michael Angell demanded for what purpose served the little short arrowes which we had in our shippe, and those in so great quantitie. I satisfied them that they were for our muskets. They are not as yet in use amongst the Spaniards, yet of singular effect and execution, as our enemies confessed : for the upper worke of their shippes being musket proofe, in all places they passed through both sides with facilitie, and wrought extraordinary disasters ; which caused admiration, to see themselves wounded with small shott, where they thought themselves secure ; and by no meanes could find where they entred, nor come to the sight of any of the shott.

Hereof they proved to profit themselves after, but for that they wanted the tampkins, which are first to be driven home before the arrow be put in ; and as they understood not the secret, they rejected them as uncertaine, and therefore not to be used : but of all the shot used now a-dayes, for the annoying of an enemie in fight by sea, few are of greater moment for many respects, which I hold not convenient to treat of in publique.

SECTION LXVII.

A LITTLE to the south-wards of the iland of Pearle, be- twixt seven and eight degrees, is the great river of Saint Buena Ventura. It falleth into the South sea with three mouthes, the head of which is but a little distant from the North sea. In anno 1575, or 1576, one John Oxman,[1] of

---

[1] Oxenham ? See page 209.

Plymouth, going into the West Indies, joyned with the
Symarons.

What the
Symarons
are.   These are fugitive negroes, and for the bad intreatie
which their masters had given them, were then retyred into
the mountaines, and lived upon the spoyle of such Spaniards
as they could master, and could never be brought into
obedience, till by composition they had a place limmitted
them for their freedome, where they should live quietly by
Their
habitation.   themselves. At this day they have a great habitation neere
Panama, called Saint Iago de Los Negros, well peopled,
with all their officers and commaunders of their owne, save
onely a Spanish governour.

Their
assistance.   By the assistance of these Symarons, hee brought to the
head of this river, by peecemeale, and in many journeys, a
small pinnace; hee fitted it by time in a warlike manner,
and with the choice of his company, put himselfe into the
South sea, where his good hap was to meete with a cople
of shippes of trade, and in the one of them a great quantitie
of gold. And amongst other things, two peeces of speciall
estimation: the one a table of massie gold, with emralds,
sent for a present to the King; the other a lady of
singular beautie, married, and a mother of children. The
John Oxman
capituluteth
with them.   latter grewe to bee his perdition: for hee had capitulated
with these Symarons, that their part of the bootie should
be onely the prisoners, to the ende to execute their malice
upon them (such was the rancor they had conceived against
them, for that they had beene the tyrants of their libertie).
But the Spaniards not contented to have them their slaves,
who lately had beene their lords, added to their servitude,
cruell entreaties. And they againe, to feede their insatiable
revenges, accustomed to rost and eate the hearts of all those
Spaniards, whom at any time they could lay hand upon.

His folly
and breach
of promise.   John Oxman, I say, was taken with the love of this lady,
and to winne her good will, what through her teares and

perswasions, and what through feare and detestation of their
barbarous inclinations, breaking promise with the Symarons,
yeelded to her request; which was, to give the prisoners
liberty with their shippes, for that they were not usefull for
him : notwithstanding, Oxman kept the lady, who had in
one of the restored shippes eyther a sonne or a nephew.
This nephew, with the rest of the Spaniards, made all the His pursuit.
hast they could to Panama, and they used such diligence,
as within fewe howers some were dispatched to seek those
who little thought so quickly too bee overtaken. The pur-
suers approaching the river, were doubtfull by which of the
afore-remembred three mouthes they should take their way.

In this wavering, one of the souldiers espied certaine And evill
feathers of hennes, and some boughes of trees, which they fortune.
had cut off to make their way, swimming down one of the
outlets. This was light sufficient to guide them in their
course ; they entred the river, and followed the tracke as
farre as their frigats had water sufficient ; and then with
part of their souldiers in their boates, and the rest on the
bankes on eyther side, they marched day and night in pur-
suite of their enemies ; and in fine came uppon them unexpected, at the head of the river, making good cheare in
their tents, and devided in two partialities about the partition, and sharing of their gold. Thus were they surprised,
and not one escaped.

Some say that John Oxman fled to the Symarons, but He flyeth
they utterly denyed to receive or succour him, for that he to the
Symarons.
had broken his promise ; the onely objection they cast in
his teeth was, that if he had held his word with them, hee
had never fallen into this extremitie.

In fine, hee was taken, and after, his shippe also was
possessed by the Spaniards, which he had hid in a certaine
cove, and covered with boughes of trees, in the guard and
custodie of some foure or five of his followers. All his
company were conveyed to Panama, and there were ym-

barked for Lyma ; where a processe was made against them by the justice, and all condemned and hanged as pirates.

Breach of
faith never
unpunished.

This may be a good example to others in like occasions: first to shunne such notorious sinnes, which cannot escape punishment in this life, nor in the life to come : for the breach of faith is reputed amongst the greatest faults which a man can committ. Secondly, not to abuse another mans wife, much lesse to force her; both being odious to God and man. Thirdly, to beware of mutenies, which seldome or never are seene to come to better ends; for where such trees flourish, the fruite, of force, must eyther bee bitter, sweete, or very sower. And therefore, seeing wee vaunt ourselves to bee Christians, and make profession of His law who forbiddeth all such vanities; let us faithfully shunne them, that wee may partake the end of that hope which our profession teacheth and promiseth.

SECTION LXVIII.

Comming in sight of the ilands of Pearles, the wind began to fresh in with us, and wee profited our selves of it : but comming thwart of a small iland, which they call la Pacheta, that lyeth within the Pearle ilands, close abourd the mayne, and some eight or ten leagues south and by west from Panama, the wind calmed againe.

La Pacheta.

This iland belongeth to a private man; it is a round humock,[1] conteyning not a league of ground, but most fertile. Insomuch, that by the owners industrie, and the labour of some few slaves, who occupie themselves in manuring it; and two barkes, which he imployeth in bringing

---

[1] Mound or hillock.

the fruit it giveth to Panama, it is sayd to bee worth him
every weeke, one with another, a barre of silver, valued
betwixt two hundreth and fiftie or three hundreth pezos ;
which in English money, may amount to fiftie or threescore pounds : and for that which I saw at my being in
Panama, touching this, I hold to be true.

In our course to fetch the port of Panama, wee put our
selves betwixt the iland and the maine : which is a goodly
channell, of three, foure, and five leagues broad, and without danger, except a man come too neare the shoare on any
side ; and that is thought the better course, then to goe a
sea-boord of the ilands, because of the swift running of the
tydes, and the advantage to stop the ebbe : as also for succour, if a man should happen to bee becalmed at any time
beyond expectation, which happeneth sometimes.

The seventh of July wee had sight of Perico : they are *The generall
certefieth the
Audiencia of
his successe.*
two little ilands which cause the port of Panama, where all
the shippes used to ride. It is some two leagues west north-
west of the cittie, which hath also a pere[2] in itselfe for small
barkes ; at full sea it may have some sixe or seaven foote
water, but at low water it is drie.

The ninth of July wee anchored under Perico, and the *The great
joy of the
Spaniards.*
generall presently advised the *Audiencia* of that which had
succeeded in his journey : which, understood by them,
caused bonfires to be made, and every man to put lumina-
ries in their houses. The fashion is much used amongst the
Spaniards in their feasts of joy, or for glad tidings; placing
many lights in their churches, in their windowes, and
galleries, and corners of their houses ; which being in the
beginning of the night, and the cittie close by the sea-shore,
showed to us, being farre of, as though the cittie had been
on a light fire.

About eight of the clocke, all the artillery of the citty

2 Pier ?

was shott off, which wee might discerne by the flashes of fire, but could not heare the report; yet the armado being advised thereof, and in a readinesse, answered them likewise with all their artillery; which taking ende, as all the vanities of this earth doe, the generall settled himselfe to dispatch advise for the King, for the vice-roy of Peru, and for the vice-roy of the Nova Spana, for hee also had beene certified of our being in that sea, and had fitted an armado to seeke us, and to guard his coast.

Note.   But now for a farewell (and note it), let me relate unto you this secret, how Don Beltran shewed mee a letter from the King, his master, directed to the vice-roy, wherein he gave him particular relation of my pretended voyage; of the ships, their burden, their munition, their number of men, which I had in them, as perfectly as if he had seene all with his own eyes: saying unto me, " Heereby may you discerne whether the King, my master, have friends in England, and good and speedie advice of all that passeth."

Whereunto I replyed : " It was no wonder, for that hee had plentie of gold and silver, which worketh this and more strange effects : for my journey was publique and notorious to all the kingdome." Whereunto hee replyed, that. if I thought is so convenient, leave should be given mee to write into England to the Queens Majestie, my mistresse, to my father, and to other personages, as I thought good; and leaving the letters open, that he would send some of them in the King's packet, others to his uncle Don Rodrigo de Castro, cardinall and archbishoppe of Sevill, and to other friends of his; not making any doubt but that they would be speedily in England." For which I thanked him, and accepted his courtesie; and although I was my selfe unable to write, yet by the hands of a servant of mine, I wrote three or foure coppies of one letter to my father, Sir John Hawkins; in which I briefly made relation of all that had succeeded in our voyage.

The dispatches of Spaine and New Spaine, went by ordinary course in ships of advise; but that for the Peru, was sent by a kinseman of the generalls, called Don Francisco de la Cuena.

Which being dispatched, Don Beltran hasted all that ever hee could to put his shippes in order, to returne to Lyma. Hee caused the *Daintie* to be grounded and trimmed ; for in those ilands it higheth and falleth some fifteen or sixteen foote water.

And the generall with his captaines, and some religious men being aboord her, and new naming her, named her the *Visitation,* for that shee was rendred on the day on which they celebrate the visitation of the blessed Virgin Mary. In that place, the ground being plaine and without vantage, whereby to helpe the tender sided and sharpe ships, they are forced to shore them on either side. In the midest of their solemnity, her props and shores of one side fayled, and so shee fell over upon that side suddenly, intreating many of them which were in her, very badly ; and doubtlesse, had shee bin like the shippes of the South sea, shee had broken out her bulge: but being without mastes and empty (for in the South sea, when they bring a-ground a shippe, they leave neither mast, balast, nor any other thing abourd, besides the bare hull), her strength was such as it made no great show to have received any damage ; but the feare shee put them all into was not little, and caused them to runne out of her faster then a good pace.

In these ilands is no succour nor refreshing ; onely in the one of them is one house of strawe, and a little spring of small moment. For the water, which the shippes use for their provision, they fetch from another iland, two leagues west north-west of these, which they call Tabaga, having in it some fruite and refreshing, and some fewe Indians to inhabite it.

Q

What succeeded to mee, and to the rest during our imprisonment, with the rarities and particularities of the Peru and Terra Firme, my voyage to Spaine, and the successe, with the time I spent in prison in the Peru, in the Tercera, in Sevill, and in Madrid, with the accidents which befell me in them, I leave for a second part of this discourse, if God give life and convenient place and rest, necessary for so tedious and troublesome a worke : desiring God, that is Almightie, to give his blessing to this and the rest of my intentions, that it and they may bee fruitefull to His glory, and the good of all : then shall my desires be accomplished, and I account myselfe most happie. To whom be all glory, and thankes from all eternitie.

FINIS.

THE TABLE

OF

THE PRINCIPALL OBSERVATIONS

CONTEINED IN THIS BOOKE.

FINIS.

RICHARDS, PRINTER, 100, ST. MARTIN'S LANE.